Ligt, Barthélemy de.
    The conquest of violence; an essay on war
and revolution. By Barthelemy de Ligt, with
an introd. by Aldous Huxley. With a new
introd. for the Garland ed. by George Lakey.
New York, Garland Pub., 1972.
    11, xi, 306 p. (The Garland library of
war and peace)
    Reprint of the 1937 ed.
    A rev. and enl. English version of the
author's Pour vaincre sans violence, originally
(continued next card)

The
Garland Library
of
War and Peace

The
Garland Library
of
War and Peace

Under the General Editorship of

Blanche Wiesen Cook, *John Jay College, C.U.N.Y.*

Sandi E. Cooper, *Richmond College, C.U.N.Y.*

Charles Chatfield, *Wittenberg University*

The Conquest of Violence

An Essay on War and Revolution

by
Barthélemy de Ligt

with an introduction by
Aldous Huxley

with a new introduction
for the Garland Edition by
George Lakey

Garland Publishing, Inc., New York & London
1972

Library of Congress Cataloging in Publication Data

Ligt, Barthélemy de.
    The conquest of violence.

    (The Garland library of war and peace)
    Reprint of the 1937 ed.
    A rev. and enl. English version of the author's
Pour vaincre sans violence, originally published in
1935.
    Bibliography: p.
    1. Passive resistance to government. 2. War.
3. Revolutions. 4. Netherlands--Foreign relations.
I. Title. II. Series.
JX1952.L6352 1972   301.6'33   76-147627
ISBN 0-8240-0402-7

Introduction

The Conquest of Violence *is a classic work in the literature of war and revolution, and it has contemporary relevance.*[1] *A young black student who read it recently told me that it made the best case he had seen for nonviolent struggle.*

Bart. de Ligt, a Dutch sociologist, faced the pervasive fact of violence and the social dynamic of injustice. A scholar of wide learning who had published a study of historic religious attitudes toward war, La Paix Créatrice *(2 vols., 1934), he wrote in Holland at a time of wars and fear of wars — a time like ours. The Spanish Civil War and the Italian invasion of Ethiopia were heavily on his mind, and a second world war was on the horizon. There is a tremendous sense of urgency in this book; it is as though there was not even time enough to footnote all the cases of nonviolent action that are recounted.*

De Ligt was keenly aware of the role of economic forces in causing war. The role of political economy is rising again in the consciousness of peace activists, and because of de Ligt's clarity on this matter his book is more relevant than much of the peace research of recent years. It is not only economic interests he faulted: it is the complacent use of force that these interests have sanctioned. In his chapter on

5

"Violence and the Masses" he showed how the bourgeoisie have taught workers (another generation in another land could read "blacks") the romance and promise of violence; no one should be surprised that the oppressed use it at last for their own cause.

The central thesis of de Ligt's analysis is that violence as a means of social revolution contradicts both the humane and the political ends of socialism, anarchism, and syndicalism. What will it gain a Russian revolutionary piloting a bomber over the Ruhr to destroy his comrades, knowing that those most responsible for fascism are most safe from his bombs? The contemporary reader can supply his own equivalent drawn from almost any continent: what will it gain Latin American guerrillas, for example, to attack regiments of peasants conscripted into the army of the regime?

The corollary to de Ligt's thesis of the reactionary character of violence is that there are nonviolent alternatives in the struggle for social justice. He cited numerous historical cases of nonviolent struggle in order to portray a practical alternative to violence. I have compared his descriptions with later researches of the Ruhrkampf by Wolfgang Sternstein and the Kapp putsch by Adam Roberts, the work of Patricia Parkman on the Samoan independence struggle, and my own work on the Hungarian independence struggle of the mid-nineteenth century, and de Ligt's accounts hold up well.[2]

De Ligt did not attribute war to a single factor. Its

causes include psychological motives, economic institutions, the rivalry of nation-states, and the cultural conditioning which in the long run makes world wars possible. He conceded that war has had useful by-products and has aided social evolution on occasion, but he considered modern war monstrous because of changes in its technology and scope.

Without saying that the only cause of war is capitalism, de Ligt nevertheless saw capitalism as necessarily resulting in violence and war: "our society is violent just as fog is wet." An army is needed to keep down unrest at home, to suppress the risings in the underdeveloped world, and for leverage in international competition for markets and raw materials. Americans used to seeing military power deployed in Washington and other domestic centers of protest, moved into the Dominican Republic, Vietnam, and other areas of the world, and used in bargaining with other states may find de Ligt's observations contemporary in implication. A capital-ist, bourgeois pacifist is a contradiction in terms, he concluded: if one truly wants peace, one cannot support a system that depends upon military power.

Conversely, a true revolutionary cannot depend on violence. De Ligt's concept of nonviolent action is the same as that used by leading contemporary scholars in the field. He shrewdly saw why nonviolent struggle is so effective when conducted on a mass basis: the rulers depend upon the compliance of the ruled, and legitimacy is essential to long-run government.

INTRODUCTION

Noncooperation is powerful because, in his words, it upsets the "whole social edifice." According to Gene Sharp in his forthcoming basic work, The Politics of Nonviolent Action, *this is the central political theorem which explains the effectiveness of nonviolent coercion, a theorem which has support even in Machiavelli's writings.*

The Conquest of Violence *is very different from another substantial work with a similar title,* Conquest of Violence, *by Joan Bondurant.[3] In the latter Gandhi is the center of attention and is approached with near reverence, whereas in de Ligt's view the Indian leader was a giant who had limitations. By making much of the perhaps dubious distinction between satyagraha and duragraha, Bondurant idealizes Gandhi and his method and puts them at a distance from the reality of today's struggles. De Ligt, by contrast, criticized Gandhi for temporizing with the empire (especially when it was at war), but yet related the Gandhian experience all the more vigorously to his European audience.*

Although de Ligt recognized the multi-dimensional character of social reality and had great clarity about nonviolent techniques as a means of struggle, still he was not a creative strategist. True, several elements of strategy are asserted confidently in his plan for opposing war: the movement must be international, opposition to war should be converted into social revolution, education and organization are important as well as action, participation in revolutionary

8

INTRODUCTION

movements is sometimes necessary for the pacifist
even though it may mean associating with users of
violence. And yet, that which de Ligt offers as a plan
is in reality a list of options. There are no priorities,
no sense of phasing or timing. It is far from clear how
a Dutch or British reader of the thirties should
proceed to put together a mobilization for peace,
much less how he might escalate the peace movement
into a revolutionary movement (although "...the
struggle against war will never be effective until it
forms an integral part in the struggle for a new
society").

De Ligt admitted the question of how the Russians
might defend themselves against Japanese aggression;
it is a fair problem, he wrote. But he digressed from
an answer with almost no concrete alternatives to war
except for the abstractions "nonco-operation" and
"civil disobedience." The same approach characterizes his treatment of the Franco attack on the
Spanish republican government. Finally, it is sad in
light of later events that the chapter in which de Ligt
considered a German invasion of Holland is so lacking
in discussion of civilian defense; there is not enough
exposition to make nonviolent resistance credible,
much less of practical use. The modern reader shares
the frustrated sense of a contemporaneous reviewer
that social revolution should be relevant to existing
social crises.[4]

Nonetheless, de Ligt's refusal to let the nationalist
frenzy of his time distort his own sense of

9

INTRODUCTION

community with all those who put humanity first remains eloquent:

> But if among the sixty-eight million Germans there was one single anti-militarist comrade — and there are many men and women there who have not bowed the knee to the Nazi Baal — this one comrade would be nearer to us than all the members of the Government at the Hague and all the Dutch militarists and imperialists. (p. 244)

In that remark de Ligt asserted a sense of community that crossed the boundaries of violence in his time and revealed a vision of humanity that crosses the boundaries marking his time off from our own.

George Lakey
A Quaker Action Group
Philadelphia

INTRODUCTION

NOTES

[1] The Conquest of Violence *was translated by Honor Tracy from the French text,* Pour vaincre sans violence, *and was published in England by Routledge & Sons in 1937 and in an unaltered edition in the United States by E. P. Dutton & Co. in 1938.*

[2] *See Sternstein's study in Adam Roberts, ed.,* Civilian Resistance as a National Defense *(Baltimore: Penguin, 1969), and Robert's article, "Resisting Military Coups," in* New Society *(June 1, 1967). The Parkman and Lakey work has not yet been published, but neither Patricia Parkman nor I have been able to track down the Argentinian general strike in 1917 against participation in the World War, which de Ligt mentions briefly on p. 142.*

[3] *(Berkeley: University of California Press, 1965).*

[4] *Walter H. C. Laves, in* American Political Science Review, *XXXII (October, 1938), p. 1009.*

THE CONQUEST OF
VIOLENCE

THE CONQUEST
OF VIOLENCE

An Essay on War and
Revolution

By
BART. DE LIGT

With an Introduction by
ALDOUS HUXLEY

NEW YORK
E. P. DUTTON & COMPANY
1938

Translated by HONOR TRACY
from the French text
revised and enlarged
by the Author

PRINTED IN GREAT BRITAIN BY HEADLEY BROTHERS
109 KINGSWAY, LONDON, W.C.2 ; AND ASHFORD, KENT

Those on whom falls the formidable task of raising humanity above the capitalist stage must be ready to try method after method until they find the one which best corresponds to their goal.—LENIN.

Civilization is an appreciation of values, gained by an accumulation of experience.—ELLWOOD.

The " war to end war " has been the obscure aim behind all human conflict.—CORNEJO.

CONTENTS

INTRODUCTION

BART. DE LIGT is the author of two books which are among the most important contributions to the literature of pacifism. The first is a comprehensive history of pacifist thought and action from the earliest times to the present day. This work has appeared in its entirety in Dutch, and a new and enlarged edition in French is in process of publication. Two volumes have already appeared under the title, *La Paix Créatrice*, and two more are to be issued in the near future. *La Paix Créatrice* is a work of wide and profound learning, indispensable to those who would study the history of peace and of " the things that make for peace ". It is much to be hoped that, in due course, it will find an English translator and publisher.

M. de Ligt's other important work is *Pour Vaincre sans Violence*, the translation of which is now being made available to the English public. This is not a work of historical research, but a text-book of applied pacifism, in which the techniques of non-violent activity are described with a sober precision of language, refreshingly different from the vague, well-meaning rhetoric of so much pacifist writing.

Particularly valuable at the present time is M. de Ligt's discussion of pacifism in relation to revolution. Those who call themselves revolutionaries believe that all militarism is wicked except their own militarism ;

that their ends are so good that they are justified in using the worst means in order to achieve them ; that they are fighting on the side of an ineluctable historical process, and that, whereas their opponents' violence is not only evil, but futile, their own brutalities are historically justified and predestined by the very nature of things to have good results.   Unfortunately, the fact is that (unless very speedily followed by compensatory acts of non-violence) violence always produces the results of violence.   In the victims, the results of violence are either resentful hostility, leading ultimately to counter-violence, or else (if the violence has been " successful ") utter, sub-human abjection.   In the perpetrators, the results of violence are the formation of a habit of brutality and a growing determination to retain power by even the foulest means.   A violent revolution does not result in any fundamental change in human relations ; it results merely in a confirmation of the old, bad relations of oppressor and oppressed, of irresponsible tyranny and irresponsible passive obedience.   In de Ligt's own phrase, " the more violence, the less revolution ".   Violence guarantees that *plus ça change, plus c'est la même chose*.   If we want it not to be the same thing, we must make our change by the methods of non-violence.

Such is the lesson, unmistakably clear to anyone who considers the evidence without prejudice, of all the violent revolutions of the past.   Ignoring this lesson, violent revolutionaries persist in asking us to make use, yet once more, of methods of change which have led, on every previous occasion, to manifestly unsatisfactory results. The apostle's advice is that we should try all things and hold fast to that which is good. The violent revolutionary urges us to try very few things and hold fast to that which is demonstrably bad. Mere common sense demands that, before accepting their invitation, we should consider the possible alternatives. In the present volume the reader will find the most promising of those alternatives clearly set out.

ALDOUS HUXLEY.

CHAPTER I

THE RELIGION OF VIOLENCE

In the world of to-day, peace is nothing
but a suspension of war.

GENERAL SIKORSKI.

WE live in a time of violence triumphant. What
does it mean ? Its etymology explains it : violation,
violate, violence—these words all mean the abuse of
strength and an offence against that which is healthy,
right and pure. They come from the Sanscrit root *gi*
(Latin *vis*, Greek *bia*) which is related to the Vedic
radical *gyâ*, best translated as invade, violate, subdue,
oppress, etc. The German and Dutch words analogous
to it are *Gewalt* and *geweld*, from the German root
waldan, used in connection with the behaviour of men
who are strong and brutal, who impose their wills
ruthlessly, love to rule and to dominate, and who use
their power in such a way as to infringe the rights of
those who come under it. In French, it is *violence*, in
Italian, *violenza*. In all these, it means an attack on
those human and civilizing values which ought to
command the greatest respect.

In our time, wherever we turn our eyes, whether it
is to Japan, Italy, Germany, Morocco, India, Indochina,
Indonesia or Abyssinia, violence is paramount.
Napoleon and Bismarck would have made more

disciples to-day than ever before. Everywhere the same cry : One man, one soldier. Might is right. Blood and steel.

In the life of nations, violence gathers strength from day to day. The noblest inventions of science are made to serve its purpose : no sooner have the scientists managed to climb to the stratosphere than their observations are placed at the service of homicidal technique.

This mentality is not confined to the countries under dictatorships. Latterly, it has even made an appearance in France. " The fashion—as well as the necessities of the time—is all for strong personalities," we read in the *Mercure de France*. So much for the idealists and pacifists of the eighteenth century ! Let us be realists. The State, heavily armed, is the personification of supreme authority, political, social and moral. Let us be sceptics as to the essential kindliness of the human animal. Let politics be based on the most profound of human instincts : pride, greed, lust for power ! The Christian religion can only be tolerated as long as it upholds an earthly authority by the suggestion of a divine : it is unacceptable in opposition. Liberty of conscience and freedom of thought can only be allowed to the individual in the degree authorized by " the common good ", that is, the State. The relations a country has, both with the outer world and with its own people, rest finally on violence. " The armed prophet triumphs, the unarmed perishes," wrote Machiavelli, in his *Il Principe*. Mussolini, prophet of Fascism, and Stalin prophet of Bolshevism, have both based their authority on force. It is not a question of just or unjust, moral or immoral. 1914 proved that the great field where, in the dream of Isaiah, the lamb and the lion, the sheep and the wolf, shall lie down together, is nothing but a senseless fairy tale. Only war can bring out the noblest qualities of Man.[1]

Even more disquieting than the actual practice of violence is the confidence people repose in it. This confidence has now become a real cult, a new religion. Usually, those who are against it—quoting the bombastic words of Mussolini : " dagger between the teeth, bomb in hand, and in the heart a sovereign contempt for all danger " or some theatrically heroic passage in the Wagnerian style from Hitler's *Mein Kampf*—console themselves with Einstein by saying that we of the Western democracies would never go so far. And yet, in some ways, it is these democracies who have gone the farthest : their nationalism and militarism no longer have even to be forced or stimulated. To the average Western mind, the national armies which have absorbed the mass of the people ever since the French Revolution, in all modern States, are the natural thing. The principle of totalitarian warfare is accepted, even by Socialists and Bolshevists. In the United States, in Great Britain, France, Belgium, the Netherlands, the brutalities of ultra-modern war are so freely admitted that it might almost seem one of the articles of a nation's code, assent to which is as obligatory as the performance of rites in official Christianity. Two religions face each other. But the cult of force is definitely supplanting that of Christ. So much so that Col. Fuller, the " military Luther " as he called himself, who wants to ennoble and reform the science of war in honour of the million British who fell in the World War and

[1] G. Peytavi de Faugères. " La Modernité de Machiavel," *Mercure de France*, October 15th, 1932, pp. 513-37.

in preparation for the next great one[1] has even boasted
that if British soldiers are superior to those on the
Continent, it is due to their having assimilated the
tactics of scientific warfare " like a new Gospel ".   In
the *Nieuwe Rotterdamsche Courant*, a great Dutch paper
which prides itself on its moderation as well as its high
intellectual and moral level, some military expert
puffs up " this attractive new creed " which gives the
strength " to move mountains".   And in spite of the
Dutch law against irreverence, the paper was not
prosecuted.[2]   In Holland, a country with very old
traditions of tolerance and liberty, the government now
prefers to persecute those who fight, by word and deed,
that absurdly narrow creed of " God, the Netherlands
and the House of Orange ", the moral level of which
is scarcely above that of the court-religion in Israel
a thousand years before Jesus Christ.

In France, *Paris Soir* enthusiastically quotes Mussolini's
declaration that all men should have their streak of
barbarism.   " We   must   be   hard."   Fulminating
against Germany's rearmament, in the *Echo de Paris*,
M. de Kerillis exclaims, " Bravo, Mussolini ! You
are great. You arm 700,000 men. You mobilize
them materially and morally. And you are wise, for
you trust only in the virtue of bayonets. You prepare
to defend peace to the roar of cannon." The *Journal*
declares that in glorifying militarism, the Duce has done
nothing but exalt an ideal common to every nation

[1] Col. J. F. C. Fuller, D.S.O., *The Reformation of War*, a book
dedicated to The Unknown Warrior.

[2] *Nieuwe Rotterdamsche Courant*, August 3rd, 1933. *Cf.* Matthew,
XVII, 20, " If ye have faith as a grain of mustard seed, ye shall
say unto this mountain, Remove hence to yonder place, and it
shall remove."

in the world. And, for a long time past, M. Paul
Boncour has been praising totalitarian warfare as the
symbol of complete democracy, and, just like the
German Major Hesse, he and Léon Jouhaux demand
for " the defence of peace " the general adoption of the
militia system, which finds favour in Switzerland.[1] And
this although Col. Lecomte openly admits in Switzerland
itself the army is, next to the Italian, the most expensive
in the world as well as being incapable of defence against
chemical, electro-technical and other modern methods
of warfare.[2] What of it ! The slogan of the past
century, " art for art's sake " has been supplanted
by that of " war for war's sake ".

At the seventeenth anniversary of the Russian
Revolution, Karl Radek, at that time still in Stalin's
good books, writing in the *Izvestia* of November 7th
heaped praises on the Machiavellian doctrines, declaring
them to be in complete harmony with those of the
Bolshevist Maximovski. Addressing the author of
Il Principe, he said : " Our workers, surrounded by
enemies, must learn from you how to combine the
politics of the lion with those of the fox, and they will
gladly read your words and carry them out in the service
of the Socialist Fatherland : when the safety of the
Fatherland is at stake, it is not right to think about
what is just or unjust, merciful or cruel, glorious or
shameful."[3] And *Travail*, a pro-Moscow Geneva paper,
mentioned on April 24th, 1935, that a great winged
gun was in process of construction in some secret

[1] See Jouhaux, *Le Désarmement*.
[2] See *La Gazette de Lausanne*, Nos. 46 and 48, 1932.
[3] See Karl Radek, " Machiavelli and Rousseau," *Lu*, November
16th, 1934.

Russian laboratory, and that it would reach a speed greater than that of the fastest plane, and penetrate farther into the stratosphere than any balloon : and, without comment, the paper went on to say : " It is not necessary to underline the military importance of the stratospherical gun in a country of Russia's vast breadth."

There is, then, no essential difference between such convictions, as fashionable in the Western democracies as in " barbarous, Asiatic Russia ", and those of the notorious German professor, Ewald Banse, who declared in 1933 that the methods and the aims of the new science of war, are " to create and to establish the foundations of an unshakable faith in the lofty moral value and usefulness of war. All must understand that war is nothing extraordinary nor criminal, is not a crime against humanity. . . . A State lives by its warlike population and dies from its pacifist population. . . . Hostilities can break out, without so much as a declaration of war, beginning simply with the destruction of the capital and chief industrial centres of the enemy country from the air "[1] and the Polish General Sikorski, in a book on modern warfare, preface by Marshal Pétain, accepts the German General Bucsineck's opinion, that modern warfare breaks with the tradition that all available strength has to be concentrated against the enemy forces . . . the objective of future wars will be the entire enemy nation, the theatre of war, the whole of the enemy territory. This Polish strategist agrees with the ideas of the German Major Soldau : " Chivalry belongs to the time of the professional armies. It is no longer admissible when

[1] Quoted by Décugis, *Le Destin des Races Blanches*, pp. 7-8.

nations fight for their very existence. So that, although after the terrible experiences of the last war, the nations may take refuge in the divine symbol of human nobility, the war to come will make mincemeat of it."

At the Anti-Gas Warfare Conference at Frankfort in 1929, an expert German chemist declared that what was so alarming in modern war was not, as one might think, the use of the most ingenious methods of killing, but the still more odious fact that modern men had come to regard it as normal to poison—at the order of some official—his fellow-men by millions, to burn and exterminate them. According to this scientist, it has already been ascertained how disastrously so murderous an outlook has influenced private crime in so-called times of peace. The gas-poisoners must really be those who are poisoned in spirit and the bacteria for war must come from infected minds. Modern society is only an extremely refined form of barbarism, which bolsters up both individual and collective insanity, and often is one with them. So that a strategist of relatively moderate conceptions, like General Sikorski, believes that in future wars, " the contamination of wells and springs by microbic cultures of cholera, typhoid and glanders, and the use of germ-laden shells, will be on a scale to cause a terrible massacre. One can never be vigilant enough in this respect " ;[1] and Dr Romieu, in the *Revue des Deux Mondes* of July 1930, as well as various experts at the French Veterinary Congress held in June 1935, surmised that in the next war, bacteria would be used against the following :

1. Potatoes, corn and other agricultural products of the enemy fields.

[1] Sikorski, *La Guerre Moderne*, p. 195.

2. Animals of the enemy country.

3. Men, whether mobilized or not.

And with a *Rücksichtslosigkeit* that one usually expects
from Germans alone, the French Commandant Velu
declares :

1. Bacteriological warfare is possible, therefore it
    will take place.

2. No International law, no pact, no ethical con-
    sideration will prevent the use of these new
    weapons.[1]

So that war now threatens to destroy not only all real
civilization, but also the lives of tens of millions of men,
leaving aside the devilish extermination of animals
and plants . . .

Nothing is harder than to break with all these
methods and impulses. It requires, as people are
beginning to see, more courage, sacrifice, initiative
and creative intelligence than war itself. Because peace
is something new : it has got to be learnt. Violence
and war are deeply rooted in the habits of men. We are
dragged into it not only politically and socially, but
morally too, and sometimes even unconsciously.

In the *Encyclopaedia Universalis Mundaneum*, edited by
Paul Otlet of Brussels, it is stated that among the
so-called historical peoples, there were 3,130 years of
war in a period of 3,357 years, beginning in 1496 B.C.
and ending in A.D. 1861, as against 227 years of peace.
So that the ratio of war years to peace years is 13 to 1.

These figures are apparently taken from the researches
of M. Novicow.[2]   Davie also estimates that the whole

[1] See the Report by Commandant Velu in *Journées Vétérinaires*
of June 16th, 1935.

[2] See Davie, *War in Primitive Societies*.

history of Africa and of many parts of India could be comprised in a history of warfare. Like Sumner, Davie explains the origin and frequency of wars by their four most powerful motivations : hunger, love, religion, vanity. It seems to us that fear and the love of danger, and of power, must be added to these.

Van der Bij has shown that the first wars were waged more on religious grounds than on economic. A feeling of solidarity towards their own clan and its dead obliged the other members, when one of their number died or was killed, to re-establish social equilibrium and pacify the terrible soul of the dead man by killing the real or supposed author of the death. Once marked out by the witch-doctor, this individual must be punished and sacrificed to the dead, a measure of collective vengeance accompanied by all sorts of religious rites, to which the spirit of the dead man himself is believed to incite the clan members by dreadful cries at night and horribly mysterious threats.

At the beginning of war, therefore, there would seem to have been a kind of religious vendetta carried on by the whole community in question, man as an individual " being unable to imagine, in these societies, any action of his own apart from that of the group ".[1]

One thing is certain, that from the earliest times war has been closely linked to religion. Cannibalism, head-hunting, scalping, human-sacrifice, wars of defence and wars of attack, and all other kinds of armed collective activity, were all undertaken with the assistance of the gods. Every war is, religiously speaking, a holy war, and all holy wars are a barbarous form of mass murder. From time immemorial, human wars have been reflected in the mythical fights of the gods, who are supposed to take part in the earthly struggles of men, sometimes for their own people and sometimes against, as Jehovah did, for example.[2]

[1] Lahy-Hollebecque, *L'Évolution Humaine des Origines à nos Jours*, 1934, Vol. III, p. 77.
[2] See Jeremiah xix. 1-15.

Official Christianity to-day continues this age-old tradition, as we saw in the Great War, when both sides implored the assistance of Heaven. We read in the *Memorial to Belgian Soldiers*, the Flemish edition of which was written by the Almoner Paul Bouillot, published by the Printers to the Holy See at Tournay and recommended by Cardinal Mercier, and which begins with a picture of the crucified Christ, as follows :

" My friend, love your country not only by word but also in deed. Be a good soldier. Be a good citizen. . . . Be a good Christian . . . by your military virtues . . . by your Christian virtues . . .

" As a Soldier, you have so many glorious patrons in heaven ! No other profession has produced so many saints. . . . To mention even the most famous would take a whole litany. In heaven, you have a host of friends and protectors praying for you."

> Protège-nous, vierge Marie,
> De nos premiers jours au trépas ;
> Dans les sentiers de cette vie
> Partout, toujours, guide nos pas.
>
> Nous voulons Dieu dans notre armée,
> Afin que nos vaillants soldats
> Luttant pour la Patrie aimée
> Soient des héros dans les combats.
>
> Sur La Belgique étends ta main bénie,
> Pour son bonheur, nos voeux montent vers toi
> Que sous ta garde, elle reste, ô Marie,
> Fidèle au Christ, à l'Église, à la Croix.
>
> Le monde sait les luttes héroiques
> Que pour la foi soutinrent nos aieux ;
> Pour mériter le nom de Catholiques
> Jusqu'à la mort nous lutterons comme eux.[1]

[1] Paul Bouillot, *God en Vaderland*, pp. 11-12, 161-2. For translation see Appendix II, p. 287.

And, as we know, the official catechism published by the Archbishop of Paris, was changed by Mgr Amette in 1914 so that the sixth commandment read " Thou shalt not kill unrighteously, in deed nor in will " instead of " Thou shalt not kill in deed nor in will " as before. In fact, the commandment of the Old Testament, " Thou shalt not kill," seems rather to have been meant for reckless motorists than for soldiers. According to the Holy See at any rate, this commandment had nothing to do with the colonial enterprises of Fascist Italy. On February 15th, 1929, the Pope composed a prayer, in gratitude for the recognition of his temporal power by the Italian Government, asking grace for the king, and the following part of this prayer was introduced into the Good Friday Mass :

" Let us pray for the king, that God may grant to him, for our perpetual peace, the subjection of all barbarous nations."[1]

So Mussolini's gamble in Ethiopia had the Church's sanction in advance. It is hardly astonishing that immediately Abyssinia was attacked, the responsible members of the Italian clergy should vie with each other in blessing this war, as civilizing as it was Christian. According to the *Corriere della Sera*, of October 29th, 1935, Cardinal Schuster, presiding at the ceremony in honour of the thirteenth anniversary of the March on Rome, declared that the Italian standard was carrying the Cross to victory on the Abyssinian field, breaking the chains of the slaves and making way for the missionaries of Christ. Meanwhile, the Pope himself declared Mussolini a Man of God, and the Bishop of Messina blessed the Italian fleet on its way to Africa. In the Cathedral of Siena, the Archbishop invoked God's blessing on the Italian troops, who were fighting for civilization, for justice and for the glory of the Fatherland, etc.[2]

[1] Suzanne Bouillet, *Comment Réaliser La Paix*, p. 200.
[2] See Daniel Hogg, " Italy, Year XIII of the Fascist Era " in *Cahiers de la Réconciliation*, Paris, May, No. 5, and " The Church and Conflict " in *Le Temps*, November 14th, 1935.

That is the official Catholic idea as regards God and war. As for the Protestant idea, it is well-known that from the very start of Protestantism, its various forms, arising at the same time as the modern capitalist state, identified themselves with nationalism. The Church of England represents an essentially English type of religion, the Reformed Church of the Netherlands the national religion of Holland, and the Lutheran church, under the Emperor, represented the official religion of the German Reich, and in many ways resembled the Cesaropapism of the Tsar of all the Russias.

To-day, too, the Officers' Christian Union, in London, organized specially for the Army, Navy and Air Force, regularly publishes a Review for Officers and Ex-Officers of the Fighting Services, called *Practical Christianity*. This Union is " based on prayer " and it " welcomes as a Member every officer in H.M. Fighting Forces whether serving or having served, who believes in prayer to God through our Lord Jesus Christ and is willing to pray for the spiritual welfare of the Services." In this paper, officers are encouraged to " hold fast the teaching of Christ without whom ye can do nothing ", and to surrender to Divine guidance. One of the greatest saints of the Old Testament, David the warrior king, intending to attack one of the cities of Judea " inquired of the Lord, saying ' Shall I go up ? ' and God immediately answered ' Go up ', and in reply to a second question indicated the place to which he was to go (Hebron) . . . Cannot the Christian nowadays expect such definite and clear guidance as was enjoyed by saints of old ? He certainly can, and the object of these notes is to help us to understand how God works in the present dispensation, and what are the rules and regulations which He has laid down for our instruction in this matter."[1]

> Lord of Battles, God of armies,
> He has gained the victory.

[1] *Practical Christianity*, January 1932, pp. 37 and 4-5.

The second factor in wars is the economic, which has grown to be the dominant factor in the course of centuries. In the beginning, it was a simple question of physical hunger, which since the growth of agriculture has changed into a hunger for land, the desire to appropriate cultivated lands and finally slaves as well, to do the hard and disagreeable work. As civilization progressed, this " hunger " was mingled with

Auri sacra fames . . .

" the gold-hunger ". Lahy-Hollebecque states that the attack on some village among the desert Arabs by pillaging tribes and the outbreak of the Great War differ from each other only in degree. " Here, a water-hole or palm grove is coveted, there, a province rich in iron, salt, or potassium, or some colony to be exploited, or a market for goods, or the road leading to the petrol fields of Mossoul."[1]

The factor of love, or rather, the sexual motive in war, which at one time in the history of mankind led to the rape of women becoming a social institution and of which the Iliad as well as the Ramayana and the Mâhabhârata are full, has long since disappeared as an ostensible reason for war. But psychoanalysis has shown that subconsciously men are still driven on to fight by such motives ; and particularly by certain sadistic or masochistic tendencies which can turn into an absolute thirst for blood.

With this is bound up the factor of vanity, a psychological motive which, like the others, has often been and still is one of the causes of war. Military vanity arises not only out of individual psychology but also out of that of the group, the man who lives by himself having no desire to cut a dash or to be admired. This need of recognition has every chance of being satisfied in war. For hundreds of centuries, groups like the clan, the tribe, the town, the nation had to be protected and defended by the physical violence of warriors. These

[1] *L'Évolution Humaine des Origines à nos Jours*, Vol. III, p. 72.

would be distinguished by their clothing, magico-religious in origin and by their technique, the purpose of which was to impress the enemy, to be recognizable in battle and to stand out among the civilian population ; and they also had to distinguish themselves in battle by acts of bravery, which in turn brought them all kinds of marks of distinction. Being looked upon as the safeguarders of the groups' very existence, the warriors were always sure of general esteem, especially on the part of women, who in most societies depended on their protection and yielded themselves blindly to their strength. This explains the almost magic attraction which military uniform and parades have for the female mind even to-day, and the close and age-long bond between Venus and Mars.

We thus begin to see yet another motivating factor in war : fear, the psychical expression of the need for security, which is indispensable to the development of human life, civilization and spiritual culture. It is chiefly collective fear which forces nations to arm and rearm and drives them to all kinds of military defence measures which, by the dialectics of military evolution must go hand in hand with aggressive measures and even with aggression, pure and simple, itself.

These different needs and tendencies make an appeal also to the love of danger and adventure rooted so deeply in every man, and gravely neglected by the traditional psychologists.

However, in order thoroughly to understand war, we must take into account the love of power, the innate passion for domination, the need of self-expression and dominance which are as typical of the great individual as of the great nation, and which are some of the deepest roots of political imperialism. The *Libido Dominandi*, the will to live and expand in order to survive, which Hobbes in his treatise on *Human Nature* characterized as love of power and which two centuries later Nietzsche christened *die Wille zur Macht*, is one of the main-springs of human passion, especially in the male. Seillière even suggested giving the single name of

" imperialism " to this psychological tendency ; a name which characterizes all those of its manifestations which for the past fifty years have been the most pregnant in consequences for society.

This " imperialism ", so essential to the living being, must be taken in an entirely psychological sense. Amongst our earliest ancestors it was combined with the religious mysticism of which we have already spoken, which is a real stimulant of human action and which very soon became the usual auxiliary to this form of *élan vital*. According to Seillière, these two primitive tendencies have worked in together for so many centuries that they have become almost instinctive and, so to speak, necessary to all planned and persistent action on the part of mankind.

This vital energy, ineradicably fixed in the living creature, but for which life itself would soon come to an end, has been for a long time more or less irrationally used by the group to achieve its ends and to-day has culminated in national and racial imperialism.

And so, for centuries past, they have been speaking of the " gesta Dei per Francos ", which means that the will of God is to be executed by Frenchmen. This messianic sentiment of the French nation has been symbolized by Joan of Arc, the Maid of Orleans, especially since the World War ; with the encouragement of catholic-nationalist priests, the French patriots have been making a real cult of her.

Across the Rhine, an idea has grown up that God wishes the German people to organize and rule the world :

> Am deutschen Wesen
> Wird die Welt genesen.

Germany, saviour of the world, redeemer of the universe. This national Messianism was one of the factors of the Great War, and, years later, of the success of Adolf Hitler, le Führer, " whose voice is the law of God ".

In Italy, Gabrielo d'Annunzio wrote to his comrades in arms, after his imperialist venture against Fiume, " Brothers, you will know henceforward what we have done with the inspiration and help of our God ! I was ill in bed ! I rose in response to the call, and not I alone, but all of us obeyed the Spirit and we felt ourselves to be cleansed of all evil."[1] And we have already mentioned how the Pope raised Benito Mussolini, the Duce, to the rank of Man of God.

In England, similar tendencies have developed since the Tudors, nationalism being invoked by Henry VIII in religion and by Elizabeth in commerce. " It was made holy by Protestantism, glorious by the defeat of the Armada, and profitable by overseas trade and the loot of Spanish galleons . . . After Waterloo, the English settled down to a comfortable belief that they were superior to all other nations in virtue, intelligence, martial prowess, and commercial acumen. Above all, they felt that, as Milton says (speaking nominally of the Jews) they understood ' the solid rules of civil government.' "[2] According to Wells, this " megalo-maniac nationalism " found always its strongest support in " the military and official castes, and in the enter-prising and acquisitive strata of society, in new money, that is, and big business ".[3] Since the publication of Seeley's famous essay *The Expansion of England* (1883), this imperialist mentality has become a serious historical force. A real Messianic nationalism, impreg-nated with war-like sentiments, it found political expression in the exploits of Cecil Rhodes, an Empire Builder whose ambition was " Africa British from the Cape to Cairo ", and its poetical expression in the racial mysticism of Kipling, amazingly akin to the National-Socialist theory : " Blut und Boden ", which means blood and soil.

[1] Quoted by Seillière, *Du Quiétisme au Socialisme romantique,* p. 15.

[2] Russell, *Freedom and Organization,* p. 395.

[3] Wells, *The Outline of History,* pp. 560-1.

Truly yet come of The Blood . . . So long as
    The Blood endures
I shall know that your good is mine : ye shall feel
    that my strength is yours :
In the day of Armageddon, at the last great fight of
    all,
That our House stand together and the pillars do
    not fall.

Fair is our lot—O goodly is our heritage !
(Humble ye, my people, and be fearful in your
    mirth !)
For the Lord our God most High
He hath made the deep as dry,
He hath smote for us a pathway to the ends of all
    the Earth !

As we see, there are no grounds for reproaching Japan
with her Shintoism, that religion of Japanese blood and
soil which inspires the frenzied imperialists in the land
of the Rising Sun. Even in the tiny Netherlands, we
see to-day a strong revival of the nationalist religion,
centred around " God, the Netherlands, and the House
of Orange ". In Holland they go so far as to identify
the Royal House with the orange Sun, which never
sets on the vast Dutch Empire, spread over the two
hemispheres. Their determination to hold this Empire
down for ever is expressed in the national motto,
" Je maintiendrai ".

We can see how much easier it is to give way to violence
than to oppose it, if only on account of the moral and
social retrogression which goes with warlike inclinations.
To fall is easier than to climb, and there are still
individuals and races who prefer to go backwards !

Even to those who see the catastrophic consequences
of such an atavistic mentality and who are seriously
trying to put an end to armed conflict, fear, that
bad counsellor, often suggests the primitive methods
of terrorism. Terrified themselves by the threat of

2

violence, they hope to avert it by terrifying their potential enemies by a super-armament, which induces these last to arm more heavily than ever, etc., etc., *ad infinitum* . . .

Even Lord Robert Cecil, the leader of the International Peace Campaign, which is supposed to express the will to peace of some hundreds of millions of people and which has recently received a considerable sum as a gift from the Nobel Peace Institute, even this passionate pacifist, frightened by the armaments of Germany and Italy, has fallen blindly back on the old philosophy of *si vis pacem para bellum*, the futility of which has been evident for centuries past, and approves the gigantic arms programme of Britain in 1937 : as long as the other countries are armed, a country cannot be unarmed or insufficiently armed. It is true that such measures are not conducive to international peace. But they afford, if not protection, at least a certain amount of confidence.[1]

Whether this may not be a misplaced confidence is a question which Lord Robert Cecil does not ask. British rearmament is justified as a temporary means of placing the nations on a footing of equality so that disarmament can be discussed. Equality ! ? . . .

Besides, the most that Lord Robert Cecil can hope to gain by his Peace Campaign is not the entire abolition of national armaments but their reduction and limitation prior to a system of national and international security, based on the right of national defence and ultimately on military sanctions imposed by the League of Nations : in other words, the maintenance of peace by war.

It was in this same spirit that Pierre Cot, vice-president of the I.P.C., expressed his satisfaction in the French Chamber that next to Russia, France possessed the most powerful air arm in the world, and congratulated the French Minister for War on the increase by

[1] " To Safeguard Peace." A speech given at the opening session of the I.P.C. at Geneva, March 15th, 1937, at three o'clock. *Journal des Nations*, March 17th, 1937.

37 per cent. of first-line military planes, by 50 per cent. in munition stocks, by 70 per cent. in armaments. " No one in the last six months has done as much for aerial warfare as we have ! "[1]

These declarations would at present have the sympathy even of such a pacifist as Romain Rolland. After being for years a real champion of peace, this great successor of Tolstoy, horrified by the advent of Hitlerism in Germany, has fallen back on the old policy of terrorism which may well be called belli-pacifism. In the paper *Vendredi*, this one-time war-resister announced that he favours a collective system of peace, based on the military collaboration of all other States against a potential " aggressor ", and aimed primarily against National Socialist Germany which, according to him, ought to be reduced to impotence by a permanent politico-strategical threat. With a lack of imagination astounding in so great a writer, Romain Rolland suggests that the other states impose on Germany their way of thinking and living, and that the Reich be forced to accept a revision of the Versailles Treaty as well as a system of European peace elaborated by them without her assistance, and with this preliminary condition, that Germany should be the first to enter into this European peace pact. In the same article, Romain Rolland emphasizes the necessity of the collective armed defence of the U.S.S.R., thus giving his moral support to the super-armament of the Kremlin as well as to the political encirclement of Germany as seen by Barthou and Litvinoff.

The famous German author Emil Ludwig, too, after having advocated immediate disarmament, refusal of military credits and of military service ever since the war, declared in August 1934, while living in Switzerland, his adopted country, " Those who have neighbours teaching and preaching openly a philosophy of armaments, and a science of war, should arm to the teeth

---

[1] *Cf.* the protest against this questionable pacifism made by Pastor J. J. Buskes, Jr., in *Kerk en Vrede*, Amsterdam, April 6th, 1937.

themselves. In our times, a new form of pacifism has come into being : the alliance of all other States against an aggressor."[1]

As if in present-day political and economic conditions, one single nation could be the aggressor ! As we pointed out, at the appearance of this Pacifism of Despair, any such aggressor, fully convinced of his own righteousness, would always find powerful allies of the same turn of mind, or at any rate accomplices. Thus it would be quite impossible ever to isolate Germany in this way either politically or militarily, as history has amply proved. In reply to this quasi-pacifist policy, Germany, feeling herself threatened and frustrated, has allied herself with Japan, Italy and various other powers of secondary importance. Furthermore, each of these nations immediately accelerated its armament programme, which has led to a new race in armaments, intensified by the activities of international armament manufacturers, the only International which remained alive and intact before, during and after the War.

The result is, that the political situation now in 1937 is more strained than it was in early 1914.

And so we find ourselves on a level with the military experts, such as Marshal Pétain, who writes : " In the present state of international relations, peace can only be maintained by force. Force only can restrain and avert (!) the war which the profound rivalries of the different States would otherwise render inevitable. Such at the present time is the true justification of force. But this Force must be organized."[2]

We are now in a position to answer the question, so often raised, as to why the above-mentioned English nobleman is willing to collaborate quite happily in the I.P.C. with the French Stalinist Marcel Cachin, an old

[1] *Cf.* Emil Ludwig, *Europeesche Leiders*, Arnhem, 1934, Introduction.

[2] Ph. Pétain, in the preface to *La Guerre Moderne*, by Sikorski.

" socialist patriot " who has never been able nor has
wanted to renounce his obstinate nationalism . . .

What will our old friend and co-worker Albert
Einstein have to say to this reaction ? he who, after
the advent of Hitler in Germany and in consequence of an easily understandable psychological
reverse, was one of the first converts to this new belli-
pacifism.

The fact that modern warfare is put at the service
of Peace does not in any way change its inhuman
character, nor its fatal effect on civilization and human
culture, which will be far worse than that of the Great
War. It is clear that mankind will never free itself
from armed conflict in this way. For special and sacred
reasons for fighting will always be forthcoming. Nothing
could be more true than General Sikorski's remark :
" As long as human groups, social or national, cannot
make mutual sacrifices for peace, they will inevitably
come to settle their differences by force. War will seem
to them a smaller calamity than the renunciation of the
spiritual, moral and material interests which the
communities embodying them represent. . . .
So that to-day peace is nothing more than an
armistice."[1]

To-day we must answer the question : total war or
. . . total peace. At a meeting of the Peace Pledge
Union, at Brussels, on August 7th, 1936, Aldous Huxley
remarked that no one, however bellicose, wants to
fight everybody. Even Hitler, that fanatic, does not
want to fight the republic of Andorra, nor the British
Empire, nor even France perhaps, but only Russia
for the moment. And in 1935, Mussolini had no wish
to go to war with the whole of Europe, but only with
Abyssinia. Even Alexander, Caesar and Napoleon
fought for peace, that is, for peace for themselves. In
other words, the most fanatical war-mongers have
peaceful intentions towards 50, 60, 70 per cent. if not
90 per cent. of the world. What then is the difference

[1] Sikorski, *La Guerre Moderne*, pp. 24-5.

between these Bellicists and those Belli-pacifists who also do not wish to renounce their 10 per cent. of war ? The only genuine war-resisters, as Mr Huxley said, are those who are 100 per cent. Pacifists; those who are willing to give up even their own 10 per cent. of war.

In brief, the choice lies between real universal peace and universal war ; and universal peace necessitates a complete remodelling of our lives, social and individual, and a permanent organization against war and preparations for war.   For in order to overcome violence and war, we must not only, to quote Professor Duprat, free ourselves intellectually, morally and practically, from a social determinism which is deeply engrained and which we find in ourselves and round us,[1] but we must bring about a new social determinism, that of personal and social liberty—a determinism which, based on a responsibility as much individual as collective, must be developed to the point where it becomes instinctive, and overcomes all traditional resistances.

This means that we, too, have need of strong personalities, but of a different kind.   For, according to this conception, only those are strong who have dispensed with war and violence.   Only those are strong who have overcome violence in themselves and have remained unaffected by the suggestions of official powers, both in the political and economic field as well in that pertaining to civilization as a whole.   Only those are strong who share in the new universal conscience and remain unshaken by the presumptuous claims of the State, that modern Moloch, and immune from all nationalization of conscience.   Only those are strong who, in a society based above all on purely animal fear and distrust of one's neighbour, stand out by virtue

[1] Duprat, *La Contrainte Sociale et la Guerre.*

of a conscience which transforms the whole world, and by their contempt of fear. Only those are strong who, instead of dominating others, govern themselves : and who, looking reality in the face, have sufficient courage to recognize the moral values in the men and the social phenomena which they are obliged by their convictions to combat.

Chapter II

VIOLENCE AND WAR IN HISTORY

> The knowledge that war is not a natural fact but an acquired habit of society is a powerful counter-argument to the war-mongers. It exists only in as far as the conditions for it exist in the life of men. Since it appeared at a certain stage of history, it can also disappear.
>
> LAHY-HOLLEBECQUE.

No doubt it is impossible to ignore the relatively beneficent rôle played by violence and war in the history of humanity, and to suppress them both by one simple pacifist gesture. In the course of the world's history, violence has made possible all sorts of civilizations, and even war, that horror, has sometimes called forth what is beautiful and noble. From this point of view there is no disagreement between the bourgeois sociologists and the Socialist Marx or the anarchist Proudhon.

But war is a historical, not a biological, phenomenon : it is not a consequence of human nature as such but of certain social, economic and political conditions which at a certain time have come into being, and which are bound later to disappear. Only spontaneous conflicts are biological in nature. But this bloody collective conflict, war, systematically prepared and waged with consummate technique, undertaken for reasons either magico-metaphysical, economic, social, political, religious or " civilizing ", this violent conflict is a comparatively recent development in the evolution of humanity. According to the most conservative estimate of modern science, Man has been on the earth for at least 500,000 years, while war dates back for only a few hundreds of centuries.[1] No doubt all kinds of passions and appetites, of aggressive and destructive instincts, even the instinct of self-destruction, have made it possible. But all the same, primitive man was more peace-loving than warlike by nature and the less developed communities of the world are so still, as long at least as they live beyond the reach of " higher " civilizations. According to ethnologists, the first weapons were used not to kill men but animals.[2]

Besides, collective violence has shown a far more primitive character in previous centuries than it does to-day. Doubtless the consequences were always terrible, for the losers especially, and countless civilizing values have been destroyed by it. But, taken as a whole, war has never in the course of thousands of years wrought the same havoc as to-day. In the history of all the tribes, races and peoples together, we find a relatively favourable relation between destructive forces and constructive forces, between annihilation and creation, between murder and civilization so that despite all the violence and all the wars, civilization survived civilizations and positive values in the end triumphed over negative. However cruel it may have been, violence has helped through the centuries towards the unification and fusion of the human race. The first barely differentiated human societies, raising themselves more by

[1] Cf. especially Ellwood, *Cultural Evolution*.

[2] Cf. B. de Ligt, " Le Détrônement de la Guerre," *Évolution*, March 1931, pp. 32-42.

war than anything else up the first rungs of evolution, were farther removed from their previous state
than a butterfly from a caterpillar after bursting its
cocoon.

War has in many ways been favourable to commerce
and trade, to art and science.   It has played an important rôle in the history of education : self-discipline
especially is something we owe not only to the ancient
wizards, priests, saints and mystics, but also to soldiers.
Courage, still so rare in our own day, was fostered
particularly by war.   Certain conceptions, such as
that of a " manly spirit " and the " male virtues ",
as well as the word " virtue " itself in the Latin sense
(*virtus*) all proceed from the ideology and mentality
of warriors.   While the instinctive combats of primitive
men all had the satisfaction of direct, immediate needs
in view—even though here already the interests and the
future of the race were at stake, often indirectly, as for
instance in the struggle for food and the conquest
of the female—war became more and more indirect
in nature, that is to say, more civilizing and was put
at the service of the social, political and cultural future :
men learnt to sacrifice themselves and renounce their
immediate interests, even joyfully.   Heroism, of which
animals know nothing, was born.

" What are the individual qualities of one man who
fights another ?   First, the will : the will drives a man
to offer or to accept combat.   It is the will of man which
exalts human force when it is used ; it is the will of
man which refuses to admit defeat, so long as it can put
up any resistance.
" In all times, armies have put first the strength of
their will-power ; their weakness has lain in the
vulnerability of their flanks and rear.

" So do not fear war (moral worth).
Take by surprise ; or be always on guard.
Strengthen the rear and flanks of the army.
Attack the rear and flanks of the enemy army.
Be strong in equipment and organization."

These are the maxims laid down by the military expert, Jean Lafeuillade, in *L'Evolution Humaine*, as being vital to the strength of any army the world over. This is why moral strength has always been studied and exploited for the exigencies of war. According to Lahy-Hollebecque, in the above-mentioned essay, the exploitation of moral courage in wartime " depends on the study of the very springs of human emotion and their adaptation to the necessities of warfare ; it is through psychic research that moral courage can be strengthened, if its results are directed towards action, or at least are given professional study. The evolution of moral forces in the army must therefore inevitably tend to introduce the study of Man, his life and actions, and to give this a more important place in the profession." According to Col. Fuller, in his *Reformation of War*, integrity, honour, justice and courage are the weapons of the great strategist, which not only demonstrates a nation's martial power, but also its moral worth. During the war, soldiers must show :

" Superiority of will.
Superiority of endurance.
Superiority of co-operation.
Superiority of speed.
Continuity of movement.
Superiority of manœuvre."

Men have to excel not only in muscles but also in mind. "As the physiological object of the fighter is ' to kill without being killed ', so is his psychological object ' to kill without being killed ' . . . In war the elemental psychological power is mind."

We must even admit that all civilizations have hitherto been based on violence and that up to a certain point they have maintained themselves by violence ;

none has ever broken completely away from it. And this is true even of the most peaceful of them ; notably of the Chinese civilization which, as a matter of fact, has for some time past, been showing a marked inclination to methods of violence. There is nothing astonishing in this, for all civilizations hitherto have been the work of the minority or the élite, governed by a small number of privileged men, whose magnificence springs from the exploitation of the always increasing masses. All civilization has built itself in the same way as the Pyramids : a golden summit, of glittering splendour, crowning a structure which rests on a very wide base, formed of layers of the oppressed and impoverished, right down to the very blackest misery. And from these dark and wretched depths the great ones of society draw their prestige and glory without pity.

Naturally, to keep such monstrous social edifices upright, one had to resort to violence. But this violence, exercised from the top downwards, inevitably brought about a counter-balancing violence. This phenomenon, which repeats itself throughout the history of the world, may be called " vertical violence ". To-day it reveals itself especially in the class-struggle : in spite of the most delightful slogans about " national unity ", the army in every country is ranged first and foremost against " the enemy at home ", that is, against the masses of labourers, petit bourgeois and industrial workers, who might at any time be driven to revolt.

Besides this, all civilizations have tended to grow at the expense of those less developed and above all, those weaker physically and materially, even though the latter may have been more advanced from the cultural point of view. War, class struggle, private property, all emerged at about the same time. And in the course of centuries the ruling classes have been able more and more to monopolize violence, using the State as intermediary (*lo stato*, a word dating from the Italian Renaissance which originally meant " the rulers and the party they represent "). They were able in the long run so to enlarge the power of the State that now— according to Carl Schmitt, a German sociologist— supreme political authority is characterized by the *jus belli*, the right to declare and to wage war, and by the right which every Government reserves to demand at any moment from every citizen, who is nothing but a subject after all, the *Todesbereitschaft und Tötungsbereitschaft*, which means, readiness both to kill and be killed in murderous conflicts against no matter whom and for no matter what cause. This typical attribute of political sovereignty has been further strengthened by the League of Nations Covenant.[1]

From all this there comes what in the history of mankind may be described as "horizontal violence", which has not failed to end up, as was inevitable, in the Great War of 1914. When we speak of "war", it is usually a question of this horizontal violence being turned against " the enemy abroad ". We also understand by this word all kinds of " civil wars ", " religious wars ", etc., which in any case often coincide with economic, political and class wars.

Funck-Bretano gives a striking example of these mixed wars : the Hundred Years War, which, according to him, was much more civil than foreign : the struggle of the artisans against the patricians, the guilds against

---

[1] *Cf.* Carl Schmitt, " Begriff des Politischen," *Archiv. fur Sozialwissenschaft und Sozialpolitik*, 1927, pp. 1-33. *Cf.* my book, *Contre a Guerre Nouvelle*, pp. 193-4.

the nobles, the Burgundians against the Armagnacs, the "Clauwerts" against the "Leliarts" in Flanders : as in Italy, the "popolo minuto" against the "popolo grasso", the Guelfs against the Ghibellines, the "whites" against the "blacks". Latin texts call them "minores" and "majores". In France, the People's Party is usually called *commun*.[1]

The kind of war with which we are here concerned has been principally "horizontal" : for the conquest of the surface of the earth. Its inevitable consequence was to destroy frontier after frontier.

Thus war certainly did contribute to the long process of unification of tribes, peoples and races. From this point of view, the deification of war (Mars, for instance) has had a certain cultural sense, and the great conquerors of antiquity did accomplish a more or less "divine" mission. Were they not looked upon as Men from Heaven ? An ever-stronger collective force was able not only to protect the more ancient civilizations from the ceaseless onslaughts of rapacious barbarians, but also to help on the interpenetration and interdependence of tribes, peoples and races. Alexander the Great, in the second part of the fourth century B.C. played an amazing part in the history of the world, uniting Asia and Europe by war (he believed himself, not entirely without justification, to be a kind of god). The Roman thirst for conquest made possible the diffusion of the noblest traditions of civilization in Asia Minor, Egypt and Greece, as far as to the barbarous coasts of the North Sea. The Crusades—however unchristian they were, and despite the atrocities committed against Jews and heathen—laid open again the West to Oriental influences and prepared the way

[1] Funck-Brentano, *La Renaissance*, p. 12.

for the Renaissance and the bourgeois Revolution. Calvinist violence safeguarded the Reformation against the Counter-Revolution. And, finally, from the Eighty Years War against Spain there sprang the liberty of the Netherlands.

Even the colonial wars of the white races, however rapacious, have contributed to the unification of the world, in spite of the countless atrocities, even if only by scourging the Asiatic peoples, sunk in their age-long lethargy, into self-realization. And we know how " out of the Europeanization of Asia came the revolt of Asia against Europe ".[1]

But let us just think how military science has developed since Napoleon above all. The technique of war seems now to have reached the peak of perfection. While modern civilization grows ever more complex and refined, thereby becoming more vulnerable, the world has put such ingenuity into increasing the potentialities of war for devastation, that the forces of destruction can be seen to gain on those of construction. Yet, the World War itself, futile as it was, had a certain civilizing value : it brought about a gigantic proletarian revolution, which, in spite of countless errors and weaknesses—especially the recourse to an unheard of violence, of which we shall speak again—gave a new impulse to the lives of tens of millions of human beings : it was favourable to the struggle for freedom of oppressed nations and exploited races, to the development of medicine and hygiene, to the emancipation of women, etc.

And what is even more, however ferocious may have been the long train of wars which threw down one frontier after another, it has brought about the growth

[1] Grousset, *Le Réveil de l'Asie*, p. 111.

of a human conscience which has steadily widened : the incessant mingling of races and civilizations has gradually given rise to the conception of " humanity ". In spite of innumerable oppositions of class, race and tradition, certain exceptionally gifted individuals have ended by grasping the idea of " the human race ", which, passing over all the official boundaries, has gone on growing ever since. Men have come to recognize their neighbour in a foreigner, in a one-time enemy, even in a slave ; they got accustomed to seeing, in the foe before them, another . . . themselves. From about 800 years before Christ, a universal and a human conscience has slowly arisen in men and women of lofty intuition and profound sense of solidarity, in the more advanced civilizations. In China, India, the Near East, in Greece, people slowly began to see that violence, not only in the personal relations of man to man, but between people and people and race and race, could only be something provisional and ephemeral : that in the history of the world, the effort must be more and more towards a civilizing unity of the globe, in the self-realization of the human race : and, for this self-realization, there was need of an intense struggle, which would nevertheless diminish in violence from the moment when violent methods could be seen to be in flagrant conflict with true human nature and the noblest goals of life.[1]

Here, stripped of all magical coverings, are the essential conclusions reached by these forerunners of the new humanity :

Violence will be piled on violence, and war on war :

[1] *Cf.* B. de Ligt, *La Paix Créatrice*, I.

Empires will tear each other in pieces so ferociously that finally war, famine and pestilence will rage as never before :

But then, the whole system of violence throughout the world will crumble, and universal peace, so fervently hoped for by the martyred peoples, will come, and justice for one and all will be established on earth.

Those who foresaw and proclaimed these future trends were the rare exception for centuries. They were held by public opinion—which clung to traditions more ancient but growing obsolete—to be Utopians, not unattractive, perhaps, but all the more dangerous for that.

At certain critical stages in history, the official powers would have them isolated as madmen, if not tortured, imprisoned or killed, as ordinary criminals.

Without a doubt, where the geographical, economical and political conditions were favourable, there did appear here and there civilizations that were relatively peaceful, where belief in the divine significance of force did not only grow weaker but died out altogether ; in India and China, for instance. But there, too, violence remained at any rate latent, ready to resume its virulence at any moment. Taking a bird's eye view of the history of our planet, we must admit that up to the present, both vertical and horizontal violence have played an extremely important rôle. There is no civilization, when we come down to brass tacks, which is not held together by violence. Every " right "—affirms Rudolf von Ihering—has been won by violence and can only be defended by it : in our times still, law is imposed and maintained by force.

Modern bellicists such as Fuller assume therefore that since " human nature has not changed " and " the duty of a nation is to survive ", war, that divine force of "creative destruction ", will continue for ever. For thousands of years, man was the hunter who had to kill for food, for warmth, for protection, while the first desire of the woman, dependent on him, was to preserve life. " Life lives on life," and cannibalism was once a normal thing. Men were always competitors, as nations are now, especially great civilized nations ; and even now, every nation is " hunting " in the world not only for food, warmth and protection, but for wealth and honour. " We are animals ; some of us gentle, others ferocious, and those of carnivorous tastes live on those who browse the tender herbs of life. We are slaves of a hunting spirit, which we may quell but cannot slay."

> . . . Nought shall make us rue
> If England to itself do rest but true.[1]

In this same spirit, Homer Lea declares that " the basic principle of war has been the same for all time and will continue so until the end of human contention. Only the immediate causes and manner of war, those last straws that break down the peace of nations, alter from age to age. In the past, it was the individual who was the predominant factor ; to-day nations ; to-morrow, races."[2]

Seeley, also, in his *Expansion of England* says that the right of a people to their land depends on force and violence, and that the Anglo-Saxons, in their conquest of Empire, were impelled by the love of force and

[1] Fuller, *The Reformation of War*, pp. vii-xv, 1-23, 57, 279-83.
[2] Lea, *The Day of the Saxon*, pp. 14-15.

covetousness. " Wars have brought about the formation of this Empire, and wars will prolong or shorten its existence."[1] All must be subordinated to the imperial-istic interests of the country which will not stop at break-ing the most sacred treaties, and will, if need be, violate territories officially recognized as neutral : " the Empire is not moved by the sanctity of neutrality"—continued Homer Lea, in 1912, two years before the Reich violated the neutrality of Belgium ; "no nation has violated neutral territory and denied their obligations more frequently than the Saxon." The occupation by the Saxon of neutral territory " is a territorial and not a moral violation . . . England and other nations violated both peace and neutrality in the beginning of the nineteenth century". It is clear that, once such a principle of international conduct was accepted, Germany had every justification for occupying Belgium, Japan for conquering Manchuria and Korea, Italy for appropriating Tripoli and Abyssinia, etc.

We must realize that, stimulated by the hunting spirit, men have for centuries made themselves Empire after Empire, until the Anglo-Saxon branch of the Nordic family attained world power, beginning in the sixteenth century. In a fanatically anti-English book[2] published in 1935, Arturo Labriolo stated that the Angles, Saxons and Jutes, after almost completely destroying the ancient British population of Roman times by those same methods which fifteen centuries later they were to employ in annihilating the population of Tasmania, were still, in the sixth century, savages given up to cannibalism ; and that according to Buckle,

[1] Homer Lea, p. 226.
[2] A. Labriolo, *Le Crépuscule de la Civilisation*, pp. 90, 94.

in Scotland, there were cannibals in the land as late as 1389 ; and that the blond Northerners remained savage until a quite recent date. " Can we really believe that sixteen centuries have been enough to cure the English of their cannibalism ? " A remark which, despite its exaggeration, contains a good deal of truth. However, the events of 1936-7 have also shown that twenty centuries have not been enough to cure the Italians of the habits of the Roman wolf . . .

In the meantime, the question must be faced whether Man can continue to allow himself to be enslaved by his savage instincts, however deeply they may be rooted in his nature.   In the last few hundred years, the complexity and universality of human civilization has enormously increased ; the interdependence of peoples and races grows daily ; the development of agriculture, of industry, of commerce and communication, as well as the individual and collective well-being of the masses, greater than ever before in history, has an urgent need of general security outside the limits of national, imperial and continental frontiers.   The development of world civilization, as its peak, is becoming more and more vulnerable.   And the satisfaction of basic needs, economic, sexual, cultural, of man, such as hunger, love, religion, science, depends as at no other time on political and social peace.   This is the reason that the desire for peace is spread over all peoples and classes.   And finally, the technical development of warfare promises such horrors to those who use them as will be equally terrible for victors and vanquished alike.

Thus Lahy-Hollebecque, the military expert : " The development of agriculture and of industry, the foundation of towns with their vast reserves of food and material goods, while responsible for the taste for material comfort in man, as also for his attachment to land and home, gives rise to new demands, of which the most insistent is the desire for peace.   We know by experience that it can be a matter of only a few hours for the labour of centuries to be destroyed.   Fear of losing the fruits of long effort, and of becoming prey to misery, at length induced in man a little wisdom.   .   .   . Beneath the double pressure of economic necessities peace begins to be organized, slowly and painfully at first, but following certain procedures which will gradually take effect on the masses.   .   .   . Perhaps the admixture of races and cultures which results from war will serve to pave the way towards harmony of groups, where economic prosperity, instead of being a cause of warfare, will be a means towards agreement.   It is possible also that war will be killed by its own excesses."

However true it may be that man has for thousands of years needed violence and war in order to survive, and to enable him to nourish and protect his family, his town, his nation, his race, the wars " hated by mothers ", *bella matribus detesta*, have never been hated by women as in our own days.   For whereas, in former times, they accepted with resignation or with complaint the fate of themselves and their children, entrusting their future to their menfolk, now that they have emancipated themselves, they are beginning to protest in thousands against the unthinkable cruelties and crazy excesses of " civilized " warfare, which threatens the civil population as much as the army, and especially the children, the coming generation, the future of mankind.

We may admit that the development of savage tribes, —through the different stages of hunter, fisher, pastoral and agricultural dwellers in the stone age, the bronze, iron and steel age, up till modern times,—that all this development from savagery to civilization could not have taken place without war. However, history itself asks us the question, whether human development can still use the methods of violence at a time when we are passing from the stage of national civilizations to that of world-wide civilization, a stage which has, as a necessary condition, universal peace.

In the last few centuries, we have been witnessing the birth of a new type of man whose special conditions and needs are such that the aspect of the whole planet is beginning to be changed.[1] " We are now in a very different position from that which our far-back forefathers enjoyed. . . . Perfection we have not, and some countries are more retarded in their growth than others, but everywhere there is a security that defies comparison with any previous period of history. In short, we have solved the problem of civil order. . . . War is not necessary. Times are changed, and we need no longer slaughter each other."[2] " Famine, pestilence and war are no longer essential for the advancement of the human race."[3]

Though in other times war was deified, being looked upon as good, for some time now we have begun to condemn it as only too human and unworthy of man. To-day the great majority of those who believe in it try to justify it as a necessary evil. The number who regard it as a useless evil, and even as *das radikale Bose*, increases as mankind becomes more humane and war more inhuman. The dream, never far from the heart of mankind, of a return to the relatively peaceful past in a

---

[1] *Cf.* Alfred H. Fried, *Handbuch der Friedensbewegung*, I, pp. 3-4.
[2] Maclagan, *International Prohibition of War*, pp. 18, 21.
[3] W. Reade, *The Martyrdom of Man*, p. 447.

harmonious future, has increased every time that war has taken on more cruel and inhuman forms. Thus bellicism provokes pacifism, and militarism anti-militarism. And at a time when the science of war is at its zenith, there is beginning a science of peace which tries to satisfy, on a higher level, the economic and social needs and psychic tendencies which in other times found their fulfilment in war.

War begins to become an anachronism. Even Napoleon in his meditations at St Helena, declared : " In the future, there lie intelligence, industry, peace. In the past, brutality, privilege and ignorance."[1] However great the progress of the anti-war movement the world over since the eighth century B.C., has been, it is still slight compared with the enormous development of collective murder. The battle for peace has hardly begun. Will it end with the foundation of universal peace ?

One thing is certain, and that is that ever since the advent of capitalism and the machine age, the collective violence of war has become monstrous.

---

[1] *Cf.* Suzanne Bouillot, *Comment Réaliser la Paix*, p. 75.

Chapter III

VIOLENCE AND THE BOURGEOISIE

Krieg, Handel und Piraterie,
Dreieinig sind sie, nicht zu trennen.

Goethe.

The old struggle of the commons to overthrow the feudal powers and to subjugate the coloured races became more and more violent. The revolutionary bourgeoisie seized more and more brutally on the monopoly of property and power and thus established its own " rights ". From this point of view, its so-called Modern History is nothing but a rehash of Ancient History in a more civilized form. In any case, the bourgeoisie has never wished to do away with the exploitation of race and class : it wants to use it for its own ends. No doubt, in its struggle against the feudal powers, it has joined forces with the very lowest strata of society : it ranged itself—often with the discontented proletariat—against the nobility and clergy. But hardly had it come to power than it shoved these allies back into the gulf. Let us call to mind the revolutions of 1789, 1830 and of 1848 in France. Similar things happened in England and elsewhere, and are happening in Chiang Kai Chek's China to-day. On the other hand, the bourgeoisie was only too ready to annex the nobility and clergy, as soon as they accepted its political, economic and moral direction. What is more, it managed by an ingenious system of social selection to skim the lower middle classes, the small peasantry and the workers, and to get hold of tens of thousands of men of the type best suited to its régime and incorporate them in its own class.[1] And now it is going in for the exploitation of class and race more intensely than ever. It is with justice that Arturo Labriola speaks severely of this civilization : " It is an *instrumental civilization*, that is to say, everything about it is subject to the need of enriching oneself, and it is even able to develop science and art on this basis, admittedly. The earth is an instrument, and man too is an instrument. Wherever it finds men weak enough to give way before violence or to accept a yoke, this civilization imposes its laws. Even to-day, when its knell is about to strike, it still tries to make man the instrument of its riches. Covet, seize, such is the law of its greed."[2]

A mentality such as this is the only thing which can explain the innumerable cruelties practised by white Christians on the coloured heathen. Is it in self-justification that we have been repeating for centuries that coloured people are usually barbarous and blood-thirsty. From our childhood we have been taught to believe, by a whole mass of literature, that the Redskins *e.g.* are exceptionally cruel as well as being born warriors. The truth is quite different, however. In the first place, war is not congenital : the Warrior Man is a myth. Even in present-day Europe, man is so far from being naturally inclined to war that the States have to force on him a special education and training in order to transform him into a soldier. Warlike education and training were as necessary for the Indians as for Europeans. They also did not resort to violence except under special conditions. The

[1] *Cf.* Cole, *Labour in the Commonwealth*, pp. 65-72.
[2] A. Labriola, *Le Crépuscule de la Civilisation*, p. 54.

mentality of the different tribes was, furthermore, so diverse that there might be more difference between such and such a Redskin than between an Arab and a Norwegian, an Englishman or a Turk.

At the time of the White invasions, the Iroquois had already got beyond the war stage. This tribe which, in the social field, had organized itself in the freest possible manner according to the methods of self-government, had created a juridico-social unity through all their vast territory, in collaboration with the Mohawks, as far back as the fifteenth century, not to mention the maintenance of a general peace unknown to the Christian Europe of that time. Lahy-Hollebecque states that this League was a particularly successful effort to realize those very methods of arbitration and co-operation which the International Court of the Hague and the League of Nations are trying—with what difficulty !—to establish to-day. We can assert that this peaceful organization of the Redskins was a presage of the great politico-social unity of the United States of America, with its frontiers open towards Canada.

There are other examples of alliances for peace in history, as for example the Amphictyonias in the pre-Christian Greece, those famous tribal assemblies, federated for political and religious ends, whose delegates or amphictyons were given the task of deliberating on the general interest and of settling whatever disputes might crop up between them. But, up to the fifteenth century, no one in Europe had ever tried to organize peace in so effective and humane a manner as the Iroquois. They attributed the foundation of their League to Hiawatha, a kind of legendary Messiah, the true incarnation of human civilization and progress, whom Hale considers as the deification of some historical personage, and about whom Longfellow wrote one of his most famous poems. According to Indian tradition, Hiawatha, the revered chief of the Onondagas, had taught them agriculture, navigation, medicine, the arts, and all kinds of magical means of subduing nature to man ; it was he, too, who had persuaded his people in the name of the Great Spirit to take the initiative in establishing a true universal peace. This peace which was to expand not by measures of violence and tyranny but by free adhesion seemed on the way to covering the whole North American continent when the whites arrived. Then, and then only, this " political masterpiece " began to decline.[1]

Besides, even the Apaches—one of the most warlike of the Redskin groups, whose members were far from being models of meekness—were accustomed always to respect the non-combatants. In most cases, they treated their prisoners of war with great consideration. If, by the force of circumstances, their worst enemy came and sought refuge with them, he became sacred through being a guest, and was religiously respected. None did him the slightest harm, whatever the hatred they felt on his account. They went so far as to give him every chance to flee and to defend himself : a horse, weapons, victuals, information concerning the route he should take, and while he remained within the limits of the sanctuary, no one raised a hand against him.

The Redskins have always had the famous practice of scalping held up against them. What is not known is, that before the coming of the whites, this usage was completely unknown to the Indians of the plains. As the Scythians did formerly in Europe, a few Red Indian tribes practised this torture, which was based on a religious superstition that the scalped warrior could not be taken to the Happy Hunting Grounds by the Great Spirit and so could not torment the living after his death. In fact, one of the first benefits brought by the civilizing Christians to the Sioux, Cheyennes and Comanches was this cruel practice. European collectors were in a great hurry, when they heard of it, to secure these hideous trophies and to buy them at

[1] *Cf.* Lahy-Hollebecque, in *L'Évolution Humaine des Origines à nos Jours*, p. 131 ; Breysig, *Vom Geschichtlichen Werden*, pp. 191-5 ; B. de Ligt, *La Paix Créatrice*, p. 367.

no matter what price ; and, with the added attraction of its commercial value, the Redskins soon came to look on the scalp as a symbol of heroism and virility. " And there go the Indians, chasing the hair of men's heads with the same good will as they hunt for furs for the Hudson Bay Company, and seeing no more harm in it." So that, thanks to the teaching of their Christian civilizers, in the seventeenth century, every Redskin knew how to scalp.[1]

In fact, it was the whites who introduced countless violences, treasons and corruptions into North America, and who must answer for the degeneration and almost complete extinction of the native population. The hateful crimes committed by European colonists against them beggar description ; they poisoned them with alcohol, which they had never tasted before ; they broke the treaties which they had made together ; they stole their lands ; they made slaves of them. " The only good Indian is a dead Indian," said the New England colonists. The Border colonists held the lives of the natives shamefully cheap. During the conquest of the Far West, right in the nineteenth century, Indian tribes who still survived were hunted down incessantly like herds of wild animals. Any excuse was good enough against the Redskins, and the slightest rising on their part brought about a pitiless massacre.

And yet, even in the midst of hostilities such as these, the old desire of universal peace never quite left the Indian mind. Once they had come into contact with Christianity, the Redskins showed themselves very susceptible to the ancient dreams of political and social harmony of the Hebrew prophets. After the Jews, the greatest number of the prophets of peace come from the Red Indians. Many of them forbade not only war among themselves but war with the whites. Taking their inspiration from Amos, Isaiah and Jeremiah, they looked on themselves as the chosen of God and awaited

[1] *Cf.* Thévenin and Coze, *Moeurs et histoire des Peaux-Rouges,* pp. 73-8.

a last world crisis which would mean the decline of the devilish whites ; after the Last Judgment of all unbelievers and malefactors, the earth would renew itself and the believers would enjoy perfect happiness in Paradise restored. Some of these prophets even demanded that all weapons should be put away at once, roundly condemned polygamy and the use of fermented drinks.[1]

That is why the Quaker experiment met with such success in Pennsylvania, a State with no army, as large as England, which maintained itself for more than seventy years without any violence whatsoever. While the Redskins, considering themselves in a state of legitimate defence, continually attacked and killed the whites, who in turn were always attacking and killing them, they spared not only all the inhabitants of Pennsylvania but all the Quaker farms in America, even the most isolated of them, whose doors were also open day and night. The " holy experiment " in Pennsylvania did not come to an end until the Quakers there had become a minority, owing to an influx of other whites into the country. Then the war habit reappeared. But the Redskins always continued to respect the members of non-violent Christian sects.[2]

The great merit of William Christie MacLeod is to have described, in his book *The American Indian Frontier* the relations between white and redskin, from the aborigines' point of view. Without falling into the exaggerated idealization of the Red Indian as Montaigne and Rousseau did, MacLeod has proved that the so-called ferocity of Indians and their warlike mentality are simply legends, and that the cruelties practised against them by the whites are infinitely worse and more thought-out. The sum of MacLeod's researches is to confirm the purely instrumental and inhuman character of modern civilization.

[1] *Cf.* MacLeod, *The American Indian Frontier*, pp. 506-7 ; Allen, *The Fight for Peace*, p. 579.

[2] *Cf.* de Ligt, *La Paix Créatrice*, pp. 313-15.

In this direction, there is still much to be done : the whole history of the discoveries of new countries— the two Americas, Africa, India, Australia—and of the attitude of white people towards coloured is one of everlasting shame to official Christianity. Since Columbus, Pizarro and Cortès, representatives of our " civilization of iron, conquest and booty " stormed the New World like true *conquistadores*, the foundations of human society have been shattered throughout the world.

In 1496, the Pope Alexander VI divided the whole world between Spain and Portugal. In 1516, Charles V granted to the Flemings the right of transporting black slaves and selling them in America. Some years later, the Holy See confirmed the doctrine promulgated in the middle of the fifteenth century by Rome, that it is permissible for a Christian to strip the heathen of all he has and to reduce him to perpetual slavery. In England, the famous negro-trader Captain Hawkins received his letters patent of nobility because he had introduced a new trade, that of the traffic in human beings, into the country. In the eighteenth century, the monopoly of hunting, transporting and selling black flesh and blood passed into English hands. A fleet of 192 ships was concentrated at Liverpool and transported 200,000 slaves every year. According to Merival, the prosperity of Manchester and Liverpool is built on the blood of slaves. The same is true of Bristol.

Nowadays, science recognizes the rich diversity of the pre-Columbian civilizations, of which many had equalled, if not surpassed, those of Europe. They give that of the Mayas, that deeply pacifist and religious race, where science and religion were one, and where they had never practised slavery and lived as vegetarians. Here again, self-government was so highly developed in them that the State, as a bureaucratic and oppressive machine, was utterly superfluous. " Unblutig und friedlich verlief überhaupt das Leben dieses Volkes," says the German author Haebler. Indeed, at the classic phase of their evolution, the Mayas were complete strangers to the idea of war.

Modern science also paints for us the civilization of the Incas, whose religious philosophy before the coming of Columbus was equal to that of the Italian Renaissance, which, in Europe, was the most sublime of the epoch and greatly superior to the narrow dogmas of the Reformation. Inca civilization, which was probably higher than that of Europe at the same time, distinguished itself especially by developing an education favourable to the harmonious growth of mind and body along parallel lines. It showed a complete balance between order and liberty, unity and co-ordination.

Arturo Labriola, in his book concerning the Occident and the coloured peoples, has painted a moving picture of the evils which white civilization has spread all over the world, one of the least known and most recent of which was the extermination in Africa of the ancient kingdom of Benin, with all its art and civilization, by the English in 1897.

We owe it chiefly to the researches of the German ethnologist Frobenius that we realize how, when the whites penetrated into the Black Continent, they found there many well-organized States, often administered to perfection, whose people were as civilized as any Europeans of the same time. But the Moroccan, Arab and, above all, white invasions have done nothing but force Africa back into a past from which she had progressed with the utmost difficulty. Portuguese, French, Dutch, English, vied with each other in hunting down the human quarry. " Thus, one continent emptied itself into another, little by little . . ."[1] A century ago, Cooper put at five and a half millions the number of Negroes in the United States, the sad relic of the 100,000,000 Africans who were the victims of this shameful trade.[2]

And we have not yet touched on the subjugation of the Indies, Indonesia, Indochina and of Australia,

[1] Ch. de la Roncière, *Nègres et Négriers*, p. 88.
[2] *Cf.* Labriola, *Le Crépuscule de la Civilisation*, p. 247.

where the Tasmanians were completely wiped out, nor on what China has had to endure since the middle of the last century, with the Christians at her side to civilize her. "Humanity and justice were virtues which were always left behind at the Cape of Good Hope by passengers for India."[1] Winwood Reade's remark is enough. At the present time, the Europeans rule over nearly 1,000,000,000 Asiatics and Africans, and the democratic England competes with Fascist Italy in hypercivilization of method for imposing and maintaining their colonial sovereignty. Let us but remember what happened in Abyssinia in 1936 and on the North West Frontier in India in 1937.

Never before has any caste, state or class resorted to violence, both vertical and horizontal, to the same extent as this bourgeoisie. Acute individual competition to amass capital (lands, means of production, money) and profits, on which its entire social system is based, turned into an even bitterer rivalry between groups (for, just as brigands band together for strength, so does one capitalist join with another) and finally became a struggle between nation and nation. For many centuries now, in social life, in the church, school, in literature, etc., a taste for rapine, greed, domination, glory, all passions that are aggressive in tendency, have been encouraged in a more and more one-sided manner, at the expense of the social instincts. These have been suppressed, falsified or misused—a process of real moral and spiritual poisoning which, in the long run, is what makes the world wars and modern methods of scientific warfare possible.

The brutal combination of capitalism and nationalism gave birth to imperialism. Since the close of the nineteenth century, the cry has always been for

[1] Reade, *The Martyrdom of Man*, p. 279.

I. Markets for Export.

II. Raw Materials.

III. Cheap Labour.

IV. Countries open to Emigration.

V. Enterprises which would show the highest return.

I. Because, in modern society, we do not work in order to supply the needs of all but to increase the wealth of those who already possess it at the expense of the masses, who are exploited both as consumers and producers ; and so, when the possibilities of agricultural and industrial production open out to the amazing extent they do to-day, the national market becomes too narrow for the national capital : however great the needs of their countrymen who do not possess any capital, the capitalists refuse to supply them if it brings nothing in, and, in spite of their ostentatious patriotism, look for their markets abroad. In the language of financiers, it is of prime importance that outlay should show a return.

II. Because, the home soil not containing all the raw materials which are needed for agriculture, for industry and, above all, for supplying the means of production, it was necessary to obtain from abroad those products which only certain climates and soils could yield.

III. Because, the opposition of the white working-classes to the horizontal violence of the capitalist class continually gaining strength, and the workers in towns winning increased wages, shorter hours, insurances, pensions, etc., the white exploiters found it profitable to obtain their labour from men of so-called inferior race, backward economically and socially and whose needs are extremely limited. In Indonesia, for instance, a native—we are not speaking of the Dutch Governor-General—" can live " according to an official statement made by the Dutch Government at the Hague, " on less than twenty-five French centimes a day ". Capitalists can therefore make infinitely more out there than at home, where the working-class standard of living has steadily risen.

4

IV. Because several capitalist nations, being less and less able to provide their growing populations with work and the means of subsistence, look round for lands to which these people can emigrate.

V. Because although the love of capitalists for their own country is naturally beyond compare if, by placing money in enterprises at home they reap a small profit and by placing money abroad, even among heathen or cannibals, they reap a large profit, it would be a poor capitalist indeed who did not export thither, even if by so doing he risked a great part of his capital, and who did not act up to the proverb : " There, where I feel at home, is my country."

The promised land of the patriotic capitalists at the present time would seem to be the international armament industry.

Efforts were made chiefly to dominate the colonial and semi-colonial territories of which there was an ever-growing need. The flag followed the capital and the capital followed the army. That is to say, the nation's defence services were placed at the disposal of its capitalists. The consequence of this was unheard of national armaments and the general slavery of conscription. An ever-increasing part of economic life was devoted to the fabrication of non-productive means of violence. That is to say, production was used more and more for destruction !

For these gigantic armies needed guns and swords by the million, an ever-increasing number of cannon, machine-guns, a larger supply of ammunition, etc. It was necessary to feed and clothe thousands of soldiers, and build them barracks and forts, all over the place, even underground. Further, they began to construct great fleets, which swallowed billions and, to crown it all, air-fleets intended for three-dimensional warfare, and which to-day can rise right into the stratosphere. Everywhere, war budgets upset the national budgets' balance. To contract more and more debts, to meet their financial obligations less and less, became the normal thing for the imperialistic powers. According to the " Stock Exchange Official Intelligence " in 1931, the national debt of forty-nine different countries amounted to 40,000 millions of pounds sterling.   Let us take Holland, not one of the great countries, whose national debt amounts to something like 400 millions of pounds sterling, to which we must add 200 millions for her Colonies.   For the most part these debts—says the *Haagsche Post* of December 16th, 1933, come from war expenses and armaments.   Of all this money, an infinitesimal part is devoted to public works, and these, if we study them, are not always of a constructive nature. As for France, Henri Décugis, in his book *The Destiny of the White Races* draws attention to the facts that her debt, national and otherwise, is 4,400 millions of pounds sterling.

And so we see a disturbance not only in financial but in moral life, in an increasing number of countries. It has become normal for men to know how to use the bayonet in a highly expert way and to spit anyone on it at the command of his government : every woman may be called on to manufacture bombs or to perform any other task in the international march of destruction. In various Protestant countries, young men are initiated into universal murder and the universal love of Christ at the same time.   One even finds special religious instruction for soldiers, for which the State pays a special fee to the pastor.   And in those Catholic countries where conscription is in force, however much the priests are in a position, as spiritual counsellors, to realize the pernicious influence of Mars and Venus Vulgivaga on the conscripts, they still continue to confess and absolve them. And so the countries are ranged one against the other, like huge camps of war. Each nation has become a permanent menace to the other. They have fallen victim to collective maladies : persecution mania and hysteria. Heaven knows what spectre has come to haunt these nations : a common anguish weighs on them day and night. An absolute mistrust of all foreign countries has become, since 1914, the basic principle of all policy ; a mistrust which is exploited in diabolical fashion by the directors of the Armaments International with the sole aim of reaping unbounded gain.

In our time, nearly every modern State is making unheard of preparations for a World War before which the imagination reels. Hence the growing tendency of States to autarchy, which makes them self-supporting economically and as independent of foreigners in war-time as possible. This economic process, thanks to which the world is divided and torn farther apart every day, is strengthened by the " structural crisis " in capitalism which is driving all the countries to solve its own social and economic difficulties artificially behind constantly rising customs barriers, to the detriment of the popular masses at home and in the colonies. And that in spite of world economic conditions so intricate that they have brought about an interdependence of every land on the globe, to the point where they will never be able to survive without constant co-operation.

So there we are, in a political and economic situation which risks to provoke a dangerous explosion at any moment, especially as the social condition of the masses of workers, small bourgeois and labourers has been growing steadily worse (bankruptcy, unemployment, etc.), becoming for some of them so wretched that they look on war simply as one way of escaping their miserable fate.

Apart from this, there are all kinds of unconscious and subconscious tensions, moral and sexual, which drive men on to collective murder in every country.

It is especially in *Sittengeschichte des Weltkrieges*, an encyclopaedic work published by Mr Magnus Hirschfeld —Director of the celebrated Institute of Scientific Sexual Research in Berlin, which was closed down by Hitler—that scholars have shown the mutual influence of sexual life and homicidal conflict, arriving at the conclusion that modern warfare is a stupendous crime against the sexual and moral life of the human race, and that every responsible man must use all his strength in the name of " jeopardized love " to prevent the return of war.

Meanwhile, in the name of the country, of God, of humanity, of Socialism or Communism, with the help of professors, literary men, historians, philosophers, journalists, politicians, pastors, priests, a whole code of honour for the universal carnage has been drawn up. Thus, the minds of millions of men have been poisoned, brought up as they were in the superstition, as stupid as criminal, that violence and war are indispensable from the practical point of view, even if they are not inevitable from the metaphysical point of view. And this moral poisoning set in at the very time when the development of modern technical warfare has resulted in weapons which strike at the conquerors as much as at the conquered : at the very time when history began to justify the age-old pacifist ideas of the more enlightened of mankind and when the requirements of the earthy utilitarianism unquestionably coincided with those of the most ardent idealism : when, finally, war, as a consequence of the growth in scientific methods of destruction had become, so to speak, impossible and had shown itself to be an activity as inept as cruel.

At the very time, in short, when " impossible-ism " went over to the bellicists !

The Greeks were wont to say in speaking of the God of War, " Ares fells the best men " and the poet Schiller cried, " Ja, der Krieg verschlingt die Besten ! (War devours the best).[1]   In fact, we may wonder if from the viewpoint of biology, eugenics and civilization itself, war has not been the cause for a long time past of a kind of inverted selection, with a downward trend. Dr S. R. Steinmetz, the well-known author of *Soziologie des Krieges* admits in the *Handwörterbuch d. Soziologie* of Ierkandt that wars have given rise to a disquieting counter-selection, above all since the introduction of conscription.   But this would be counter-balanced by the fact that the healthiest men are not always the most gifted, that in modern scientific warfare the intellectuals are sent less and less into the trenches, that a great part of the soldiers have already done their *Gattenpflicht*, that is to say, they have got their descendants before sacrificing their lives, so that the future of the race is assured—and that altogether it seems probable that the more healthy and gifted nations will survive thanks to a kind of collective selection.[2]   But this thesis must be disproved.

Even in the nineteenth century, Darwin expressed his anxiety at the fact that in every modern country, the armies seized on the best : "   .   .   .   the finest young men are taken by conscription or are enlisted. They are thus exposed to early death during war,

[1] *Cf.* O. Kraus, *Der Krieg, die Friedensfrage und die Philosophie*, p. 18.

[2] *Cf. Handwörterbuch der Soziologie*, pp. 281-2.

are often tempted into vice. . . . On the other hand, the shorter and feebler men, with poor constitutions, are left at home."[1]   And when Darwin wrote that, he was very far from vizualizing the technique of war on the lines along which it has steadily developed ever since.   In a recent book, *Le Destin des Races Blanches*, Henri Décugis has shown and proved how the Great War was in effect an attack on humanity itself from the biological, eugenic and cultural point of view.   Marshal Lyautey was right when he said that " the war of the whites " had cost them very dear.   No doubt the millions who fell in the Great War have already been replaced, but " the average quality has dropped atrociously, which goes to show the absurdity of Von Bernhardi's theories about the regenerating effects of war.   Yes, the natural selection of the weak and ill ! "[2]   The American Professor N. M. Butler, one of the most eminent scientists of his country, and one who has given the question of war some careful study, has not hesitated to declare that a new World War would constitute a national and international suicide—a statement which contains no exaggeration.   " It is enough to analyse one branch after another of the economic and social situation in the different countries of the world and of Europe in particular, to be convinced of this."[3]

[1] Darwin, *Descent of Man*, 2nd ed., p. 134, *cf*. Decugis, p. 5.

[2] Maurice Martin du Gard, " Le Destin des Races Blanches," *Les Nouvelles Littéraires*, April 6th, 1934.

[3] Décugis, p. 10.

Chapter IV

THE ABSURDITY OF BOURGEOIS PACIFISM

> Those who, in all good faith, imagine they
> are defending peace when they defend modern
> society against us, are really, without wishing
> it or knowing it, defending the standing
> possibility of war.
>
> Jaurès.

It must be said that, thanks to the Christianity of
certain sects and heretics, to the humanism of the
Renaissance and the *Aufklärung*, to the ideals of the
bourgeois Revolution and to the principles of revolutionary Socialism, the public conscience of the more
civilized nations has at last reached a level where the
uselessness and the wickedness of war is openly recognized. The voice of this conscience was seconded by
that of reason, which in turn was more and more
influenced by economic considerations. In the face
of the dire consequences of the Napoleonic Wars there
arose a pacifist movement during the nineteenth century
which steadily gained ground, and from one continent
to another and from congress to congress war was
condemned as contrary to reason and morality.
Although at the beginning of the twentieth century
the modern States were all engaged in an armaments
race greater than any before, there were even then
millions of people—and a great many of bourgeois
outlook among them—simple enough to believe that
a great European war of the kind incessantly prophesied

by military experts and revolutionary sociologists together was less and less probable, civilized man having become, according to them, too reasonable to commit such a crime and his habits being too refined for him to fall back into such savagery.

It was even said, with premature enthusiasm, that before the twentieth century was reached the abolition of all armed conflict would be seen. " In the nineteenth century, we will see the end of war, of the scaffold, of hatred, of frontiers, of dogmas : and Man will live ! " cried Victor Hugo.

As if the reasoning and the feelings of a certain number of well-meaning men and women could do anything about it ! As if the economic and social trends of the world were determined by the refinement of manners in certain circles. In spite of all pacifism, however well-meaning and widespread it may have been, the World War broke out in the August of 1914. In spite of the most eloquent zeal in favour of the League of Nations, and the Briand-Kellogg pact, the nations have become more and more strangers to one another ever since the Treaty of Versailles, and, as we have already stated, have shut themselves up behind tariff walls which are always growing higher. Never in the history of the world have the nations taken to arming themselves so frenziedly as they have been doing ever since the World Conference on Disarmament (1932) ! Just as once it was said, " The nearer to Rome, the farther from God," so now we might say, " The nearer Geneva, the farther from peace." The whole talk of our time is of war and rumours of war.

Neither God nor the Devil can do anything : the underlying cause of modern war is the character itself of modern society. Violence and war are primary factors in the system of bourgeois capitalism. Our society is violent just as fog is wet.

There are three main reasons why violence is indispensable to it :

First, the rivalry between economic groups, each united by a pretended patriotism and composed of *entrepreneurs*, great business men, financiers, politicians, diplomats, military men of high rank, etc., grows more and more intense. National expansion conflicts with national expansions. To find markets, raw materials, cheap labour and excessive profits, etc., the national capital goes abroad, in furious competition. The capitalist nations, the national capital, bubbling over in a hell-broth, submerge a greater and greater part of the world. The result is that the earth becomes too small for this senseless competition. But the economic system demands for each part of the national capital and for each capitalist nation infinite possibilities of expansion and an always larger and faster sale of merchandise. Otherwise, profits come to a full-stop. And in a society such as ours, it is far more important to assure the profit of small but powerful coteries who own the money, the land and the means of production, than to satisfy the needs, physical, moral and spiritual, of the whole population of the world. And since to-day capital yields everywhere a smaller return, the one idea of each group of capitalists and imperialists is either to keep what it has or to seize what little still remains to be conquered.

We see, too, that owing to widely varying geographical, economical, political and social conditions, the face of the earth is divided up between the nations in a most capricious, not to say, arbitrary way : some have too much, others not enough : some have been lucky, others have got there too late. During the World War, I drew attention to the difference which exists between the satiated imperialist powers, who are therefore on the defensive, and the unsatisfied imperialist powers, who are on the aggressive. In the first category, now, are England, France and the Netherlands, for example. They are all more or less pacifist, that is to say, except when the *status quo*, which it is their first interest to preserve, is threatened, they do not seem anxious to enter into war with anyone. As is generally the case with those who have great possessions, they are conservative and hope to keep things as they are. Of course, they always remain ready for war. But their attitude is always more defensive than aggressive because they only want to keep what they have. These happy possessors are quite convinced that they hold their goods as a trust in perfect legitimacy ! " Our little Holland," for instance, is actually, as the map shows, a powerful imperialist State : she has a population greater than that of Germany, of which more than 60,000,000 men, women and children belong to the exploited races. She rules over an immense kingdom of tropical isles, which conceal within them inexhaustible riches and which are inhabited by " the poor heathen " who have to be raised to the level of Christians ! In the East Indies she controls the petrol springs of Djambi, Borneo, etc., and in the West Indies a flourishing port which is at the service of the petrol trade. She owns too, like any real great Power, cruisers, submarines and bombers, which she will use as occasion demands. The Dutch Lion, who seems in Europe

like a little pug-dog in Great Britain's lap, in the East
behaves like a wild beast towards the defenceless
coloured people and even towards its own sailors when
they do not bow to its laws. Remember the aerial
attack on the rebels of the " Zeven Provincien ", that
Dutch " Potemkin " ! For the Dutch Lion, too, must
defend its " right ", according to its motto, " Je
Maintiendrai ". But it goes without saying that it
does not want a war with the powerful German Eagle
or the really terrible British Lion !   .   .   .

Belgium, too, with her Congo, is completely pacifist,
just like France, whose one desire is to maintain the
stipulations of Versailles but who does not mind—nor
England either, for that matter—attacking the natives
of Africa and Asia with the most atrocious weapons
of modern warfare, and this in order to " defend justice
and peace " and to do her duty as guardian of the
" backward peoples ", the well-being and development
of such people forming—to quote Article 22 of the
Covenant of the League of Nations—a sacred trust
of civilization.

But neither Germany nor Italy nor Japan consider
themselves satisfied. Their imperialistic appetite remains
unappeased, and, like beasts of prey, they demand a
revision of the map of the world. They entered modern
history too late, and since the beneficiaries of the
present state of things have no intention of sharing out
their cake, these new imperialists are inclined to be
aggressive and bellicose.

And while London, which, is only, so to speak, a
point keeping the immense circle of the Empire concentrated in itself by enormous effort, and the United States,
whose strength rests on very wide and solid foundations,

try prudently and with great tact, sometimes by adopting an aggressive attitude and sometimes a defensive, to extend their economic domain as far as possible without having recourse to violence ; at the same time, to be quite secure, they make ready for a scientific war as no one ever has done before, in order to be able to defend their interests. Hence, for example, the clearly defined strategic line which crosses the Pacific Ocean from the Panama Canal right to the Philippines, passing by the island of Gouan.

Meanwhile, thanks to the unheard of development of scientific homicide, modern war requires such a technical, economical and financial effort that it has revealed itself as an impossibility for the small States, and become the privilege of the great Powers. Is there even one of these who would dare to undertake it alone ? That is why, since the World War, in spite of the League of Nations, the Briand-Kellogg Pact, and congresses and conferences of every sort on Disarmament, national and international tension has brought about a new system of alliances, coalitions and semi-alliances in which a group of small countries revolve about a certain great Power like planets round a sun. The great Powers continually try to attract each other's satellites into their own system. Here again, everything is based on bitter rivalry.

Even at Geneva, the prevailing principle is : each for himself. At the Disarmament Conference, one of the most honest of States, " neutral Switzerland " tried to keep as means of legitimate defence those weapons which were most adapted to her own strategic interest, but insisted on the international abolition of all other methods of war ! Holland did the same. Since every State politely waits for the other to enter the Temple of Disarmament the first, and since they all refuse this honour, they remain outside engaged in pointless discussion. Disarmament therefore remains impossible.

And here is the basic cause : without war, or at any rate, the threat of war, the capitalist system does not work. In the course of international negotiations, each State can only count in the eyes of the others in as far as she can make herself feared. Violence is one of the first rules of the imperialist game.

The second reason why violence is indispensable in modern society is, as we have said, that without it the ruling class would be completely unable to maintain its privileged position with regard to the exploited masses in each country. The army is used first and foremost to hold down the workers, small bourgeois and labourers when they become discontented. Above all, it is directed against " the enemy at home ", even when it is only an army of militia : Karl Liebknecht showed in 1907 how nowhere in the democratic world have national armed forces been turned against the citizens of the country more than in Switzerland—the Switzerland whose military system is always quoted as an example by the Paul Boncour school of pacifists.

The third reason why violence is indispensable to modern society is that the colonial empires have an ever greater need of it to rule the masses of coloured people. The colonial Powers, including Japan, are parasite States, living at the expense of 800,000,000 oppressed men and women in Africa and in Asia. Those who, at Geneva, declare themselves ready under special conditions to renounce the use of all kinds of destructive weapons in the event of a war with other States, reserve the right to use these same weapons in case they find it necessary to " restore order " in their colonies, in their capacity as " guardians of the peace ". The Dutch Government who, at Geneva, pleaded for the abolition of aerial bombardment in the event of war with other States cannot, as we have said, do without its bombers to uphold the " right " among the colonial peoples under its Christian protection.

As if all that were not enough, certain economic powers—who are specially interested in envenoming international disputes, exacerbating chauvinist sentiment and pushing on the armaments of the various States to extremes—are collaborating more and more closely together, over and above all frontiers and in spite of all wars. We speak of the bloody International of armament makers, whose pernicious influence makes itself felt in the very Disarmament Conferences, and who control a great part of the world's Press and politics. In 1914, while the Christian and the Socialist Internationals lamentably collapsed, this was the one International to maintain itself and even come out of the War strengthened.

One thing is certain : there is no essential difference between the policy of the so-called Christian States and that of the heathen States, between the principles which guide the imperialism of the English, the French, the Italian, the American, the German, the Dutch or the Belgian, and that which we find at the back of Japanese imperialism.

The most humane policy, that with a certain universal tendency, is to be found nowadays more in China and India, that is to say, among heathen people and among certain Zionists, or Jews. As for the others, it is six of one and half a dozen of the other.

By school and university, by church and Press, by cinema and politics, the same nationalist education, whose shades only vary in the different countries according to cultural traditions and secondary politico-economic conditions, is drummed into the youth and the working-classes. As soon as any tension arises in the relations between one country and another, all powers available are brought into play to encourage the masses to sacrifice themselves blindly for the national defence : *dulce et decorum est, pro patria mori!* How noble a duty, to die for the Mother Country, even if this mother enslaves her children by the million, impoverishes them and deprives them, either gradually or all at once, of their social and political rights.

All of this goes to show that bourgeois pacifism is in itself untenable. Even the Dutch bourgeoisie, of so peaceable a tradition, would cease to exist the moment it renounced the horizontal and vertical violence the nature of which we have defined above.

War, capitalism and imperialism, therefore make a common chord, like the three notes, tonic, third and fifth.

War, capitalism and imperialism form a veritable trinity.

War, capitalism and imperialism are co-substantial one with another, like the Father, Son and Holy Ghost.

And this latter holy trinity is freely invoked by the former profane one every time there is need of it.

Manuel Devaldes has laid great stress on the fact that one of the most important causes of war is of a demo-graphical nature.[1]   According to him, war is a social

[1] See also Allendy, *Capitalisme et Sexualité*, p. 239.

or international peculiarity proceeding from the struggle for existence, so that it does not arise from armaments but from surplus population and the psychological state of mind inherent in this—in the surplus population which, by necessitating war, also necessitates the armaments with which to make it. The production of human material calls for that of inhuman material. According to Devaldes, Mussolini has summed up this truth with the words : Expansion or explosion ! We must admit that in Germany and Japan, the pressure of population is enormous and that in Italy, the increase of population among the masses is encouraged by the Government, with a view to a possible war. The greater the population of a country grows, the greater its economic needs become and the more it feels the need of expansion. At last it happens that the surplus population produces all kinds of shortages, and the words of Malthus are borne out : " A shortage of necessities may first give birth to warlike habits and these again will contribute greatly to the diminution of the means of subsistence." Was not this phrase a prophecy of the entire World War and its consequences, asks Devaldes.

We must indeed admit that up to the present the pacifists have been too ready to neglect this point of view in considering war, especially since the development of modern hygiene has so greatly reduced mortality among the peoples. Even in ancient Greece, one of the principal causes of war was over-population.[1]

On the other hand, war cannot be explained in this way only. It would really be too simple, for instance, to try to account for all the Napoleonic wars by the fact that at that time France was the most thickly populated country in Europe. Anyhow, the reduction of surplus population becomes steadily less of a problem to the European and American countries, birth control having there become so widespread that it threatens dangerously to weaken the intellectual and moral

[1] *Cf.* Raglan, *The Science of Peace*, p. 94.

élite.[1] However great the growth of the German and Italian populations may be for the moment, the number of births in Berlin has already fallen below that of Paris, and in Italy Mussolini vainly tries to force up the ever descending curve of the birth-line.[2]

In France, depopulation, mainly of the countryside, threatens to become a cultural danger. And yet this country continues a dangerous imperialist policy impossible to account for by really demographical reasons.

In Germany, Hitler has won a remarkable though temporary victory in this direction : the number of German marriages in 1934 surpassed that in 1932 by 40·5 per cent., the second year having touched the lowest point in the curve ; the number of births in 1934 had surpassed that of 1933, when the birth-rate had been at its lowest, by 23·4 per cent. The reason for this recrudescence in birth, far from being of a demographical nature, is psycho-political : moved by a crazy enthusiasm, the young Nazis rushed by thousands blindly into marriage and procreation in honour of the Führer, who, although himself a bachelor, has cheerfully put a premium on matrimony. It may be foreseen, however, that this raising of the birth-rate will drop off as and when the German people, disillusioned by the economic and moral experiences of the new régime, recover their critical sense . . .

Anyhow, the evolution of industry, of agriculture and of the means of transport have completely changed this aspect of the question since the days of Malthus. " Over-population " is always a relative matter : it changes according to the economic, political and social circumstances of the peoples, and varies with the extent of their needs. In our time, although privations do certainly still exist, they are in flagrant contradiction to the immense possibilities of modern technique. They are one of the consequences of the lack of social and moral

[1] See Décugis.
[2] There is much of interest relating to this question in *Berichte zur Kultur und Zeitgeschichte*, January 27th, 1935, Vienna-Leipzig.

order which is typical of capital-imperialist régimes, whose goal is not the due satisfaction of mankind's needs but the piling up of profits for the ruling classes. The capitalists will even go as far as to create artificial shortage when these seem to them to be more profitable than plenty. The restriction and voluntary destruction of industrial and agrarian produce of these latter years, which in their way are premeditated crimes against humanity, have aroused the anger of all men and women of heart ; they are, in fact, a real self-accusation of the economic system in action. Thanks to modern science and technique, we have reached the point where the earth can produce infinitely more of the necessities of life than could be used by the whole population of the world.

In a word, the cases of over-population in the modern world are more political and economic in shape than biological or demographical. Yet the problem presents itself differently in each country, accordingly as they are highly industrialized (Europe, America, Japan) or as agriculture is still of the first importance.

It is above all in Asia that the struggle for the control of population opens up a new avenue towards universal peace. In India, for instance, where there is a population of 253 millions, this has in fifty years increased by 39 per cent. And yet the earth would be fully equal to providing for these immense numbers if it did not suffer the yoke of two different exploiters : native (the princes and great landowners) and colonial (foreign capital). Besides, the Neo-Malthusian propaganda, especially from America, is gaining a good deal of ground. The Neo-Malthusian League, founded in 1928, recruits its Indian members particularly from among the more cultivated classes. Even a large number of Christian missionaries shared in the views expressed at the last Lambeth Conference, when the English bishops admitted the social value of birth control.[1]

[1] De Zending in Britisch-Indie, *Nieuwe Rotterdamsche Courant*, May 22nd, 1935.

However, even in Asia, over-population is not the prime motive for war, nor usually the most important. The social determinism which unleashes war is generally much more complex. It consists as we have seen in the interplay of a multiplicity of causes which are demogogic, economic, psychologic, etc. In modern imperialism, the question of " national honour " can absorb a people to such an extent that they are willing to put aside their economic interests. On the other hand, we may be menaced by racial wars, caused chiefly by the feelings of inferiority, produced among coloured people by the contemptuous attitude and the brutalities of the white people.

On this point, the reader will find some interesting observations in Strowski's *Nationalisme ou Patriotisme*, although the author is rather too biased in favour of France and appears to ignore the classical exposés of Ferrero on " Napoleon and his Wars " and on " Militarism and Caesarism in France ".[1]

It is therefore very much to the point that the psychoanalysts and the psychologists should have applied themselves to the study of war and peace. The Dutch psychiatrist, Groeneveld, has looked into the aggressive tendencies hidden behind every war and every military attitude[2] and the English doctor Glover has studied war from the point of view of sadism.[3] The views of the latter, however, are as one-sided as those of Devaldes. Just as the latter is blinded by the problem of surplus population, so Glover exaggerates the psychoanalytic side of the question. Glover does not even seem to be sufficiently well up in the history of the working-class movement.[4] Besides, the importance of the psychological

---

[1] Ferrero, *Le Militarisme et la Société moderne*, pp. 71-198.

[2] Groeneveld, " Das Problem d. Aggressivität," *Bericht über den VI allgemeinen ärtzlichen Kongress für Psychotherapie in Dresden.*

[3] Glover, *War, Sadism and Pacifism.*

[4] Glover even says that never in history has direct action prevented war ! See farther on, pp. 137-8.

side of the struggle against war has been clearly shown by Vergin, in his capital book.[1] In an article on the struggle against war and psychoanalysis, M. Giltay appealed to all those who are interested to band themselves together for a systematic study of the psychological causes of war.[2]

[1] Vergin, *Das Unbewusste Europa.* See too H. Damaye, *Paix et morale par la Science, Psychiatrie et Civilisation.*

[2] See *Évolution,* March 1932, pp. 231-41.

Chapter V

VIOLENCE AND THE MASSES

> Men are small : up to a certain point they
> are able to disturb the course of things : by
> doing so, they can only hurt themselves.
> Humanity alone is great, is infallible. Now,
> I believe I may say in its name : Humanity
> wants no more war.
>
> Proudhon.

Both the individual and the mass must, then, always
be ready to die for an idea, " to sacrifice themselves
for the community ". It is not to be wondered at if
a number of these exploited men and women at last
resolved to use violence no longer in an alien cause but
in their own, which was also the cause of humanity.
Again, it is not to be wondered at if they drew inspiration
for their own revolution from the example that the
revolutionary bourgeoisie once gave, which is incessantly
glorified by schools, churches, the Press, literature,
art and science. Nothing to wonder at, once more,
if idealists of noble or middle-class birth, exasperated
by the iniquitous behaviour of their own class, came to
reject it and to devote themselves whole-heartedly
to imparting their own faith in the liberating virtues
of violence to the rising proletariat. If countless
numbers of the disinherited and the disillusioned have
been brought to take up those very arms which were
legally imposed on them against their own private

70

" enemy at home "—the ruling class—the responsibility lies less with them than with their pitiless masters, who have educated them in this direction for centuries past.

It is the bourgeoisie, too, who, upheld everywhere by the last vestiges of the feudal system, has spread the romantic ideology of violence right down to the lowest strata of the lower middle classes and proletariat. They are the ones who, ever since the French Revolution, have forced the sons of the poor to undergo military training by the million and who poured them out into the trenches in 1914. They have divided the entire world into national camps, ready to tear each other to pieces at any moment. They have developed scientific warfare, beginning with the powder and shot which was used against the armour and the castle-walls of the nobility, until they have now come to the point of throwing gas and incendiary bombs on defenceless crowds, women, children, sick people, animals. They have corrupted the people's spirit by a disciplinary system unworthy of human beings, in factories, barracks, prisons, etc. They have introduced, with the Church's consent, warships, cruisers, submarines, bombers and military airships, and have carried the art of murder into the very stratosphere. And so it is the bourgeoisie, helped always by those representing the ancient spirit of the nobility and clergy, who have given the proletariat a taste for using these tools of destruction, encouraging them to employ them more and more in civil and revolutionary wars against their real social enemy, the ruling class. If the white working-class and the coloured peoples believe in the efficacy of violence to further their own noble cause, the blame must be put on the international bourgeoisie, who, what is more, are still attacking all who fight for justice and liberty with the most fiendish weapons.   Look at what has happened in Spain since 1934 !

To the essentially parasitic bourgeoisie, the use of this violence comes naturally, as we have said.   On the other hand, the Bolsheviks, Socialists, Syndicalists and Anarchists, who wish to do away with every kind of parasitism, exploitation, and oppression, are battling for a world from which every form of brutal violence will be banished.   That is why, when once the old means of violence are used by them there appears a flagrant contradiction between such means and the goal in sight.

For it is a fixed law that all means have their own abiding end, proceeding from the function for which they came into being, which can only be subordinated to other, loftier ends as far as the latter are attuned to the essential and, as it were, innate end.   Besides, every end suggests its own means.   To transgress this law inevitably brings about a tyranny of the means. For if these lead away from their intended goal, then the more people use them, the farther they get from the objective and the more their actions are determined by them.   For example, it is impossible to educate people in liberty by force, just as it is impossible to breathe by coal gas.   Life must have fresh air.   And freedom must be awakened and stimulated by freedom and in freedom.   It can never be born of violence. At the most, we may seek liberty as an antidote to our bondage, just as we cry out for fresh air when we are threatened with asphyxiation.

And so, when those who struggle for the abolition of class and race exploitation automatically employ in their revolution—the greatest and noblest in history—

those very means of horizontal and vertical warfare that the capitalist class once employed against the feudal powers, aggravating them further by mediaeval cruelties such as inquisitions and tortures, abhorred by the bourgeoisie itself for a long time past, the result is a tragic contradiction. To take an example, the free organization of labour which the Workers' Soviets had in mind in the Russian revolutions of 1905 and 1917 can never be realized as long as the following are in force :

Absolute government and secret police, borrowed from Tsarism ; Inquisitions and Jesuitism, borrowed from mediaeval Catholicism ; Nationalism and militarism, created by the bourgeoisie ; *Étatism*, bureaucracy and Parliamentarianism, so characteristic of political systems under capitalism ; and all other methods proceeding from these.

Bolshevism, whenever it used these methods to attain its revolutionary goal, strayed from its first principle : the Soviets of Workers and Peasants. It blundered into a State Socialism, or rather, a State Capitalism, tainted by the feudal spirit, and became more and more involved in the Machiavellian politics of the imperialist world. This is shown by Litvinoff's opportunist policy of coalitions, based on that fairy-tale of security in armaments, which is now driving mankind towards a gigantic war, the consequence of which can only be the end of justice and liberty.

Modern capitalism, no longer able to justify itself from either a practical or a moral point of view, inevitably finished up by adopting the methods of Fascism. Even in the most democratic countries, the middle-classes, in order to impose their will, found themselves often unwillingly obliged to resort to all kinds of feudal expedients which once were repugnant to them. In our time, freedom of thought, of speech, of the Press, of organization and association, is being more and more curtailed, even in the classic lands of liberty like England, France and the Netherlands. There is not a single act to-day at which the capitalists will stop short in order to safeguard their " authority " and maintain the " right ", that is to say, the privileges of the bourgeoisie. Those beauteous devices with which the bourgeoisie had so proudly adorned itself in its rise, have fallen away ; and, stripped of those deceitful garments, it is seen for what it is and always has been.

Fascism, that is, a politico-economic state where the ruling class of each country behaves towards its own people as for several centuries it has behaved to the colonial peoples under its heel ; Fascism, which takes from its victims one after the other, the few political and social rights which they enjoyed ; Fascism which is always lowering wages and reducing human beings, men and women, to a state of slavery ; Fascism is the last despairing stand which imperialist capitalism must inevitably make, unless the working-class opposes it with all its might. It is, we have reason to hope, the last effort of the upper middle-classes to check that social evolution which threatens to sweep away the selfish regime they have instituted. From the point of view of social psychology, we are up against the policy of despair and a system which takes advantage of the people's increasing misery to seduce them by a new Messianism : belief in the Strong Man, the Duce, the Führer. This condition of hopeless misery explains the brutality and cruelty of Fascism : on both sides, the upper classes and the down-trodden masses alike, people are no longer themselves, *i.e.* no longer human.

It may therefore be said that Fascism in a country is nothing but imperialism the wrong way up, turned against its own people, and that imperialism is only Fascism the wrong way up, turned against foreign peoples. In both cases, the essence of the thing is violence.

While capitalism has come by its very nature to Fascist methods, Socialism on the other hand must never fall back on them ; to do so would attack its very roots. The violence and warfare which are characteristic conditions of the imperialist world do not go with the liberation of the individual and of society, which is the historic mission of the exploited classes. The greater the violence, the weaker the revolution, even where violence has deliberately been put at the service of revolution. The greater the revolution, that is to say, the social construction, the less there will be to deplore of violence and destruction. To create a really new order, violence can never be anything more than a *pis aller* and a counsel of despair, it " is never, from the revolutionary point of view, essential to the change ".[1]

The modern revolutionary therefore must : either accept the conclusion which, at the Anti-Gas Warfare Conference at Frankfort, in 1929, was vociferously proclaimed by Bolshevists, both men and women : " Against the armies of women reactionaries, we must have armies of women Reds ! Against the poison gas of the Whites, the poison gas of the Reds ! Against the White bacteria, the Red bacteria ! " and so direct his whole system of production and the whole community

[1] Aron et Dandieu, *La Révolution nécessaire*, pp. ix-x.

life steadily towards general destruction, as before . . . or else he must break with all that, in principle and practice, and hold to those fighting methods which are essentially in harmony with his goal of general reconstruction.

Some revolutionaries of the last century were naive enough to think that war, political or national, might easily be turned into war, civil and revolutionary, though Proudhon, in his immortal book *La Guerre et la Paix* (1861) had already concluded, from the Napoleonic wars and events of his own time, that the collective violence of the modern world would lose more and more of its civilizing bent, and would conflict with the character of modern Socialism : by reason of the technical and scientific warfare being evolved, every constructive work found itself threatened with destruction : it was therefore necessary, according to the Saint-Simon ideal, to change the military society into an industrial society as swiftly as possible. Nowadays, war, thanks to the scientific means of slaying available, presents a character so negative, not to say, nihilist, that to use it is impossible for a real revolutionary[1] unless he is willing to load his conscience with the mechanical mass-murder of men, women, children and animals ; the complete destruction of towns and plains and their inhabitants, and plants ; the diffusion, impossible to regulate, of gas and microbes, which would blindly annihilate friends and foes, comrades and adversaries— a way of action even more barbarous than that of the Old Testament God against Sodom and Gomorrah— and the odious crime that this would mean against Socialism and mankind in general.

[1] *Cf.* Léo Campion, *Le Noyautage de l'Armée.*

Let us imagine a community of Socialists or Communists more highly developed than that of the U.S.S.R. which for convenience we will call " Russia " and which, like the Russia of the present day, was surrounded by imperialist States. At a certain moment, this community was attacked by a State, let us say, " Germany ". Let us suppose that our imaginary Russia had not taken part in any coalitions comparable to those which bind the U.S.S.R. to non-Communist states such as Turkey and France, that is, in accordance with the principles of Lenin, she had been careful not to group herself with rival capitalist States. This Russia would have accepted the risk of having to defend herself single-handed, against all modern weapons. Let us admit that she would be in a better position to do so than modern Russia, even though the latter—to refer to the declarations of Pierre Cot, French Minister for Air, who was given an official reception in Moscow— possesses a perfect modern military machine, and notably a model Air Force, so that powerful military planes can leave Moscow at any moment to go and blot out some far-away enemy town. According to modern strategy, such a war requires that the nerve centres of the State machine, that is, the town where the Government is in residence and the industrial and traffic centres of the enemy country, should be attacked first (and let us remember that we are not speaking of some country in the abstract, such as is shown on the map, but quite simply of the life of millions of living creatures).

Imagine, then, that the German Air Force has come to attack Moscow. According to modern strategy, the only possible way in which Russia can defend herself is by reprisal, that is, by going and dropping bombs on Berlin.

But in our hypothesis, the airman hovering in his plane over Berlin with his bombs and his gas, on the verge of executing the orders received from Moscow, is a real revolutionary. If he faces squarely up to the reality of his act, will he be able to carry it out ? Down below, under him, live hundreds of thousands of proletarians, among whom are tens of thousands of comrades, secret members or sympathizers with his own Communist Party, besides women, children, babies, invalids—his own sort, in a word, of whom the great majority do not desire war with Russia, or not really, at least, but only because they have been deceived by their Government, their church, their press or their political party.

" But aren't the real culprits down there as well ? "

It is more likely that they have already taken refuge. One thing we may be sure of, and that is that they will be the best protected. As to the Government, everyone knows that as soon as it feels in danger it hastens to take shelter as far away as possible. Remember the Exodus from Paris in 1914 ! Besides, where are the real culprits, those who shelter behind the Government ? It is a fact that the ones who are most to blame are always the hardest to get at, while the innocent— millions of men, women, children—are in the greatest danger. If the airman in question is fully alive to the criminal act he is on the verge of committing, it will not be possible for him to carry it out.

Let us imagine another Communist airman, flying above the Ruhr district, that proletarian ant-heap, and above countless machines, the marvels of modern technique. Can he ruthlessly destroy all this ?

And again, we have assumed the hypothesis of a purely defensive war, brought about by insurmountable political difficulties which have obliged the Government in question to act against its will. Actually, things are not so simple. The policy of present-day Russia, for example, is the same as the old imperialist diplomacy and traditional Machiavellianism, and is collaborating in the preparation of military coalitions of one set of imperialist powers against another. Having formerly favoured the secret armament of Germany and rendered countless services to Turkey and Italy, she is now working in with France along the lines of Barthou.

Now, many revolutionaries are beginning to grasp all this. Yet they hesitate to break with the traditional methods of violence. Why?

In the first place, by a false shame with regard to their own moral feelings. For morality has gone out of fashion with us. As we have said, there are few things so hard as to remain outside the " nationalization of consciences " and not to be carried away on the powerful current of belief in violence, which has permeated the working-class movement. Bourgeois-feudal-barbarous violence can congratulate itself on having obtained amazing results, thanks to its powers of seduction. Great strength and great courage is required to resist its appeal, for, besides the insidious language which it speaks, to do so brings down on one Fascists and Bolshevists, Socialists and bourgeois Nationalists, practically everyone. Fist-shaking, shrieking, vociferating, marching through streets with flying flags and beating of drums —such is the behaviour of the thing to-day. What do the reasons for the agitation matter, provided one has a strong, heroic step and can howl loudly enough to persuade oneself? Such things have already stunned a great number of revolutionaries, who no longer venture into the breach for their own humane and humanitarian ideas, especially when these are trampled underfoot by their own revolutionary officials. There are even some—not so few of them, either—who blindly drift from the Bolshevist camp into the Fascist, and from the Fascist camp into the Bolshevist.

Secondly, people will not reject violence, because they believe by so doing they will also be rejecting the results expected from it.

" What shall we do, if we do not reply to the violence

of the reactionaries with our own ? Are the methods
of defence not decided by the methods of attack ? Must
we not convince the ruling classes with their own
arguments ? "

At a most contradictory conference, a Dutch worker
flung the following remark at me : " We cannot send the
bourgeoisie packing with a wave of the fan. We do
not make war on Hitler with toothpicks. Against
reactionary violence we must use methods that will
work."

Certainly, we need methods that will work. But
there is no greater fallacy than the generally accepted
dogma, always propagated by the nobility and the
bourgeoisie, that a righteous cause must be defended by
force, and that war will decide between the two sides
like a trial by ordeal. Ever since mankind took to
war, in every one there have in reality been two waged
by one side against the other. A great number of these
armed enterprises have been indecisive ; and indeed,
victory, as that truth-lover M. de la Palice would have
pointed out, can belong only to one of the belligerents.
So it follows that of all the wars the world has seen,
there have been more undecided or lost than won.
And among the latter, very few of those undertaken
for some holy cause can be reckoned. Most of the wars
which ended up in victory have been waged in the service
of an unjust rather than a just cause. However that
may be, in modern wars at least the righteousness of
the cause weighs less and less in the balance. Napoleon
declared long ago that God was always on the side of the
heaviest cannon. One thing can be definitely asserted,
and that is that the Boers, fighting at the beginning of
the century in so heroic a manner for a holy cause,

Bible in one hand and rifle in the other, were the losers in the fight against " perfidious Albion " in spite of their God and their weapons. The bourgeoisie of to-day has even built up a whole world of injustice and oppression by means of its violence, both horizontal and vertical. Right up to the present minute no righteous cause in the world has ever had the tenth chance of conquering by violence. And nowadays would it have even a hundredth chance ? It would have none at all, for, as we have shown, the methods of modern warfare make even the justest cause unjust, since those who allowed themselves to be dragged into it cannot do other than descend to the same level of brutality as those they fight. Even were they to triumph, they would be doomed to safeguard the fruits of victory by a system of force which would always be developing and therefore growing less human, and to sink ever more deeply and inescapably into the mire of destruction. Catholic moralists[1] are beginning to see at last that consequent upon the developments of modern technique, and having regard to the nature of modern politics, a " just war " cannot even arise.

In any case, it is wrong to suppose that violence is the only weapon suited to a just cause. For the exploited white masses and the oppressed coloured peoples, armed warfare is no longer practicable, since the scientific means of destruction are in the hands of well-paid experts, —who for the most part are profoundly reactionary in temperament,—and since the working-classes have at their disposal neither aeroplanes nor poison gas nor death rays nor bacteria. All this is the monopoly

[1] See *The Catholics and War*, published by the War Resisters' International.

of a group of professionals, devoid of all scruples and all sense of human responsibility.   And even if the masses had such weapons at their disposal, they could not use them without committing a monstrous crime against themselves, since the results of chemical, bacteriological, electrotechnical, stratospherical warfare cannot be regulated.   Like the wizard's apprentice, the masses would let loose a storm of uncontrollable forces on themselves, and they would be the chief victims.

Meanwhile, from the revolutionary side, vehement reproaches are uttered against their opponents for using those same methods which they reserve the right to use themselves.   The Swiss paper *Le Travail*, which is much in sympathy with Moscow, reveals indignantly that Mussolini and Hitler are fighting anti-Fascism with methods so barbarous as to recall those of the mediaeval Popes.   But this revolutionary paper glosses over the fact that the very same repressive methods are used against the anti-Bolshevik opposition.   According to the Dutch paper *Fakkel*, we must fight Fascism by all available means : " Tread this vermin underfoot the instant you have the necessary strength, and do not waste a moment.   A war of aggression against Fascism is not only permissible : it is a duty, an unavoidable and sacred duty ! "   French, Swiss, Belgian, Danish, Dutch, English and Czech Socialists are preparing, just as Albert Einstein, and Emil Ludwig did, to oppose the Nazi violence by a " democratic " violence.   As if modern warfare did not bring with it an era of Fascism and dictatorship, even in the so-called democratic and possibly victorious countries.

" Those who desire the end must also desire the means ", we hear on all sides.

Yes, but only the means which are suited to the end. And for genuine revolutionaries, these means can never be " any means ", because most of the latter are bourgeois, feudal and barbarous, and conflict with Socialism and with humanity.

It is of the first importance to note that, in neo-Marxist circles, they are coming at last to understand the mistake made by Marx and Engels in automatically accepting the horizontal and vertical use of violence as a means of bringing about the social revolution.

In the *Critique Sociale* of November 1933, Simone Weil recognized that the Marxists have as a rule blindly followed the traditions of revolutionary violence begun in the great French Revolution. In this respect, they have quite forgotten that " the materialist way is to examine a given fact of human life much less in the light of the end pursued than of the consequences necessarily implied by such means as are brought into play ". To judge of the efficacy of war in relation to the social revolution, one must first of all examine the mechanism of military conflict, that is to say, analyse the bearing it has on existing technical, economic and social conditions.

The author quoted above proves how the revolutionary wars since 1792 which play such a legendary rôle in revolutionary ideology were really the result of provocation on the part of the Court and the upper classes, plotting against the people's liberty.

First, it was not long before the French people were forced by conscription to take part in the wars of the bourgeoisie. These wars also made inevitable the introduction of a centralized political machine, the institution of a bloody terror and the annihilation of every liberty the people had, and thus prepared the way for the military and bureaucratic despotism of Napoleon.

The clearest minds saw this coming with great anxiety. Saint-Just wrote " Only those who fight the

battles win them, and only the powerful profit from it."
Robespierre himself recognized that war, without
freeing any foreign people, could only deliver the
French over to the slavery of *Étatism*. According to
him, war was only good for " officers, the ambitious,
the grafters, for those in executive positions : one does
not bring freedom at the bayonet's point ". In spite
of the apparent success of the Revolution, Robespierre
understood that a military despotism must follow it
as night follows day, to the great detriment of French
peasants and workers.

Simone Weil also states that as a result of the development of lethal technique in modern war, this differs from
all previous wars. Just as Marx shows how the modern
economic system is the subordination of the workers
to the means of production, which belong solely to the
owner class, so does modern war consist of the subordination of the soldier to the instruments of war,
which belong to the ruling class. As the machine of
national defence cannot function unless the masses are
compulsorily sent out to their death, the war of one
State against another is primarily a war of the political
and military machine against its own Army : " War
appears finally to be waged by the State machine and
General Staff together against all the able-bodied men
of military age together."

It seems to us that since modern warfare is total
warfare, we must go farther and say that it now is
waged by the assembly of State machine and General
Staff against the whole people, women and children
included, so that in every country the political and
military directors are absolutely the enemies of the
entire population.

Not to have drawn this conclusion was the fatal
mistake made by Lenin and other leaders of the workers'
revolution in Russia. The Soviet Constitution, proceeds
Simone Weil, has undergone precisely the same fate
as the Constitution of 1793. " Lenin had abandoned
his democratic doctrines and established the despotism
of a centralized political machine, just as Robespierre

did, and was in fact the forerunner of Stalin just as Robespierre was of Bonaparte." And this although Lenin knew that, according to Marx, the dictatorship of the proletariat cannot allow of an army, nor of police nor of a permanent bureaucracy.

"Revolutionary war is the grave of revolution," concludes Simone Weil. By the very workings of modern armed conflict it must either succumb to the blows of counter-revolution or transform itself into counter-revolution. It is the same for a war calling itself anti-Fascist. It must end either in the victory of the Fascism which is fought or in such an *État*-ization and militarization of the revolution defended that this would be undermined at the very roots.

We are glad that on this point, the neo-Marxists have come to conclusions which are as radically anti-*Étatist* as those of the anarchists and revolutionary syndicalists. Logically, anti-*Étatism* must also of its very nature reject all forms of war both horizontal and vertical.[1]

---

[1] See also, Simone Weil, "Ne recommençons pas la Guerre de Troie ", *Nouveaux Cahiers*, of April 1st and 15th, 1937.

CHAPTER VI

THE EFFECTIVENESS OF THE NON-VIOLENT
STRUGGLE

> Non-violence is the law of our species as
> violence is the law of the brute. The spirit lies
> dormant in the brute and he knows no law but
> that of physical might. The dignity of man
> requires obedience to a higher law—to the
> strength of the spirit.
>
> GANDHI.

How much more noble non-violent methods of struggle
are than the violent ! And how much more effective,
when they are well prepared.

In the Transvaal, a country which in spite of the
justice of its cause, the religious fanaticism of its people,
its famous marksmen and a favourable position was
unable to hold out against the brutality of British
imperialism—in the Transvaal at the beginning of the
century there lived a group of Hindu immigrés, subject
to harsh and special laws, which shackled them socially
and economically and were profoundly offensive to
their dignity as human beings.

Indian coolies were employed in the mines of Natal
and elsewhere in South Africa, and they were tied to
their work by five-year contracts. As a rule, they were
very industrious. A great number of Indians, once
their contracts had expired, stayed behind in the

country to set up as small peasants or tradesmen.   At the beginning of this century, there were 12,500 in the Transvaal.   The white people, although they themselves had formerly penetrated into the country by violence, soon began to look on these peaceable rivals as undesirable intruders.

In 1906 these Indians were placed on the same footing as criminals : every one of them had to report regularly to the police and have his finger-prints taken. On the advice of their fellow countrymen, Gandhi, a Hindu lawyer at Pretoria, some thousands of them decided to ignore the new regulation and to bear the penalties incurred by this infraction in a dignified manner.   Meanwhile they continued to look on those who were treating them with mistrust and cruelty as their fellow men and only appealed to their human feelings.   They did not wish to overcome by violence, but by *satyagraha*, or sacrifice and moral force, according to the methods of civil disobedience.

The Government met this entirely non-violent rebellion with severe imprisonments.   The non-violent combatants were even threatened economically.   But enthusiasm was high and solidarity great, the more so as the whole movement was based on the ancient Hindu tradition of *ahimsa*, the religious belief in non-violence.

Gandhi, who had already been in prison, went to London in 1910 to make a personal appeal to the British Government.   But they would not yield.   In 1912, all marriages according to Hindu law were declared illegal, with the result that all offspring of these marriages were considered to be illegitimate and therefore unable to inherit.   Further, an extraordinary tax was imposed on every Indian living in Africa. Up till then, the struggle had been carried on only by the small bourgeoisie—peasants and tradesmen. Now Gandhi called on the Indian workers as well, on the coolies working in the mines. Indian women made demonstrations in the mining districts and urged their countrymen everywhere to stop work until the wicked measures of the British Government were done away with. And so it was that the strike was added to the non-co-operation. The Government was on the verge of relaxing and promised to do away with the poll-tax, but the Hindus wanted this to be done immediately and further demanded full recognition of their rights. They organized a great demonstration which spread all over the Transvaal.

Large detachments of police were mobilized. Gandhi was arrested. But his non-violent army went on its way without a leader. Once more, Gandhi was released but when he rejoined his comrades he found that large numbers of the demonstrators were being seized upon, packed into trains and sent back to their own country.

But they had attained their object : public opinion was shaken. Gandhi had just been sent to prison for the third time, for a period of fifteen months, when the Government finally gave in. In 1913, the poll-tax was abolished, the validity of Hindu marriages was recognized and the Indian immigrants obtained the same rights as the other South African citizens. The one-time Boer general, Smuts, who had declared in 1906 that he would never abolish the special laws had to acknowledge himself morally defeated.

One thing is indisputable, and that is, that if this little handful of men had offered armed resistance to the violence of the British, they would have been crushed, and more fearfully than ever the Boers were—for these had been more numerous, better equipped and much more favourably placed from the strategic point of view, than the Hindu immigrants.

And besides, such an attitude was no novelty for the Indians. For example, when the British Government had introduced an extremely unjust tax in 1912, the population of Benares retaliated by practising non-co-operation and paralysed the life of the community, by simply refusing to work for their rulers. The natives obeyed the leaders they had chosen under a free discipline. The British Government had to give way and the tax was abolished.

The Indians have often used similar methods in their struggle against native tyranny. In 1830, in the State of Mysore, the entire population refused to work in the fields or to pay their taxes, leaving their villages and retiring to the forests as a protest against the intolerable exploitation of a native despot. Nowhere—as the official report of the British Government stated—was their any disorder. None resorted to arms. " The natives understand very well the use of such measures to defend themselves against the abuse of authority. The method most in use, and that which gives the best results, is complete non-co-operation in all that concerns the Government, the administration and public life generally."

How much more effective non-violence is than violence as a means of carrying on a struggle, especially when it is against heavily armed powers, is shown by what happened at the beginning of the century in Bengal. There again, under the leadership of Aurobindo Ghose, sprang

up an energetic non-co-operation movement to combat
the scandalous measures of the British Government.
They ignored the entire administration systematically,
by ceasing to co-operate with the Government in any
department whatever. At the same time, they boycotted all British goods. Tagore, by his passionate
songs, inspired his countrymen to sacrifice possessions
and life itself for the liberation of their country. They
built up stakes and burnt everything English on them :
woven materials and other merchandise. Ghose
wished his people to be so independent that they could
supply their material and spiritual needs without
paying tribute to a foreigner.

As the British Government refused to give way, the
Bengalese turned against the British régime as such.
Ghose called on his compatriots not only to ignore
official authority but also, and above all, to help themselves in order that they might thereby demonstrate their
fitness for political and economic independence : they
were to fight against bad hygienic conditions, found
schools everywhere, establish a network of roads,
develop agriculture, etc. But the masses had become
impatient, let themselves be carried away by fanatical
leaders and fell back on violence. The British Government asked nothing better. They seized the opportunity of pitilessly crushing this movement, which had
begun so well.

So it was not surprising if, in 1917, the peasants
of Champaran resorted once more to non-violent
weapons. They were forced by law to plant indigo on
three-twentieths of their land and subjected to all kinds of
oppressive measures on the part of the planters. Gandhi,
who had returned to India, set about examining the

situation of the peasants.   Much disturbed, the planters
demanded of the authorities that Gandhi should be
expelled from the country.   They did actually order
Gandhi to leave the district at once.   To which Gandhi
replied that he had come on purpose, from a sense of
duty, that he had done nothing but state certain facts
perfectly calmly and that he would remain in the
district to finish his task, being at the same time ready
to undergo the punishment incurred by his disobedience.
Without letting themselves be intimidated, he and his
friends continued their campaign.   But thenceforward,
police officials were present and took notes of all that
went on.   Gandhi and his collaborators organized
their work in such a way that in case the leader was
imprisoned or banished, two of them were able to
carry on the inquiry, and if these were imprisoned in
turn, two others would replace them and so on.

Gandhi was called before the court.   He confessed
he was guilty in the eyes of the law and declared that
there was a conflict of duty in him.   Should he obey
the law, or his own conscience and serve the truly
humane purpose for which he had come to the country ?
It was left to the British administration to assume the
responsibility of eventually turning him out.   The
authorities deferred judgment and before it was pronounced the Lieutenant-Governor gave orders that
Gandhi should be set free to pursue his inquiry.   The
Governor, having himself had a discussion with Gandhi,
set up a Governmental Commission of Inquiry, of
which Gandhi was a member.   This Commission was
not long in recognizing that the law about indigo and the
exactions of the planters were unjust.   The law in
question was abolished and the peasants had gained

their cause without any violence whatever having been used.

In 1918, the peasants of Kaira, wishing to oppose some very oppressive taxes, also consulted Gandhi. He suggested that they should pay nothing at all, and bear with dignity whatever punishment might ensue. Hundreds of peasants were imprisoned, but the population persevered until the taxes were abolished.

In similar fashion, the population of a Kolgarth village in the Himalayas succeeded in 1921 in freeing themselves from the harsh fatigues called " bugar ", which was nothing else than a system by which any representative of the British Government, or European whatsoever for that matter, was entitled to demand all kinds of services, such as carrying luggage, taking messages, etc., from the natives, for whatever length of time suited these gentlemen.

We saw again in 1924, how the Untouchables of the Vykom village, in the Travancore State in South India, carried on, under the guidance of Gandhi and his friends, a struggle against the Brahmans, who for reasons of caste had forbidden them the entry of a certain raised route which was of great importance for trade. At that time, Gandhi was lying ill a hundred kilometres from the above-mentioned village. But the leaders of the movement came to get his advice on their plan of campaign, and kept in touch with him by letter and wire. These leaders, accompanied by some of the Untouchables, proceeded along the forbidden way towards the Brahman quarters. They were cruelly beaten by their enemies : one of them was grievously wounded, but refrained from offering any violence in return. A number of them were then arrested by the police for having incited the Untouchables to break the law. They were sentenced to penalties which went up to one year in prison. But immediately, and from all parts of the country, volunteers surged towards the forbidden road to take their place. The Government made no further arrests and enjoined on the police that they were to prevent any of the " reformers " from crossing the road. Then, at the instigation of Gandhi, the " reformers " placed themselves before the police cordon in the attitude of prayer. In six-hour shifts, they kept up this singular struggle for months, in order to soften the hearts of the Brahmans. More than once these non-violent combatants found themselves plunged up to their necks in water after a downpour, while the police maintained their cordon in boats above the water. At such times the Untouchables would relieve each other every three hours.

This action, seemingly so naïve, had nevertheless the effect of making this vexed question discussed through the whole of India. At last, in the autumn of 1925, after six months' struggle, the Brahmans gave way, perceiving that they could not hold out against such moral force. And the Untouchables were allowed to use the road, to pass the temple and to cross the Brahman quarters. This was the first of a whole series of reforms with regard to the caste system.

And finally in 1928, the peasants of Bardoli Taluca, in the Bombay province, numbering 90,000, opposed by non-violent methods an agrarian tax which was swallowing up as much as 60 per cent. of their revenues. The Government ignored all protests. Under the direction of Vallabbhai Patel and the inspiration of Gandhi, the peasants refused to pay their taxes although

State representatives confiscated their goods and sold
their lands.   Insults, threats, even terrorization on the
part of the Government did nothing but strengthen
the moral combativity of the peasants who went on
to a complete boycott of everything of an official nature.
The local newspapers could speak of nothing but this
enterprise, and sympathy was aroused throughout India.
The matter was not only debated in the British administration in India, but even in the London Parliament.
After six months of non-violent struggle, the unjust
taxes were abolished.

In like manner, we have often seen forming in India
what has been called the " Diamond Front ".   And
often with remarkable success.   This was notably the
case in the struggle of the Virangan and the Ahmedabad
workers to better their economic conditions.

In 1921, India gave, under Gandhi's guidance, its
first great example of national civil disobedience.   We
know the character of such an undertaking : a social
group, a class, a people, acts in many circumstances
as if the Government did not exist and ignores it
systematically in the whole of economic and social
life.   The schools stand empty, the laws are not carried
out, taxes do not come in, etc.   Above all, obedience
is refused to certain decrees or laws the abolition of
which is the primary aim.   Very often, such a full-stop or
check in the life of the community is accompanied
by strikes as well as by a refusal to sell or buy those
goods the sale of which is a profit to the enemy.   In
India, for instance, it is salt, alcohol and English woven
materials.   And so, joined to non-co-operation, we
have the boycott, a method of struggle which is of the
greatest efficacy, as China has been showing for 3,000

years past. Drawing their inspiration from age-old religious and moral conceptions, the Indian non-co-operators bear even the most cruel attacks of police and army, and the punishments laid down for breaking the law, with resignation, prepared as they are to suffer endlessly for the triumph of their cause. One can persecute them, ill-treat them, throw them into prison, they only hold the faster to the moral and spiritual forces by which they are ruled, rising above the base violence their enemies use, although they still appeal to them as their fellow men.

Even more remarkable than the abstention from any kind of violence in the unarmed combatants is the absence of all fear before the aggressor and the absence of all hatred against the enemy. Even they go so far as to show profound confidence in the better feelings of those against whom they are struggling.

The world knows for the best part how much of moral and spiritual force was shown by the awakened India in this struggle, and how, in the course of non-violent demonstrations and picketings before the shops, alcohol booths, etc., men and women—women especially —the young and the old, vied with each other in heroism. The British Empire had to give way : India won its first great victory. This country, which did not possess a single military means of defence, would never have won such a victory by non-pacific methods over the hyper-modern violence of the adversary.

"However, the Indians are still far from being free !"

But why do they always judge non-violent methods of fighting in a different way from the homicidal methods ? Even in war the first victory is seldom the decisive one. A struggle, whether violent or otherwise,

as a rule goes on for years.   It is made up of luck and
ill-luck, of victories and defeats, and only in the more
favoured cases does it end in a decisive victory for one
side or the other.

In spite of some temporary successes, how remote
a hope of success the Netherlands seemed to have, in
their War of Independence against Spain in the
sixteenth century.   It took them eighty years (1568-
1648) to achieve their goal, and success was very far
from being complete even then, since they had to give
up the whole southern part of the land.   The Indian
struggle for independence will certainly take less time.
The thing which is indisputable is that by employing
the non-violent methods of struggle, they have assured
themselves of successes which otherwise they could
never have had.   If India, who did not possess " the
material or the training for organized violence ",[1] had
made war on the British Empire since 1921, she would
be utterly smashed by now.   Now, after fifteen years
of non-violent struggle, it is impossible for the British
Lion, armed to the teeth, to keep the Indian Government still what Lord Curzon called it—" a subordinate
department of Whitehall ".[2]   In 1932, by simply
threatening a hunger strike, Gandhi managed to give
a constitutional orientation to the negotiations with
England.   After the provisional settling of serious
disputes, the new Constitution of 1937 may function
for a certain time.   Nevertheless the difficulties will
continue to exist, and it is certain that England, in order
to avoid a break, will see itself obliged to grant many a

[1] Nehru, *India and the World*, p. 33.
[2] C. F. Andrews, The New Indian Constitution, *Reconciliation*,
May 1937, p. 120.

demand of India, for the latter is sure of her strength to carry on the fight. Again Gandhi, the non-violent, dominates the scene. " He represents a flame which, having smouldered several months, may at any moment break out and inflame the whole of India."[1]

"But, you will object, Gandhi is a Hindu. He follows a religious tradition that is hundreds of years old. He is a saint, an ascetic. How does such an example affect us ? In India, non-violence is a traditional form of religion, while our Christianity is impregnated with violence through and through."

We can reply that other Indians, who do not reject violence in principle and follow utterly different religious and moral traditions from those of Gandhi, have been so impressed by the efficacy of his fighting methods that they have adopted them. As is known, the British Army of Occupation in India recruits chiefly from among the Sikhs. These people, whose religion goes so far as to forbid them to lay down their sabres, had a serious quarrel with the Government during the period 1922 to 1924 on the subject of the control of certain properties belonging to some temples. Unable to solve the matter by violence, they decided to try direct, non-violent action. Proud and immovable, the sword at their side but their arms crossed, they put up with the most brutal behaviour on the part of the British police and Army without offering the slightest physical resistance, until they had obtained what they wanted.

This shows that non-violent methods of struggle are not bound up with the person of Gandhi in particular, nor with any special form of religion. This is shown

[1] Paul F. Hegi, in the *Tribune de Genève*, of April 29th, 1937.

still more clearly by what happened with the Pathans, in Northern India. These tribes are well-known for their passion for revenge. Very touchy, intolerant of the slightest offence, the Pathans were accustomed to respond immediately with violence. That is, until 1930, when Abdul Ghaffar Khan, a Mahometan leader of the Puritan Revolution, the " Khudai Khitmatgars " or Servants of God, and therefore outside the ancient Hindu tradition of non-violence, managed to convince them of the efficacy of unarmed resistance. From that day on, the British Government tried in vain to shatter the collective action of the " Red Shirts ". This movement, which in April 1930 had 500 members, had 40,000 three months later and, towards the end of the year, 300,000.[1] Persecutions, imprisonments, executions without trial, so far have not shaken their courage.

In August 1934, several leaders were set free after two years of prison, among others Abdul Ghaffar Khan himself, the " Gandhi of the frontier provinces ", though he was not allowed to go back to the Punjab or the north-west district. In December 1934, the papers announced that Abdul Ghaffar Khan, " that fine man and true, beloved of millions "[1] had again been sentenced to two years imprisonment, on account of a speech he made at Bombay, where he remarked that the part played by the British police was not to protect the Indian population but to persecute them and make false charges against them. He had further stated that in the northern provinces, some Hindu soldiers had refused to fire on a quiet and unarmed crowd, and that some British troops had then opened fire, killing more than 200 people in a few minutes.

[1] Nehru, *India and the World*, p. 76.

The " Red Shirt " movement, which according to Abdul Ghaffar Khan is " non-violent, and based on freedom, love and truth ", carries on its struggle even though officially it has been banned.

Like Subhas Bose, we may raise serious objections to the opportunism of Gandhi and deplore that this leader, so devoutly obeyed, should so often have seen fit to hold up the national struggle from motives that were essentially subjective.   Bose, who insists on tactics which are objective and scientific as well as revolutionary, sees that Gandhi's chief fault lies in his repeated attempts to reach a premature compromise with the British Government.   That is why Bose considers that the Mahatma, instead of renouncing the non-violent struggle as he has done on various occasions, ought to have pursued it with redoubled energy. Although for his part he in no way rejects the principle of armed conflict, he admits that in these cases Gandhi could have obtained far greater, and indeed unprecedented, results. This is a criticism not of non-violent methods but of the way in which Gandhi used them.   He was at fault again, according to Bose, in systematically neglecting the method which consists of winning over the enemies' soldiers, even though these were Indians too.   He reproaches him also with having deliberately refrained from showing his solidarity with the mutineers of the Garwhali regiment, who were so severely punished by the British authorities for having refused to fire on their countrymen.   All of which goes to demonstrate Gandhi's almost instinctive tendency to respect the political authority of the British Government as much as possible, as well as his dislike of purely revolutionary methods.   But these remarks in no way reflect

on the efficacy of the tactics in question.   If Gandhi
had only done all that Bose reproaches him with having
left undone, the practical sense of his non-violent
tactic would have revealed itself more strikingly still.

The Communist Sumyendranath Tagore has recently
published a study of Gandhi, which is a regular indict-
ment of him.   A fanatical Bolshevist, the author
declares, and quite rightly, that from the economic,
social, moral and religious points of view, there are all
sorts of conservative and even reactionary tendencies.
Tagore reproaches Gandhi with being a thinker as
naïve as mediocre, understanding nothing of sexual
life nor of revolutionary universalism ; and as for his
attitude with regard to the British Empire, the Mahatma
has shown an untimely opportunism which has actually
been harmful to the struggle for independence of his
country, and he seems to have an instinctive dislike
of the modern working-class movement.   The criticisms
of Sumyendranath Tagore are so bitter that the reader
will be astonished to find Tagore admitting in the last
pages of the book that Gandhi has some " eminent
qualities " : great personal charm ; an extraordinary
capacity for work, indomitable courage ; utter absence
of self-interest ; a rigid self-control and a gift which is
almost miraculous for divining popular feeling, which
has developed in the course of his many years contact
with the masses.   Because from the very first page, the
reader gets the impression that this damned Gandhi
is nothing but a cunning intriguer in the service of the
Indian and British rulers !

The author has in fact done nothing to explain the
complicated and even contradictory character of Gandhi,
nor the important part he has played in the history of
Indian emancipation and the world significance of his
experiences in the non-violent struggle.   Tagore goes
so far as to say that " the bourgeois world has recognized
Gandhi as its prophet " and that it is Gandhi who
" has furnished the ruling classes of the world with
their weapon of pacifist ideology ".   Which is just

silly. Everybody knows, in any case, that the prophet of the bourgeoisie to-day is more likely Hitler or Mussolini—if not Franco—and that, in the eyes of the ruling classes in the " democratic " countries as well as in those of the Fascist dictators, nothing is more detestable than the doctrine and especially the practice of complete pacifism. Everywhere, those who oppose violence, whether horizontal or vertical, are vigorously persecuted. And if Gandhi has been able more or less to gain the confidence of a certain section of the English bourgeoisie, it is just because, at certain critical moments, he renounced his pacifism in order to take part in the colonial and national wars of the British Empire.

How much better founded is the judgment of Jawaharal Nehru, the best qualified man to speak in this case, when he says in his book *India and the World* that the Mahatma has been able through nation-wide action to mould the millions and change them " from a demoralized, timid and hopeless mass, bullied and crushed by every dominant interest, and incapable of resistance, into a people with self-respect and self-reliance, resisting tyranny, and capable of united action and sacrifice for a larger cause. He made them think of political and economic issues, and every village and every bazaar hummed with argument and debate on the new ideas and hopes that filled the people. That was an amazing psychological change . . . The only practical solution of the problem came from Gandhi. Whether that was a final solution or not remains to be seen, but it did combine the Sermon on the Mount with effective action .   . . In spite of the abundance of " nons " in his movement (non-violence, non-co-operation, etc.) it was not a negative, passive affair. It was an active, dynamic, energizing drive. . . . Of course there were lapses and bitterness and hatred, but the surprising thing is that they were so few and that within a short term of years he could have worked this astounding change."[1]

[1] Nehru, *India and the World*, pp. 173 and 223-4.

The first to try to understand, from the point of view of social effectiveness, the significance of the non-violent methods of struggle as used by Gandhi in Africa and India, was the American professor Clarence Marsh Case, who in 1923 published a remarkable study entitled *Non-violent Coercion*, in which he deals with non-violent methods of struggle from the point of view of history, of social psychology, and of their practice, interesting himself chiefly in what had actually been done in India.

In 1934, another very remarkable book was published by Richard B. Gregg, an American lawyer who had collaborated in 1923 with the Committee Chairman of the Federation of Railway Shop Employees in a huge strike which spread over the whole of the United States. During this movement, at a moment of the highest tension, an article on Gandhi fell into the hands of Mr Gregg. A few words spoken by the Mahatma made such an impression on him that he began to study everything he could get that concerned him. After a few years, having thoroughly digested the subject and being well-versed in the agrarian question, he went to India. There, he met Gandhi and his chief colla-borators, and studied the economic, political and social condition of the country. Back in the States, in 1928, he published various interesting articles on India, and at last, in 1935, his work on *The Power of Non-Violence*. In this book the author has tried to lay the foundations both psychological and moral, of a possible non-violent strategy. According to him, violence has been tried out for thousands of years without settling anything ; " why not try non-violence, in the search for social truth ? "[1]   Gregg's book is indispensable for all those who are interested in this subject, for as well as the principal contents there is a large amount of psychological and sociological information added in the appendix.

One thing is certain, and that is that since the Great War, the self-respect and the fighting-spirit of the

[1] Gregg, *The Power of Non-Violence*, p. 112.

Indians has increased to an incredible degree, and that the Indians are already in a position where they can proudly refuse the considerable concessions which the British Empire has had to grant them.

The non-violent methods of struggle are not bound up with any one person, nor one particular race, nor with any separate country, nor with one sole conception of life or of the universe : at the Anti-Imperialist Conference at Brussels in 1927, we heard the Zulu Goumed declare that the blacks, in their fight for liberty, could not do better than follow the example of India.   Yes, indeed ! for how could they ever rival the modern armaments of the whites, armaments which are closely connected too with a whole social and technical organization which is absolutely foreign to them ?

At the Conference of Non-Europeans, which was held at Port Elizabeth in South Africa in April 1934, a resolution was passed among others asking the whole non-European population to boycott all goods manufactured or sold by establishments which refused to employ native workers.[1]

Gandhi himself admits that he has come round to his tactics not only through the influence of certain Hindu religious traditions, but also :

through the Jewish legend of Daniel and his friends
through the Sermon on the Mount
through the ideas of the Englishman, Ruskin
through the teaching of the Russian, Tolstoy
and above all, through the words and actions of Thoreau,
        the American revolutionary of French origin.

Let us note that the technical term " civil disobedience ", which Gandhi likes to apply to his fighting

[1] " In the same way as Gandhi," *Lu*, May 11th, 1934.

methods, has been consciously borrowed by him from the immortal speech Thoreau made in 1849, in which he gave a classic *exposé* of his ideas concerning individual and collective refusal of military service, and, in certain circumstances, of all social service and payment of taxes.

According to Thoreau, every responsible citizen should utterly ignore the public authorities, laws and institutions, when a truly human interest requires it, and so prevent his Government from committing crimes in critical moments. Co-operation with all people and institutions which lean towards the good, non-co-operation the minute there is a question of promoting the bad, such is the maxim in which one could sum up Thoreau's theory, which he himself put into practice in exemplary fashion. The few hundred people who knew him during his life in America, looked on him as a rule as a cranky idealist, if not a pleasant simpleton, with whom practical dealings were impossible. To-day in Asia, millions of his fellow men have put his tactics, as simple as effective, into practice with surprising results.

Thoreau knew besides—like his friend Emerson, whose speech *On War* in 1838 should at least be mentioned here—the doctrine of that gifted young Frenchman, Etienne de la Boétie (1530-63) to whom Emerson dedicated one of his most outstanding poems.

In his essay called *Of Voluntary Servitude* Etienne de la Boétie threw a light on the whole social edifice and showed that a ruler only has power in as much as the people allow it to him. The power of the ruling class lasts only as long as those who are subject to it recognize it in principle and in fact—that is, as long as the governed people consent to give their respect to those who require it.

Official authority, the power some hold legally over others, is more moral than physical in character. It rests less on violence than on respect, that is, on the belief in the right to govern of those in power. The day the masses learn to free themselves of their veneration for those who hold them down, the authority of the ruling classes, no longer being recognized, will vanish at once, and they will lose their power immediately.

No despotism, tyranny, dictatorship or public authority of any kind exists except thanks to the submission of the masses. As soon as the people realize that the public authorities are essentially parasitic in nature and take from them the power which formerly they had granted, the whole social pyramid topples. The one advantage, declares la Boétie, that the ruling class has over the subjugated masses is the right these masses have conceded them to hold them in slavery. From where come the police, the spies, the soldiers? From the people, who, putting themselves at the service of all branches of official authority, fight amongst and destroy themselves. When, with their heavy tread, the soldiers go forward over fields and towns, it is the people crushing the people, at the behest of the established powers, declares Boétie once again. Domela Nieuwenhuis, a Dutch anti-militarist, was to say, several centuries later, " A people in uniform is its own tyrant! "

Another thinker to be deeply impressed by la Boétie's essay was Tolstoy, who quotes a striking passage from it in *The Law of Violence and the Law of Love*. The great Russian's *Letter to a Hindu*, which was so to influence Gandhi and to prepare the direct non-violent action of his countrymen in India, bears witness also to a strong influence from de la Boétie.   The German Socialist and lover of freedom, Gustav Landauer—whose tomb was one of the first to be violated by the Nazis—made a stirring summary of " Of Voluntary Servitude ", which became the pivot of his classical essay, *Die Revolution*.

Let us pass over the impressive history of the direct non-violent action of Christianity in the first centuries and that of religious sects, both mediaeval and modern, as well as the remarkable anti-war movement which is being led by an ever increasing number of Protestant clergymen in Europe and America, reaching a figure of thousands at the present time—a history which we have dealt with at length in another book.[1]   Because, if we were to quote these, the Western workers would immediately reply : " That has nothing to do with us, it's religion."

Well then, let us leave out the Christians, whether modern, mediaeval or primitive, and go back to pagan Rome.   In 494 B.C. even she gave us an unforgettable example of non-co-operation.   As we know, the plebeians—that is to say, the small peasants who, although free, were excluded from political power—were suffering out of all reason from the iniquitous laws.   The patricians—that is to say, the great landowners, who occupied the State offices—had all the rights ;   they possessed enormous fortunes.   On the other hand, the plebeians, who were very poor for the most part, were shut out

---

[1] See *La Paix Créatrice*, II.   For what concerns America, read Van Kirk, *Religion renounces War*.

The official organ of the Fellowship of Reconciliation, *Reconciliation*, a monthly review of things which belong to Peace, 17 Red Lion Square, London, W.C.1, gives a regular account of the present development of Peace Work in the Churches.

of all position and public duty. The patricians had seized all the common lands, which had been a survival of communal ownership, and drew vast profits from them. They continued to force the people to equip themselves at their own expense for war. These people, resorting more and more to loans to maintain their families, got deeper and deeper into debt. Crushed beneath the weight of these debts, they were subjected to a cruel system of imprisonment. But aware that in society, the wealth and the victory of the upper strata only exist thanks to continual support of the lower classes, they decided at a certain moment to withhold their forces from this iniquitous social system. Driven to the end of their tether, they left Rome to found an independent community on Mons Sacra, *sine ullo duce*, without a leader[1]—they had no use for Führers ! They declared that they would not return until they were granted a share in the government and in the common lands. Livy describes how this exodus took place in exemplary order and how these peasant-soldiers organized a camp on Mount Aventine and installed themselves there. Such a *secessio in montem* must have been repeated more than once.[2] At last, the patricians were forced to comply with the demands of the plebs because, with their warlike policy, they needed them. In the fourth century B.C., therefore, the plebs acquired considerable advantages both economic and political. Case affirms that this " secession ", the first effective action by the proletariat, took place without any disorder or violence.[3]

[1] Livy, II, p. 32.
[2] G. de Sanctis, in *Propyläen-Weltgeschichte*, II, pp. 260-1.
[3] Case, *Non-Violent Coercion*, p. 303.

The expression " proletariat " must, however, be taken in a wider sense than the usual. Beer states, rightly, that the distinction between patricians and plebians, or " proletarii ", did not constitute a distinction of class, and that the plebeians did not propose to set up a new economic and social order. " It was not a different conception of the world which they defended against the patricians. Their conception rested like the others, on slavery and the exploitation of foreign peoples." It was a question of a certain stratum of a warlike society which, not being able to conquer those above them by violence, resorted to non-violent methods to bring about, not a revolution, but a simple social reform. Non-violent methods of struggle are not to blame for this, since in any case they proved their complete efficacy.[1]

Wells considers the Roman plebs to have been the inventors of the general strike;[2] but it is really a question here of a kind of non-co-operation or civil disobedience.

In Livy, too, we find a description of how, in 375 B.C. the people of Tusculum " averted the vengeance of Rome by an obstinate peace, which they could never have done with their arms ".[3] See the different forms of Gandhi-ism which appeared even in pagan Rome ! We must admit that the non-violent methods of struggle are not at all foreign to a Western conscience. Did not Mirabeau, who has been praised as one of the thinkers who were most alive to the different times, declare at the Assembly of the States of Provence, " Take care, do not despise these people who produce everything, this people who, to be formidable, have only to stand motionless." Opposing in this way the

---

[1] Beer, *Histoire Générale du Socialisme et des Luttes Sociales*, I, pp. 130-42.

[2] Wells, *Outline of History*, p. 225.

[3] Livy, VI, pp. 25-6. See *La Paix Créatrice*, I, p. 43.

" strength and the law of the producers " to the privileged " sterility of the nobles ", he gave " the most powerful and striking formula of what we now call the general strike ".[1]

In the middle of the last century, the French revolutionary Anselm Bellegarrigue, as a consequence of his social and political experiences in the United States and in France, lost all confidence both in the Governments whose very nature is violence and in revolutions from the moment they allow themselves to be involved in bloodshed : in one case as in the other, everything rests in the final analysis on oppression and murder, and once caught in this trap there is no way of getting out. The barricades, in his view, are usually raised by those who wish to rule against those who are ruling. Let us do away with all forms of Government and govern ourselves in reasonable fashion, and henceforward all barricades will be superfluous for ever.

" In the end," Bellegarrigue goes on, " there are no tyrants, only slaves." The Socialist movement has only arisen from the profound thirst of humanity for freedom. The exercise of power, even in the name of Socialism, can only kill it. A people is always too much governed.

That is why Bellegarrigue spread the idea of a *refusal of assistance*, which is identified with the principle of non-co-operation and civil disobedience. He developed a whole " theory of calm " which opens up possibilities of overcoming even the most powerful regime " by abstention and inertia ". Everything must succumb to the power of Abstention : social privileges, unjust taxes, spy systems, military hierarchies, must all give

[1] Jaurès, *Histoire Socialiste*, I, La Constituante, pp. 58-9.

way before it, when the masses withdraw their support
from the régime of violence and concentrate on their
own moral force. A conception which clearly corresponds to the spirit of Shelley's immortal poem, "The
Mask of Anarchy", which was inspired by the massacre
of the Peterloo workers in 1819, and describes almost
literally the attitude which, a century later, the Indians
were to take up against British violence under Gandhi's
direction.

Bellegarrigue, returning from America, went back
to France in February 1848. Soon after, he remarked
that the tragic thing about revolutions is that they are
always robbed of their fruits by the governments they
set up. While in America, there was a minimum of
government, in France everything was growing more
and more centralized, in order that it might pass
through the hands of the State. In his brochure,
Au Fait, au Fait (1848) he described how the whole of a
people's living was eaten up by bureaucratic administration. There is the modern Minotaur, who sucks
the masses' blood and swallows up whole milliards !
Nothing is actually changed when Socialist Governments replace the bourgeois, all *Étatisme* being in
flagrant contradiction with self-government, which
is the essence of all true revolution.

So the non-violent methods of struggle are not
bound then either to a particular religion or to a special
race or people. European and American lovers of
freedom discover its worth just as much as Hindu
mystics, rebellious Negroes and warlike Sikhs. Besides,
the general strike, practised as much by English,
Russian and Scandinavian Socialists as by French,
Italian, Spanish and South American anarchists and
syndicalists, and regarded since the beginning of the
century as a typically proletarian means of struggle,

is in itself a way of action foreign to the traditional violent methods. No doubt, the propaganda by general strike, as made in the revolutionary centres of Europe and America, did not envisage a complete non-violence. Many adherents to these methods even declared in so many words that they were unthinkable without a certain amount of violence. However, in the General Strike brochure, distributed in great numbers in 1901 by the Group of Propaganda by Pamphlet, Song and Poster in Liége, it is stated that general strikes are the best weapon in the fight for working-class emancipation ; it renders all bloodshed on the workers' side unnecessary and does away with all risk of defeat for them ; the time for barricades is over and it would be absurd to continue the mistakes of the past since the working-class now has a far more effective means of combat. General strikes have been discussed at the Workers' Congress of Bordeaux (1888), of Tours and Marseilles (1892), of Nantes (1894), of Rennes (1898) and of Paris (1900) ; they became the rallying cry of the working-class forces. This strike method must extend into the very barracks to paralyse the army. During the last strike at Creusot, the soldiers refused to march and at Dunkerque, a sergeant appealed to the men not to commit any hostile act against the workers. " Before triumphing, we must fight, and in order to fight we need brains which are free of all prejudice and sophism ; we need conscious individuals who will not be towed along by just anyone. The General Strike is the grandest gesture of revolt of the modern masses . . . it offers to all the pariahs of the factory and the workshop the opportunity of enforcing their claims."

In this same year of 1901, the Committee of Propaganda for General Strikes, elected by the syndicalist Congress of Lyons, concluded its manifesto by this appeal : " Comrades ! it is indispensable that we should leave the field of theory, in which we are stuck, and enter resolutely into that of action. The general strike, a pacifist weapon, will be the only effective way to oppose our class enemies."

People were singing the song of the General Strike everywhere, in the homes, at meetings, in the workshops :

> O toi, qui penches vers la terre
> Ton front pali par la douleur,
> Redresse-toi, fier prolétaire,
> L'avenir apparaît meilleur !
> Ce n'est pas à coup de mitraille
> Que le capital tu vaincras.
> Non, car pour gagner la bataille,
> Tu n'auras qu'à croiser les bras !
>
> Pour la chute fatale
> Des exploiteurs tyrans,
> La grève générale
> Nous fera triomphants !
>
> Le meilleure arme pour abattre
> Les détenteurs du Capital,
> Cette affreuse engeance marâtre,
> C'est le chômage général   .   .   .[1]

In adopting similar tactics in the social war, the most militant section of the Western proletariat showed itself to a certain extent Gandhi-ist before Gandhi himself !

[1] For translation see Appendix III, p. 287.

Let us not forget, by the way, that Gandhi is no more than the most part of European revolutionaries an " absolutist ", or dogmatist, in non-violence. According to him, it is better in certain circumstances, when one is not able to defend a righteous cause in non-violent ways, to defend it with arms sooner than abandon it in cowardly fashion. For essentially opportunist reasons, Gandhi has already taken part three times in the imperialist wars of the British Empire and, in August 1914, he renounced his super-national point of view in favour of the holy Union, like most of the supporters of the Second International. In 1918, he had become so to speak the real recruiter for the British Army in India ![1]

The revolutionary syndicalist Sorel, a well-known atheist, whose doctrine is anything but a plea for non-violence, has clearly defined the difference between " Bourgeois force " and " Proletarian violence " (we should say : bourgeois violence and proletarian strength). Sorel sees in the general strike a sublimation of war, a method of fighting which is fundamentally in keeping with the dignity of the proletariat. To fight against the terror of the bourgeoisie, which rears its system on the ruin of its enemies and whose political inquisition claims more victims than the old Holy Inquisition ever did, there is no need for the proletariat to institute a counter-terror. It must, also, oppose all wars of conquest, a crime typical of bourgeois rapacity. The proletariat has a very different task to perform than aping the bourgeois fighting methods, a thing which Sorel reproaches Marx for having too easily forgotten : " Too often, he follows inspirations

[1] See my correspondence with Gandhi, of which a French translation appeared in *Evolution*, Paris, in 1928, 1929 and 1930.

which belong to the past : in his writings, he even includes a good deal of old rubbish."[1]

That Western egotist Max Stirner, a well-known atheist who in no way adhered to the school of absolute non-violence[2] did nevertheless recognize that the greatest power the workers had lay in the possibility of their withdrawing their working-power from the bourgeoisie and feudal powers. The State only rests, according to him, on the enslavement of labour. The instant labour frees itself, the State is lost. That is why he, too, urges the necessity of general strikes.[3]

And in many popular meetings in the West they recited this verse of Herwegh :

> Mann der Arbeit aufgewacht
> Und erkenne deine Macht !
> Alle Räder stehen still
> Wenn dein starker Arm es will.[4]

The German libertarian, John Henry Mackay, of Scottish origin, a supporter of extreme individualism, based on egoism, also regarded passive resistance as the only means the masses had to defend themselves effectively against aggressive violence.[5]

Mackay was deeply influenced by Benjamin Tucker, who, while he admitted the right of each man to defend himself by violence, had come by way of purely utilitarian considerations to the conclusion that passive

---

[1] Sorel, *Réflexions sur la Violence*, p. 266.
[2] *Cf.* Basch, *L'Individualisme anarchiste.*
[3] Stirner, *Der Einzige und sein Eigentum*, p. 148.
  [4] Working Man, awake !
   Learn your own power,
   All the wheels are still
   If your strong arm so wishes it.
[5] See his novel, *The Anarchists.*

resistance was the best means of defence for the oppressed masses. He considers it to be the only way of breaking both the political bureaucracy and the military discipline. Violent revolt is usually crushed very easily by the brutality of the Government. But there is no army capable of overcoming peaceable men who do not run out on the streets but who, for instance, simply abstain from voting at the elections and refuse to do their military service or to pay their taxes.

First of all, Tucker examined the method of non-payment of rents and taxes on the occasion of the fight of the Irish Land League for Home Rule, a league founded by Michael Davitt in 1879 which was a sort of agrarian movement for secession. Henry George describes in *Irish Land Questions* (1881) how the Irish Catholic peasants refused to pay their rent to the landlords, who usually were very rich Englishmen. While one section of the movement, led by C. S. Parnell, went in for the lowering of the rents and the creation of small Irish properties, the other members of the League, under the direction of Davitt, insisted that the land should go to the people. The Government mobilized 15,000 military police and 40,000 soldiers, but the Irish Land League got the upper hand in the country by boycotting the peasants and tradesmen who had taken sides with the Government. Doubtless, there would have been a certain amount of violence in this, for the Irish people have never been educated for unarmed struggle, but in principle and in practice, the methods used were far above the usual level of the masses in revolt. The British Government took extraordinary measures to imprison all who seemed to it " suspect ". But each offensive act of the police or the army was met by the population with a strong passive resistance. Just like the Indians later on under Gandhi, the Irish were ready at this period to let themselves be imprisoned *en masse* and to replace their imprisoned countrymen in the struggle and in communal life.

This great battle which fired the whole of Ireland was strongly upheld by the numerous Irishmen in America. On both sides of the Atlantic, the Catholic clergy threw themselves enthusiastically into the movement. Bishop Nulty of Meath even sent a communication to the priests in which he declared that " the land of each country is a gift from God to the people of that country, a patrimony offered by their common Father " which was to serve as their physical support and as their pleasure. " For this reason, the land of each country is the common property of the people of that country."

One would have said that the old communist conceptions of the Early Fathers were coming back to life ! which gravely displeased the ecclesiastical authorities of the time. These gentry inclined more to the capitalist point of view, with the result that the Bishop of Meath had to hold his peace. But it was impossible to prevent another priest, the Rev. McGlynn in St Stephen's New York, from continuing this " seditious propaganda ". The slogan, " The land for the people ", soon began to be looked on as a Gospel, to be preached in all its purity and not only in Ireland but in England too, and in Scotland and America and in all parts of the earth.

Some American Catholics supported the Irish movement to the best of their ability, chiefly with funds, and in 1882 the victory of the I.L.L. seemed near. But the popular masses had only the vaguest idea of what they were claiming. Parnell, the leader in chief and his followers, whose views were very moderate, came round to negotiate with the enemy and withdrew the " No-Rent Manifesto ". Thus the movement ended in a vulgar compromise which was actually a defeat, when Parnell accepted the Home Rule Bill of Gladstone in 1886.

Why is it that in critical moments it is always left to the leaders to make the final decision ?

Let us not give ourselves up blindly to any leader whatsoever. Let his work be supervised, his arguments examined, and then, when decisions have to be made, let each man trust only in himself.

" But the masses are no more infallible than anyone else ! "

Do not place a blind confidence in the masses any more than in the leaders or in yourselves. In this world, no one is infallible. But the important thing is, that in critical moments you should not put your fate and your future in the hands of other people. And all the more so when these people, by their political and social functions, are adapted more or less to the regime under attack, or even completely hardened in it. How often the Socialist masses have been betrayed by the Second International ! How many times the Bolshevist dictators have confessed themselves to have been mistaken, at the expense of millions of living creatures ! The great merit of the anarchist movement is that in 1914 it did not follow leaders like Kropotkin, Cornelissen and Malato, when they betrayed internationalism but sided deliberately with Domela Nieuwenhuis, Malatesta, Emma Goldman, Rudolf Rocker, etc., who refused point blank to join in any kind of national truce. A truly revolutionary movement only exists in the measure that its participants work together in a responsible manner, each in harmony with the others ; where the masses constantly control the leaders, and the leaders the masses, so that there is a continual process of collective self-control ; so that in times of crisis, each is prepared to rely on himself alone for the conduct of his affairs.

In an article entitled " Passive Resistance ", Tucker had described the Irish Land League as one of the most instructive movements in the whole of history : although it was wrecked by the unscrupulous politics of Parnell, followed blindly as he was by the over-simple masses, the collective resistance of the Irish peasantry went far enough to show that the British Government is helpless when confronted with such an enterprise : had it continued, by now there would not have been one single landed property in Ireland.

As regards taxes, Tucker thinks that in America it is easier and more effective to refuse State taxes than ground-rents. For this reason, he encourages all countries placed in similar circumstances collectively to resist taxes. " If one-fifth of the people were to resist taxation, it would cost more to collect their taxes, or try to collect them, than the other four-fifths would consent to pay into the treasury . . . ' Passive resistance ', said Ferdinand Lassalle, ' is the resistance which does not resist.' Never was there a greater mistake. It is the only resistance which in these days of military discipline resists with any result. There is not a tyrant in the civilized world to-day who would not rather do anything in his power to precipitate a bloody revolution rather than see himself confronted by any large fraction of his subjects determined not to obey." For nothing is easier for modern Governments than to crush revolutionary violence. " Neither the ballot nor the bayonet is to play any great part in the coming struggle ; passive resistance is the instrument by which the revolutionary force is destined to secure in the last great conflict the people's rights forever."[1]

We must admit that the Irish have always shown a marked taste for violence. So that, during several centuries they have fought against the hard domination of the British with the most brutal and even treacherous methods. But, being unable to attain their ends in this way, towards 1880 they tried to practise a boycott, though in a sufficiently violent manner. The very word " boycott " is of Irish origin, although it describes a fighting method which, as we have already said, has been in use for thousands of years in China, and of which the efficacy has been proved many times by the United States, England and Japan.

We have already seen how Gandhi himself admits that he owes a great many of his ideas to Tolstoy. If we do not linger much here over the ideas of the great Russian relating to non-violent direct action, both individual and collective, and the international influence which they have had, it is because we assume they are already well-known to the reader. What is not generally known, is that the great general strike to happen in Russia, in 1905, the only one of the three which was truly successful, was absolutely peaceable and of the sort Tolstoy had been urging for years.

" Workmen, clerks, professional men, even Government employees and dvorniks (janitors converted into spies and informers) simply dropped their tools, briefs, documents, and what not, and refused to carry on the activities of industrial and political life. The result, on the Government's side, was panic. A constitution was granted ; a whole series of reforms—on paper—followed.

---

[1] Tucker, *Individual Liberty*, pp. 78, 244-7.

" The second strike was called when the circumstances were unfavourable, and the causes distinctly
doubtful in the opinion of the majority of the Government's enemies. It failed, and the consequent bitterness and apprehension led to a third strike, with an
appeal to arms at Moscow. That appeal was most
unfortunate ; the revolutionary elements had over-
estimated their strength, and greatly under-estimated
that of the autocratic-bureaucratic machine. The
army was loyal, and the ' revolution ' was crushed.

" Of course, human nature is human nature, and it
were both idle and unfair to blame the distracted and
exasperated Russian radicals for the turn events have
taken. .   .   .   Still, the fact remains that, had the
policy of strictly passive resistance been continued,
and had not the strike and boycott weapon been too
recklessly used, the cause of freedom and progress in
Russia would to-day rejoice in much brighter prospects."

That is the conclusion reached by Tucker with regard
to the events in St Petersburg in 1905-6, set down in
his American paper " Liberty "[1] where he developed,
à propos of the non-violent methods of struggle of the
working-classes, exactly the same point of view as that
upheld by Tom Mooney, during the hearings of the
Tom Mooney *habeas corpus* proceedings, closed finally
in San Francisco on August 18th, 1936: "Violence is the
weapon used by the employers. .   .   .   Violence wins
no strike .   .   .   only education and organization."[2]

Again, we have seen how Gandhi carried on his
struggle against the British Empire almost exactly

[1] Tucker, *Individual Liberty*, pp. 79-80.
[2] Tom Mooney Molders' Defence Committee, Press Service,
August 26th, 1936.

after the ideal of the great poet Shelley, which he expressed in his poem " The Mask of Anarchy ", written on the occasion of the massacre at Manchester in 1819, where a meeting of thousands of workers had been attacked by the King's troops, with the result that hundreds of dead and wounded lay scattered about the ground :

> Stand ye calm and resolute
> Like a forest close and mute,
> With folded arms and looks which are
> Weapons of unvanquished war,
>
> On those who first should violate
> Such sacred heralds in their state
> Rest the blood that must ensue,
> And it will not rest on you.
>
> And if then the tyrants dare
> Let them ride among you there,
> Slash and stab and maim and hew—
> What they like, that let them do.
>
> With folded arms and steady eyes,
> And little fear, and less surprise,
> Look upon them as they slay
> Till their rage has died away.
>
> Then they will return with shame
> To the place from which they came,
> And the blood thus shed will speak
> In hot blushes on their cheek.
>
> Rise like Lions after slumber
> In unvanquishable number—
> Shake your chains to earth like dew
> Which in sleep had fallen on you—
>
> Ye are many—they are few.

Which means that in England too, and for a long time past, the loftier spirits have been able to raise themselves above the age-old warlike traditions of the West, to prepare the way for a new social and political order.

In this way John Ruskin, without believing in non-violence on principle—indeed, this anarchistically inclined spirit sometimes showed an imperialist nationalism in its most extreme form[1]—stressed the responsibility which exists with regard to all work to be done and advocated the refusal of all work which is harmful. During the Franco-Prussian war, while English industry was reaping huge profits from munition making, Ruskin urged the British workers not to take part in this shameful business, nor to do any work which was unworthy of men.

" The first reason for all wars, and for the necessity of national defences, is that the majority of persons, high and low, in all European nations, are Thieves, and, in their hearts, greedy of their neighbours' goods, land and fame. But beside being Thieves, they are also fools. . . . And the guilty Thieves of Europe, the real sources of all deadly war in it, are the Capitalists. . . . The Real war in Europe is between these and the workman, such as these have made him.

" You are to do good work, whether you live or die. It may be that you will have to die ;—well, men have died for their country often, yet doing her no good ; be ready to die for her in doing her assured good : her, and all other countries with her. Mind your own business with absolute heart and soul ; but see that it is a good business first. That it is corn and sweet peas you are producing,—not gunpowder and arsenic. And be sure of this, literally : you must simply die rather than make any destroying mechanism or compound.

[1] See Bertrand Russell, *Freedom and Organization*, 1814-1914, p. 461.

" There is no physical crime, at this day, so far beyond pardon,—so without parallel in its untempted guilt, as the making of war-machinery, and invention of mischievous substance.   Two nations may go mad, and fight like harlots—God have mercy on them ;— you, who hand them carving-knives off the table, for leave to pick up a dropped sixpence, what mercy is there for you ? "

So John Ruskin wrote in July 1871, in his VIIth Letter to the Workmen and Labourers of Great Britain.

By a happy chance, a Dutch translation of these words fell beneath the eye of the author of this book while he was still adolescent, and they have been an inspiration to him throughout his whole life.

Ruskin was one of the rare Europeans who are against all forms of vengeance and retribution (an eye for an eye).   Although he did not reject certain kinds of punishment, he pleaded for non-retaliation, just as Gandhi did.   In the same letter to the British Workers as we have just quoted, Ruskin wisely charges them never to take revenge for injuries.[1]

In his book *Time and Tide* (1867), a series of twenty-five letters to the Sunderland workers, Ruskin deals in the last two with the task of the soldier and urges the transformation of military warfare into social and cultural works :   " Our whole system of work must be based on the nobleness of soldiership "[2] and, a real precursor of the civil service, he tries to awaken a love of risk among the workers with a view to all kinds of daring enterprises to make unhealthy countries healthy, to fight famine, infectious diseases, etc., so that in all parts of the earth, the vision of Isaiah may come true :

[1] John Ruskin, *Fors Clavigera*, II, pp. 15-20.
[2] Ruskin, *Time and Tide*, Letter XXV.

> " And they shall beat their swords into plow
> shares and their spears into pruning-hooks : nation
> shall not lift up sword against nation, neither
> shall they learn war any more."   Isaiah ii. 4.

That gifted workman, William Morris, poet and
thinker at once, deeply influenced by Karl Marx and
Pyotr Kropotkin, condemned all horizontal violence,
whether foreign wars or colonial, and accepted only
the social war, the class struggle, in which, according
to him, the violence used by the oppressed masses could
only be an accessory.   In his Utopian story, *News from
Nowhere* (1890) he describes how, during the social
revolution, the workers used a weapon which they
thought stronger than street fighting, the general strike,
against which the ruling class, however well-armed,
could not even use its troops, and which led to a glorious
victory on a lofty plane.

Morris also establishes a clear distinction between
useful work and useless toil.   In his essay *Useful
Work versus Useless Toil* he attacks the conception
generally adopted by the ruling class that work is useful
in itself, especially for the exploited class, as a vulgar lie.
For there is work which is useful and also work which
is both useless and harmful.   " The first has hope in it,
the other has not.   It is manly to do the one kind of
work and manly also to refuse to do the other " ;[1] the
first has a creative and emancipating significance, the
second is only the shameful work of a slave.   As for
war work, Morris declares in his essay *How We Live
and How We Might Live* : " I won't submit to be
dressed up in red and marched off to shoot at my
French, German or Arab friend, in a quarrel that

[1] Morris, Centenary Edition, p. 604.

I don't understand : I will rebel sooner than do that."[1]

Morris was one of those who, in England, held that " British Socialism is not a purely materialistic criticism of economic theory, but behind it there is a basis of ethical criticism and theory ".[2]

This view was also held by Bruce Glasier and Keir Hardie, the founder of the Independent Labour Party, which, during the World War, upheld internationalism above the mêlée, together with the Russian, Italian and American Socialist Party. The essentials of their conception may be summed up in this one word : humanism.

In their struggle against English capitalism, they were in fact valiantly defending human dignity. And in 1902, during the Boer war, they took part with all their might in the " Stop the War " movement. For them, anti-militarism was an integral part of all true social struggle. Without condemning national senti-ment, in as far as it agreed with the justifiable social aspirations of mankind, they encouraged harmony in international interests and international co-operation between nations whose only rivalry lay in the bettering of society. According to them, a real Internationalist must refuse to take part in any war whatsoever, Socialism being in the first place a universal effort to bring about world peace.

In the same way, the I.L.P. at the International Socialist Congress at Copenhagen (1910) proposed an amendment to the resolution concerning the fight against war, demanding extra-Parliamentary action,

[1] Morris, p. 581.
[2] Bruce Glasier, *William Morris*, p. vii.

especially general strikes, in industries that supply war material, as one of the methods of preventing war ; and Keir Hardie declared that the point of view of labour had not only to be anti-war but anti-military, because militarism and freedom could not exist side by side. Keir Hardie did not expect that the workers were at present ready to strike against war ; but they never would be ready to do so unless we helped to educate them by pointing out to them their duty.[1] " The Nation that has the courage to be the first to throw away its arms will win for itself one of the greatest names in history," he declared.

This same tradition was carried on by the English writer, Miss M. P. Willcocks, who was inspired as well by the ideas of Tolstoy and Maria Montessori. In her remarkable book *Towards New Horizons*, Miss Willcocks states that the great mistake of the Teutons—Germans and Anglo-Saxons equally—has been to believe that the only force by which one can maintain political and social order is violence, while really there exists another force, more secret and fatally neglected ; that is, confidence. If, from childhood, we develop in each individual the power to conduct himself in continual co-operation with his fellowmen, all external authority will soon prove to be superfluous. It is for women, above all, those who are now entering the scene of world history, to undertake the task of maintaining—in the face of the imperialist crimes of modern capitalism— this *bonté impérieuse*, which has brought about a free and spontaneous discipline not only in schools but even in certain modern prisons; there are still too few of them. It is for women to prove the truth of the old Russian

[1] W. Stewart, *Keir Hardie*, pp. 298-302.

proverb, which says that real powerlessness is real God power, and it is for them to prepare the way for an epoch in which, according to the old words, " the meek shall inherit the earth ". The more men emancipate themselves individually and collectively in this direction, the less they will be able to tolerate the yoke of the State, even of the best organized State, and the less they will resort to violence. For " self-determination means ultimately no State structure at all, but liberty for every man to follow the bent of his will as decided by nothing but the authority of the God within himself. . . . Love, free and sovereign, shall become the world's religion."[1]

In Holland, it was the late Dr Clara Meijer-Wichmann, an eminent sociologist of German origin, who, inspired by Marx, Hegel, Tolstoy, Sorel and the French syndicalists of the beginning of the century, developed in particular the thesis of a compelling harmony between the goal to be reached and the means to be used in the revolutionary study. The maxim that the end justifies the means can only be allowed in one sense, according to her : a sacred goal demands sacred means. Since Socialism coincides perfectly with humanity—the human feeling in men—its methods must never be at variance with, nor offend against, this humanity. For this reason, revolution ought to bring to the human race the noblest of moral qualities, that of solidarity. A real revolutionary can never be an enemy to his enemies nor a criminal to criminals, the more so as criminals are in the first place victims of society. The revolution demands not only the renunciation of all violence in regard to nations and classes, but also to individuals.

[1] Willcocks, *Towards New Horizons.*

Complete anti-militarism transforms itself in this way into a new individual and social education which, combining with modern psychological knowledge and psychotherapy at last renders the barracks as unnecessary as the prisons.

It was by no mere chance that in Holland Clara Meijer-Wichmann took the initiative in creating a Committee of Action against the traditional ideas on crime and punishment.   She was not only the head of the Judicial Department in the Statistics Bureau at the Hague, but she was also married to Jo Meijer, one of the bravest of conscientious objectors who himself had to undergo terms of imprisonment.

The question of the treatment of the victims of common law presented itself in Holland in the same way as in England.   There, too, the imprisonment of a large number of advanced men and women, who had refused to take any part in the War, faced these anti-War believers with one of the most burning questions of the day : the fate of criminals—especially as they themselves had experienced it.   In England it was notably A. Fenner Brockway who, after undergoing severe punishments during the World War, simply because he remained faithful to International Socialism, became the champion of this cause.[1]

In Holland, it was Clara Meijer-Wichmann again who declared that in the history of civilization, criminal law is one of the branches which has stayed centuries behind compared with the advancement and transformation of the others.   While modern psychologists and pedagogues have recognized the inefficacy and the injustice of all kinds of retaliation and intimidation, justice is still a kind of social vengeance whose aim is to intimidate and to put out of harm's way.   The widespread criminality that we meet with nowadays has always been a symptom of abnormal times, the degree of criminality being more or less determined by the

[1] See Fenner Brockway, *A New Way with Crime*, 1928.

relative order or disorder of the society in question. A great number of the degenerates who fill the prisons come from unfavourable surroundings where alcoholism, scrofula and syphilis, flourish, that is to say, these criminals are first and foremost victims of hereditary and social blemishes, and they should be treated as victims to be rescued and succoured, and no longer be driven out from among their fellow men as scapegoats. The fight for entire revision of the treatment accorded to criminals must be supplemented by the struggle for social justice and for physical, moral and mental hygiene.[1]

And here are some remarkable conclusions reached by Henrietta Roland Holst, one of the best-known theorists of modern Socialism, after a long life of revolutionary activity. A friend of Rosa Luxembourg and Karl Liebknecht, she belonged, even before the war, to that group of neo-Marxists who worked out a new kind of tactic against modern imperialism. Madame Holst, after the experiences of the Russian revolution in 1905, became a firm believer in direct action on the part of the masses and in non-co-operation as regards national defence. During the Great War, she joined the Zimmerwald movement with Lenin, and when the Russian revolution broke out, she was extremely enthusiastic. At one time, she even maintained the view that to ensure the success of the Revolution the end justifies the means, and that, in case of failure, the revolutionary must give up even the highest demands of his conscience. This was all the more remarkable because, some years ago, Madame Roland Holst had published a long historical and sociological study on the revolutionary action of the masses, in which she had

[1] Meijer-Wichmann, *Misdaad, Straf en Maatschappij ; Mensch en Maatschappij ; Bevrijding.*

laid great stress on the importance of the moral factor in the battle for a new society.[1]   And there had even been a debate, which became a classic, between Clara Meijer-Wichmann and Henrietta Roland Holst, on the subject of social revolution and violence.[2]   But the way the Russian revolution went, its militarization, its bureaucratization, the violent injustices it perpetrated in the name of revolutionary justice—a whole string of these errors at last brought Madame Holst to break with Moscow.

Under the title of *Sterft gij oude vormen en gedachten*, which is a line taken from the Dutch version of the Internationale meaning " Let us raze the past to the ground ", she published a pamphlet on the occasion of the defeat of the Austrian Socialists in their attack against Fascism in February 1934.   In these pages after honouring the courage of the Social Democrats, who had been defeated weapons in hand, she warns her readers against the halo of romantic heroism which had already sprung up round this tragic episode.   According to Madame Holst, Austrian Socialism had fallen through using political and strategical methods which were obsolete, and through the traditional faith it put in collective violence.   One thing, she says, must be noticed, which is that in modern Socialism there are two contradictory tendencies, one which is in favour of confidence in all that is human and humanitarian, the other which accepts war, dictatorship and even terror. The first, which at the beginning seemed very strong, has been more and more neglected while the second

[1] Roland Holst, *Revolutionnaire Massa-Aktie*.

[2] See *Gewalt und Gewaltlosigkeit*.   A Handbook of active Pacifism, published by Franz Kobler.

has grown at its expense.   The masses in Austria, as elsewhere, had been educated with a view to a final armed struggle, beside which general strikes, non-co-operation and other forms of non-violent struggle were held to be of secondary importance.   But " it is unhappily a law that the energy which one uses in one kind of fight is just so much energy lost in another . . .   The Austrian workers who resorted to arms had remained enslaved by the technique of modern war. . . .   Modern armaments have reduced the armed revolts of the masses to absurdity, and they are doomed simply to become a vulgar copy of the system they are attacking."   The essentially humanitarian aims of revolutionary Socialism can never be realized by arms, Madame Holst goes on.   Even if victory is gained by this means, it can only be maintained by dictatorship, terror, etc.   The tragedy of the modern Socialist movement is that when it comes up against Fascist violence, it lacks training in the effective application of non-violent methods of fight.   The sacrifice and bloodshed of courageous men and women in Austria will only be justified if the international working-class movement draws the inevitable conclusions from it.[1]

In 1937, Madame Holst expressed her satisfaction over the fact that non-violent action had taken on a new form, that of the sit-down strike, of which the first example was given in October 1934 by 1,200 coal miners in the Hungarian town called Pecs.   During a wage conflict, these miners refused to leave the mine and said that unless their economic conditions were improved they would starve themselves to death.[2]   In 1936, millions

[1] Roland Holst-Van der Schalk, *Sterft, gij oude vormen en gedachten !*
[2] See Gregg, *The Power of Non-Violence,* pp. 15-17.

of workers in the French industries used the same methods. " No blood was shed, and hundreds of thousands of workers thus took a step towards a higher humanity. And they did this solely by their own moral strength. Even in the United States, the sit-down strike in General Motors, which lasted whole weeks, took place without violence and had a great moral repercussion throughout the country. Thanks to this new method of fight, American syndicalism is now beginning to be recognized by the heads of gigantic businesses which hitherto have ignored it. And so, finishes Madame Holst, a certain quietness of mind and self-control bring about the most favourable conditions for the social and revolutionary struggle.[1]

There is a surprising agreement between the latest conclusions of Henrietta Roland Holst and those of the Russian revolutionary J. Steinberg, one time People's Commissar for Justice, in the first Bolshevist Government. Steinberg had accepted his commission in the hope of directing the Russian Revolution towards really humane ways of battle. Against his will, he found himself dragged into terror. In his book on violence and terror in revolution, he has described how certain methods drag inexorably on those who use them to the point where they are completely lost and at sea, how these methods are in contradiction with the proposed aim : the revolution is bound to perish when, for purely utilitarian motives, it neglects the moral factor or acts according to the childish maxim " since the others are doing it, we can too.". According to him, every kind of terror should be banished from the methods of revolutionary struggle, and violence can only be

[1] Henriette Roland Holst, in *Vrienden van India*, April 20th, 1937.

given the smallest place. A revision of the whole revolutionary tactic is called for.[1]

It was a Swiss Socialist, Charles Naine, who declared on September 24th, 1903, before the Military Tribunal of Fribourg, in his capacity as conscientious objector, that " the awakened proletariat would not grant a man, a gun nor a sou for the army ", the only war to be waged being the social war, an infinitely more peaceful one than that between nations.[2] The revolution is essentially pacifist in character and the social struggle has nothing of that " hideous war in which, without even knowing him, one man rips up another's belly with a bayonet " ; it is a war with words and ideas, and still more with new organizations and institutions. Since capitalist governments cannot disarm we must refuse to get them the money to continue their arming, we must " found an understanding between nations and, the day the Governments want to start their throat-slitting, proclaim a general strike."

As for the social revolution, Naine first of all praises " the pacifist means because they are more normal than the violent and because they lead more surely to the goal. . . . Violence, not to mention the reaction it provokes, develops in those who use it qualities which are the opposite of those needed in a Communist regime."[3]

Nothing is more superficial and more false than the statement of Edouard Berth :

" Yes, war between States or war between Classes— the question is put and the dilemma insoluble : and

[1] Steinberg, " *Gewalt und Terror in der Revolution ; Als ich Volkskommissar war.*"
[2] Naine, *Plaidoirie*, p. 14-15.
[3] Naine, *Journaliste*, I, pp. 37, 99, 79.

revolutionaries are only pacifist when it comes to war between States : they consider that war between States has had its day and must give way to the Class war : a complete pacifist would be a man who denies both and supports peace international and social : but such a man could only be a Buddhist ascetic or a Christian or a Tolstoyan. A man of this sort renounces the world, withdraws into his cell or the desert, and, fundamentally, cuts himself off from life ; for life is battle : is not only resistance, but also attack, aggrandizement, triumph. Life is essentially expansion, conquest, imperialism, annexation, radiation, and if possible, victory. It is surely great hypocrisy or great ignorance, or weakness or cowardice, for a revolutionary to call himself a pacifist ; bourgeois pacifism is a great hypocrisy, but working-class pacifism not less so."[1]

For we mean something entirely different : a revolutionary anti-militarism, a continual social struggle in which the aggressive instinct affirms itself on the highest level and which opens up the way to victories and triumphs that the working-class movement would never obtain by any kind of homicidal " class-war ".

Berth's great mistake was to think of war as " the absence of peace ", a conception against which Erasmus once took his stand.[2] From this point of view, Emmanuel Mounier is right in maintaining the thesis that true peace is the expansion of all human powers : " Peace, true peace, is not a feeble state in which Man gives up. Neither is it a reservoir indifferent to good and evil alike. It is strength." As de Montherlant says, " Bring about a peace which shall have the same

---

[1] Berth, *Guerre des États ou Guerre des Classes*, p. 80-1.

[2] "Upon the whole it must be said that the first and most important step towards peace is sincerely to desire it. They who once love peace in their hearts will eagerly seize every opportunity of establishing or recovering it." Erasmus, *Querela Pacis*, ed. Grieve, p. 71.

spiritual grandeur as war. Bring to peace the war virtues." " Peace is not declared, it comes from within. . . . It is on the way to this peace you will find the battalion of pacifists."[1] To the negative pacifism which would renounce the world, and even life itself—and which, by the way, has nothing in common with the revolutionary pacifism of a Tolstoy—we oppose this pacifist battle, which, using methods which 'are both new and truly worthy of men, creates a harmonious commonwealth over and above all frontiers.

As is known, in the North Western provinces of India, there are turbulent frontier tribesmen, proud yet thievish, whose enormous country is too poor to be cultivated to any purpose. This scattered population is extremely impoverished, and frequently they are driven by want to invade the prosperous valleys of the Indus. In vain the English Government organized a number of military expeditions against them between 1848 and 1900, of which sixty-four were since 1879, the year when the British Empire officially annexed the territory. In April 1937, the English Government felt obliged to send a strong force of some ten thousands of soldiers against this people and to let loose the horrors of modern warfare on them.

It has recently been said that such troubles are provoked, or at least encouraged, by Moscow, and that they are symptomatic of the traditional imperialist tension between Russia and the British Empire. It is probable. But what would Bolshevism have been able to do there if the native population had not been in the grip of an age-old misery ?

When, at a meeting held in London, on February 4th, 1936, under the auspices of the Indian Conciliation Group, Nehru was asked : " What alternative method would you use for dealing with the situation on the North-West Frontier ? " he replied that these endless,

[1] Mounier, *Révolution personnaliste et communautaire*, pp. 247-8.

bloody skirmishes could at once be stopped if the English Government would only have the courage to try conciliation plus some kind of effort to deal with the problem on economic lines, because fundamentally the difficulty of the frontier men is scarcity. These people live in a hard country and they come down in search of food and loot. Even the Tsarist Government, who in the nineteenth century had similar frontier problems to solve, had the sense to act in this direction, and all their difficulties cleared up. But the British Government pursues a policy with regard to these people which obliges it to organize every year or every other year, a military expedition with slaughter and bombing and all the rest of it, and without any results at that. The only possible way to solve this difficulty would be to give the population in question some chance of leading a normal life under better conditions. " For the rest, obviously the approach must be friendly and not like the recent approach of the Italians in Abyssinia." Such methods would never answer, because like most mountain people, these frontier tribes are very brave and very fond of liberty.

That another solution is possible is highly probable, especially in view of the fact that Gandhi himself has been asked by these tribes to go and talk to them for some years past and that his name is very popular among them. Often, indeed, the Mahatma has wished to go there, but the British authorities gave him to understand that they would not favour such action on his part.

There is another man who might be able to deal with the question in a way as effective and as humane, and that is Abdul Ghaffar Khan, the great Mahometan leader, who, however, seems destined by the official authorities to spend his life in prison. Instead of laying the foundations of stability and applying economic remedies, the British Government continues to squander blood and money, and that for over a century.[1]

[1] Nehru, *India and the World*, pp. 238-9.

In fact, the violent methods of modern imperialism are the least effective and the most inhumane.   On the other hand, to attack social and political problems according to non-violent methods is to assure results satisfactory in every way, and at the same time to gratify the innate desire of Man to expand, to radiate, and to triumph.   But instead of doing this at his neighbour's expense, he is helping others as much as himself and following the profound psychological tendency towards communicativity, which is the true source of every human community and the essential condition of all sane settlement of political and social questions.

CHAPTER VII

LESSONS OF HISTORY

> I do not think that we must acquiesce in every
> evil thing that violent men may seek to impose.
> There are, I think, methods other than war
> by which we may seek to promote what we
> believe to be good ; and these methods may
> involve quite as much individual heroism as is
> called for in war.
>
> RUSSELL.

THE methods of non-violent struggle are therefore
not confined to any special person, or race, or moral
or religious idea. They are universally human and
much more effective in the West than people, poisoned
by the usual teachings of the bourgeois catechism of
violence, generally think. Here are a number of recent
events of which we hear but little in official historical
instruction, although they are harbingers of the new
epoch to which all nations aspire :

1861-1867. In the middle of the nineteenth century,
the Hungarian people suffered under the yoke of the
Imperial tyranny of Vienna, which was symbolized
by the hated " Bach system ". Under the leadership
of the Catholic leader Francois Deak, " the nation's
wise man," they started a great movement of non-
co-operation. Completely ignoring Austrian institutions
and laws, they decided to organize their education,
agriculture and industry for themselves—which is

obviously in harmony with the ideals of the Indian Ghose. All Austrian goods were boycotted and the payment of taxes refused. It cost the Government at Vienna more to get in the taxes than these amounted to—which bears out Benjamin Tucker's assertion. The Viennese Government declared the Hungarian boycott illegal, but they paid no attention, so that there were not enough prisons to house the innumerable delinquents that the law, swamped out and in despair, kept sending. But the will of the population was unshakable. The Imperial authorities then billeted Austrian soldiers on the rebels. The Hungarians consented to take them in, that is to say, gave them bed and board, but apart from that treated their guests with such contempt that they could not stand it and complained to their superiors. In vain the Viennese Government tried to force Deak and his followers to compromise. Then, the Emperor Franz Josef decided to impose conscription on the Hungarian people. But, with one accord, they refused to submit to it. The result of this pacifist action was, that in January 1867 Bach's system was abolished, and Hungary freed. She had triumphed by non-violent methods in a fight which she surely would have lost by arms.

1871. On March 18th, in the Monmartre district of Paris, the troops fraternized with the people. Instead of firing, they raised their rifles butt uppermost. The officers took to flight, the Government fell. The Commune arose.

Meanwhile, Bismarck was demanding an indemnity of 6,500,000,000 francs and the fortress of Belfort from the defeated France. Thiers replied that he would sooner see the whole of France occupied than comply with such demands. Bismarck gave it up as too risky.

1875. France, defeated, is again threatened by Bismarck. Decazes, Minister of Foreign Affairs, replies that, rather than yield, he would allow France to be occupied by the German armies. Once again, the Iron Chancellor gave up such a risky enterprise.

1878-1890. Bismarck having decided to fight the emancipation of the German working-class by a law against Socialism (Sozialisten Gesetz) and to oppose to it a policy of blood and iron, the Social-Democrats organized themselves for action on a large scale by passive resistance and secret propaganda. Although hundreds of leaders were imprisoned, thousands of papers and journals confiscated, tens of syndicates dissolved and the whole official organization of the Party annihilated, the Socialist movement did not resort to violence, save in a few isolated cases. All the persecution did was to strengthen their morale, and in one decade the movement had increased tenfold and created " a generation of leaders of strong character ready for any personal sacrifice for their ideals and their convictions." This period was so to speak " the heroic age of Social Democracy " and even gained the respect of its enemies. It was in vain that reaction did its best to force Socialism into the streets.[1] On September 30th, 1920, the anti-Socialist law was revoked, and in the following year Liebknecht was able to say before the Socialist Congress : " He (Bismarck) has had at his entire disposal for more than a quarter of a century, the police, the army, the capital, and the power of the State—in brief, all the means of mechanical

[1] H. Herkner, in *Propyläen Weltgeschichte*, p. 439.

force. We had only our just right, our bared breasts to oppose him with, and it is we who have conquered ! Our arms are the best. In the course of time brute power must yield to the moral factors, to the logic of things. Bismarck lies crushed to the earth—and social democracy is the strongest party in Germany ! . . . The essence of revolution lies not in the means, but in the end. Violence has been, for thousands of years, a reactionary factor."[1]

1891. The Shah of Persia imposed a very heavy duty on tobacco and the people boycotted it, so that the Shah had to give way.

1902. Finland refused to submit to the conscription imposed on her by the Tsar, and that august Power, Caesar and Pope in one, found himself forced to bow to the popular will.

1905. The Socialists of Norway and Sweden prevented a war between their two countries by direct action.

1905. Successful general strike in Russia.[2]

1906-1913. Effective non-violent struggle of the Hindus in South Africa, according to the principle of *satyagraha* and the methods of civil disobedience.

1909. The population of Spain showed strong opposition to their Government on the occasion of the Imperialist adventure in Morocco.

1914. The manifest will to non-participation in this fearful bloodshed expressed by a million Spanish workers, anarchists and syndicalists, prevented the

---

[1] See Hunter, *Violence and the Labour Movement*, p. 226 ; Case, *Non-Violent Coercion*, pp. 227-8.

[2] See above, page 119-20.

Government in Madrid from entering the War on the side of the Allies.

1917. The working-class movement in the Argentine, by means of a general strike, forced the Government to abandon a plan hatched in Parliament to enter the War, against Germany.[1]

1917. The British Government wished to impose conscription on Ireland. Ireland refused, and there was no conscription.

1917. Victorious non-violent struggle by the peasants of Champaran.

1917. Successful organized mass non-violent resistance in the Ahmedabad mill strike, conducted by Gandhi.

1918. After the Armistice, the German Admirals wished to take out the fleet to prevent peace from being concluded. The sailors refused to move the ships from port. The fleet was paralysed.

1918. Non-violent victory of the peasants of Kaira.

1920. The German workers, by decreeing a general strike, smashed an attempt made by the military caste to rule the country (Kapp-Putsch).

1920. The English workers force the British Government by direct action to send their mobilized troops home, to withdraw their forces from Russia and Siberia and to give up their avowed intention of fighting with Poland in her war against Soviet Russia.

1920. Beginning of the non-violent struggle of India for national independence, under the direction of Gandhi, " immensely successful in awakening that country with its population of 350,000,000 people to

[1] See, B. de Ligt, *La Patrie humaine*, January 12th, 1934.

desire freedom and to work concretely for its attainment "
and altering profoundly " the entire political situation
in India and thereby in the British Empire ".[1]

1920-1936. Heroic non-violent struggle, carried on
by the population of Western Samoa against the New
Zealand Government, and finally crowned with
success.

1923-1925. By occupying the Ruhr, France hoped to
make the recalcitrant Germany meet the heavy economic
obligations imposed on her by the Treaty of Versailles.
The Coal Syndicate moved its seat to Hamburg ;
the German Government ceased all payment of repara-
tions to France and Belgium, and organized non-
co-operation and strikes in the Ruhr in reply to the
foreign occupation. Although this unarmed battle
gravely undermined the German finances and seriously
aggravated the economical crisis, the French Government was not long in grasping the limits of military
pressure in the economic field.[2]

If ever—says René Gérin—there was an expedition
which resembled an aggression, it was the invasion
of the Ruhr ordered by Poincaré. " The result—
because Germany organized a passive resistance—
what was it but a painful defeat for France and a
brilliant victory for Germany ? "[3]

If Germany, who at that time was really disarmed,
had resorted to arms, she would certainly have lost
and the resulting misery and destruction would have
been enormous. Gérin is absolutely right when he
affirms that Germany's security was far greater when
she was disarmed than in 1935 at the moment when
she was boasting of her ultra-modern rearmament.

---

[1] Gregg, *The Power of Non-Violence*, p. 18.
[2] *Encyclopaedia Britannica*, under RUHR.
[3] " L'Erreur d'Adolf Hitler," *Le Barrage*, March 21st, 1935.

1923. Successful non-violent mass resistance at Borsad, India.[1]

1924-5. Non-violent victory of the Untouchables at Vykom.

1927. The Egyptian minister Ziwa and the British High Commissioner were forced by the direct action of the people to withdraw a reactionary electoral law.

1927. Successful mass non-violent action at Nagpur.[2]

1928. Non-violent victory of the Bardoli peasants.

1930. After the World War, the New Zealand Government passed a law putting all youths from the ages of fourteen to eighteen under a system of military instruction. But many parents encouraged their children not to join in, in spite of imprisonment. The Government imposed on all who supported their sons in this way a fine of eighty to ninety pounds. Nevertheless, 50,000 young men, with the backing of their parents, refused to take any military instruction and, in the same year, the Government had to do away with the law.

1934. Successful hunger strike and sit down strikes of the Hungarian coal miners in Pecs.

1936-7. Numerous sit-down strikes all over France, for the betterment of the workers' economic conditions, and all successful.

1937. Many successful sit-down strikes in the United States.

If I have not mentioned the English general strike of 1926 in this list of such important dates, that strike in which 3,000,000 workers took part with a complete absence of violence, it is because it finished in a painful

[1] See Gregg, *The Power of Non-Violence*, p. 18.
[2] *Ibid.*

defeat. The reason for this failure is not to be found in the mentality of the workers, however : " Despite considerable provocation to violence by the Government, the striking rank and file of labour were, almost without exception, non-violent and orderly in action and speech, and throughout the entire nine days of the strike were astonishingly good-humoured, loyal, solid and staunch. They were full of enthusiasm and faith in their cause." The reason for their failure was the lukewarm attitude of the leaders, and the fact that they were not prepared either mentally or from the point of view of organization for a struggle of long duration. While the masses were ready for great sacrifices, the General Council, without even consulting those workers and miners for whom this great movement of non-violent direct action had been begun, put themselves in communication with the Prime Minister and made an unconditional surrender ! Suddenly they called the strike off and sowed confusion and disillusion among the masses. The result was that the position of the Labour leaders was greatly strengthened in capitalist society, while there was " much victimization of labour by employers and heavy losses of legal powers and self-confidence of the unions."[1]

Concerning the events of April 1926 in England, Alexander Berkman states that the general strike is the social revolution by its very nature and that, from the outset, the British Government was aware of this fact. If the masses could have continued their non-violent struggle in a manner as calm as unshakable, the authorities, with all their army and their fleet, would have been " powerless in the face of the situation ".

" The strength of labour is not on the field of battle. It is in the shop, in the mine and factory. There lies

[1] Gregg, *The Power of Non-Violence*, pp. 13-16. See above, pp. 117-18.

10

its power that no army in the world can defeat, no
human agency conquer. . . . You can shoot
people to death but you can't shoot them to work.
The labour leaders themselves were frightened at the
thought that the General Strike actually implied
revolution.

" British capital and government won the strike—
not by the strength of arms, but because of the lack of
intelligence and courage on the part of the labour leaders
and because the English workers were not prepared
for the consequences of the General Strike. As a matter
of fact, the idea was quite new to them. They had
never before been interested in it, never studied its
significance and potentialities. It is safe to say that a
similar situation in France would have developed
quite differently, because in that country the toilers
have for years been familiar with the General Strike
as a revolutionary proletarian weapon.

" It is most important that we realize that the General
Strike is the only possibility of social revolution. In
the past the General Strike has been propagated in
various countries without sufficient emphasis that its
real meaning is revolution, that it is the only practical
way to it. It is time for us to learn this, and when we
do so the social revolution will cease to be a vague
unknown quantity. It will become an actuality, a
definite method and aim, a programme whose first
step is the taking over of the industries by organized
labour.

" I understand now why you said that the social
revolution means construction rather than destruction,"
your friend remarks.

" I am glad you do. And if you have followed me so
far, you will agree that the matter of taking over the
industries is not something that can be left to chance,
nor can it be carried out in a haphazard manner. It
can be accomplished only in a well-planned, systematic
and organized way. You alone can't do it, nor I, nor
any other man, be he worker, Ford, or the Pope of
Rome. There is no man nor any body of men that can

manage it except the workers themselves, for it takes the workers to operate the industries. But even the workers can't do it unless they are organized and organized just for such an undertaking."[1]

Now let us go back to the non-violent struggle of the native population of Western Samoa against the New Zealand Government, already mentioned in the list of historic events. The 40,000 Polynesians who inhabit this archipelago are simple, chivalrous, hospitable and brave fighters : they are the best representatives of their race. Their conception of life has something Paradisal about it. Their speech has been called the Italian of the Pacific for its musical sonority. Their religion is a remarkable mixture of pagan and Christian. Their economic life is flavoured with Communism. From November 14th, 1899, this part of the archipelago of the Samoan isles was under the German rule, and the Germans treated the natives with a certain amount of consideration. But in August 1914, it was occupied by the New Zealand fleet and in 1920, on December 17th, New Zealand received a mandate from the League of Nations over the islands, without the feelings of the natives themselves being taken into any account at all. From the first, the New Zealand Government wished the natives to fall in with their imperialistic and capitalist ideas. They refused. Not being able to reply with violence to the violence of the enemy—the powerful white Government—they resorted to passive resistance.

New Zealand sent warships, aeroplanes, soldiers, and fired on unarmed demonstrators. Tamasese, the famous chief of the movement for resistance, a true

[1] Alexander Berkman, *What is Communist Anarchism ?* pp. 247-9.

hero of meekness, was killed. But the struggle continued. And, for sixteen years, New Zealand, in spite of its great military and naval strength, and of having to do with a few thousands of " backward natives " without contact with modern technique, was not able to bend the rebels to its will.

All honour to the Socialist Party of New Zealand for having opposed the cruel colonial policy of the Government from the beginning. And when it came into power in 1935, the first thing it did was to send some of its members to Western Samoa with the new head of the Administration, in order to discuss with the Samoans themselves the ways and means of righting their wrongs. This Goodwill Mission promised the population all the liberty it could possibly give and promised that New Zealand herself would take on the cost of obtaining this liberty, since the mandate was to be exercised in the interests of the people in the mandated country.

And so, the foreign policy of New Zealand with regard to these natives was suddenly modified as if by a miracle. Annulling the decisions of its pre-decessors and using the economic improvement of the country, the Socialist Government went even farther than the Samoans had asked them to do, so that their heroic non-violence struggle finished in victory, without inflicting any defeat on the opposing faction. Indeed, there were two victories : on one side, that of the Samoans, whose struggle had at last gained its ends and, on the other, that of the Socialist government of New Zealand, who had overcome the imperialist tendencies of its country and who (as their representative Berendson was able to state before the Permanent Commission

of Mandates on November 4th, 1936) now could count
on the loyalty and support of every section of the native
population.

To suppose that such an attitude would be pleasing
to the Commission of Mandates would be a mistake.
In this institution, where they have a habit of looking
at things from the colonial rather than the human point
of view, the exemplary settlement of this conflict aroused
some anxiety. Instead of unreservedly congratulating
the New Zealand Government on its radical change of
policy, various members of this body reproached it with
a " lack of continuity " in its attitude to the native
population, because they had quashed the decisions of the
their predecessors at one go.   Although this Commission
admitted that the attitude of other New Zealand
Governments had not been very brilliant, they were
afraid that the humane outlook of the present Government might create a dangerous precedent in showing
excessive favour to the colonized peoples ! They
even went so far as to see in it a dangerous way of speed-
ing-up the " slow march of history ".[1]   That " hasten
slowly " has become the slogan of the League of Nations,
we know only too well, for example, in the matter of
disarmament.   As for us, we can only congratulate
the Socialist Government of New Zealand on having
rejected the brutal methods of colonial tradition.

Here are some details about what has happened in
Western Samoa since 1920.

When the imperialist powers, Germany, England and
the United States, began to take an interest in this
paradisal archipelago, the natives started a movement
called O le Moa, which is, the Community of the
Righteous, including 95 per cent. of the population
under the leadership of the Royal House and the

[1] See the proceedings of the Thirtieth Session of the Permanent
Commission of Mandates, held at Geneva on October 27th to
November 11th, 1936, comprising the report of the Commission
to the Council, and the proceedings of the Third Seance of the
Ninety-sixth Session of the Council, held on January 25th, 1937,
at Geneva.

nobility. This movement possessed its own police, distinguishing them from those of the State by special uniform. They also had special buildings of their own, for use as law courts, meeting- and assembly houses. In 1930, the New Zealand Government officially forbade the Moa to go on. But it continued in secret. It became even more powerful than before. The President, by the name of Faumuina Fiame, was a man of genius as well as of great good will and energy.

One of the best loved leaders of the organization was the Prince Tamasese Lealofi, of Vaimoso, who had often been molested by the mandatory functionaries. In 1924, the Governor-General, Sir George Richardson, demanded suddenly of Tamasese that he should cut down the great hedge of hollyhocks which went round his property. As is known, the leaves of this plant are the national emblem of the natives, who make crowns of them for their festivals and religious rites. Tamasese refused outright to comply with this brutal order, with the result that he was exiled to the isle of Sawai. Protests, both written and spoken, on his part came to nothing and he finally left the island and rowed all the way to Apia to seek audience of the Governor. Furiously angry, Sir George condemned the innocent prince once again, divested him of his title and sent him back to Sawai.

After several years of suffering, Tamasese was allowed to return to his home. But when, in 1928, he refused to pay an unjust tax, he was sentenced to six months' imprisonment, to be served in Auckland. Heavily shackled, he was transported like the most dangerous of criminals. This behaviour aroused the indignation not only of the entire population of the archipelago but also of the natives in Australia. The Maori minister, Sir Apirana Ngata, declared to the Parliament of New Zealand, " It goes without saying that our sympathy is with the population of Samoa, and everyone knows it."

Although there was a regular hail of protests, the Government's official attitude remained the same.

Was it extraordinary, then, that when Tamasese returned to Samoa in 1929, he should be received like a national martyr ? The enthusiasm of the Moa was greater than ever, and their leaders addressed a moving appeal to several European powers.

On December 28th, 1929, the natives waited in the port of Apia for the return of Mr. A. G. Smyth, a white man who had been deported for two years on account of the part he had taken in the Moa movement. When the procession was passing a military police station, twelve policemen suddenly rushed out upon the crowd, revolvers in hand, and started blindly firing into the ranks of the perfectly orderly demonstrators. Tamasese ordered his countrymen to raise their hands in token of peace. But the police went on firing, presently even with machine-guns, and tens of men, women and children were wounded and fifteen natives were killed. As for Tamasese, he also died, his breast riddled with holes.

All the native men withdrew after that into the bush. The Catholic clergy and the Protestant missionaries protested. Some white lawyers who took the part of the natives, defending the honour and praising the calm courage of the Samoan women in particular, were imprisoned by the new Governor, Colonel Allen. He was finally obliged to resign and was replaced by General H. E. Hort.

All these injustices were made known, without effect, to the world, in official documents such as " The Samoa Petition, 1931 " which was presented to the Foreign Secretaries of England, Germany and the United States, and " The Case for Samoa, 1933," presented to Governor Hort.

By way of example, here are some of the natives' grievances :

That the Governors of Samoa, without their knowledge, contract heavy debts which can never be repaid. These Governors rush into senseless experiments which waste money, but, when it is a question of something necessary, they say they have no money.

That the natives are forbidden to practise the medical profession, however clever they may be, and that preference is given to white doctors, often inefficient, who earn £500 per year.

That less is paid for the natives' copra than for that of the whites. Justice there is a matter of the colour of one's skin. The native population has been banished and imprisoned in hundreds and thousands, for no other reason than for remaining faithful to their national traditions.

The Moa continued to demand freedom for all political prisoners, all those who have been expelled or deported. It claimed damages for all the unjust measures, whether affecting life, liberty or property, from which the people had suffered. It asked for freedom of circulation within the country, and for the right to go to the eastern isles of Samoa in order to keep in touch with the native civilization. It asked also for a peaceful settlement of all conflicts with foreign powers through the Court of Arbitration at the Hague.

An officer of high rank in the American Navy, Dr Felix M. Keesing, has stated in his pamphlet, *Samoa Islands of Conflict*, published in the " Foreign Policy Reports ", that the natives will never go back on the traditions of their civilization. Indeed, these people carried on their passive resistance quite implacably and with amazing courage. " We are not saying that we have won our war with New Zealand, but we do wish to put on record that our men have been killed in cold blood, although we had no weapons of our own and have not put up any violent resistance," they say, in *The Case for Samoa*, and they were absolutely determined to carry on the struggle.

One thing is certain, and that is that the brutal violence of the then Government of New Zealand was powerless to shake the heroic will of these natives. They knew they had put their struggle on an infinitely loftier plane than that of their white oppressors. On March 5th, 1930, the venerable Aloali Tuimalealiifano addressed himself to an assembly of thousands of natives as follows, his speech couched in the poetic language of his country :

" I am very old—I am eighty-four—my heart overflows with love for my people, when I see what has inevitably come about since New Zealand took up Samoa. You, sirs, the mandatory officials, you say, ' New Zealand does everything for the best, and with good will,' but I, I answer to that, ' From the very fact of your holding a privileged position, you should be just before all.' You have said that the Government of New Zealand is good. But I see what goes on around me, and I can tell you, no, it is not good.

" Samoans, thousands of Samoans, are lying beneath the ground. Listen to me, officials, for I am saying to you : let justice reign, and truth, and act as Christ has taught us all. Let it be a point of honour with you to speak the truth. Why do you lie ? The Gospel of Truth has been with us for a long time, for over a hundred years ; it was you who gave it, we had it from you. You threaten to ban the Moa and to abolish it. For us, the Moa is like a vessel with its cargo. If the vessel comes happily into port, of course we shall relieve her of her charge. But not before !

" I had thought, Mr Officials, you would have cared for our national interests, worthily and honestly, and that you would have treated us with sympathy. How is it then that you are slaying the members of the Moa like mere beasts ? That is the serious thing. We know the ways of civilized countries : when a man raises his hands, you never fire upon him. . . .

" What I want, is to uphold the Moa until it obtains what it demands. And, as for the uniforms worn by the members of our movement, how can they hurt the Government ? they are not decorated with dangerous firearms. Let us therefore wear our uniforms until our claims are satisfied. For this lovely country will never cease to be our land, our own, the land to which we belong."[1]

[1] See Hellmut Drans-Tychsen, "Die Gemeinschaft der Gerechten," *Berliner Tageblatt*, October 6th, 1934 ; " Hibiscus und die Hand Neuseelands," *Berliner Tageblatt*, October 11th, 1934.

Now, let us take Russia and see how, ever since 1918, Bolshevism, whose military strength is well known, has come up against the passive resistance of the peasants. Without sharing the Kulak's point of view in any way, one must admit objectively that the enormous mass of unarmed peasants has been able to hold its own against the iron dictatorship of Moscow for more than twenty years, and has forced it to make all kinds of concessions.

Further, one of the strongest arguments in favour of non-violent methods of struggle is the history of the Russian Tolstoyans. These men and women, numbering several thousands, scattered over the vast territory of the U.S.S.R., have continually declared themselves ready to collaborate with the Bolshevists in every humanitarian task. But they have steadfastly refused to submit, even as Marxists, to the two aspects of violence which we have qualified with the adjectives horizontal and vertical and to take part in compulsory military service. Although these Tolstoyans have been treated by a Government supposed to be Communist even more cruelly than they were under the Tsarist régime, the Red dictators have not been able to conquer them. What does it matter if the Moscow Government incessantly tries to disperse their colonies and push them farther and farther into Siberia, even as far as the Chinese frontier ! As soon as there is the slightest break, the Tolstoyans at once reconstruct their free, Communist organizations, with the most primitive resources, if necessary.[1]

Even those who reject the religious and ethical

[1] See Paula Birukoff, " A Colony in Siberia," *Évolution*, Paris, May 1933, pp. 306-16.

conceptions of these mystics have to admit that if such
methods of struggle could be used not by a few hundreds
of men and women but by millions, there would be no
power in the world able to resist them.   On the other
hand, if this handful of people had risen, weapons
in hand, against the Moscow Government, they would
have been wiped out, while, thanks to the attitude
which they did actually adopt, they still have some
influence of a moral sort on the cultural life of Russia,
whose conscience in a manner of speaking they are.

So there is nothing to wonder at if those who, in
Indonesia, fight to deliver themselves of the Dutch yoke,
although for the most part Mohammedans and by no
means non-violent on principle, they are becoming more
and more convinced that the only way in which they
can meet the vertical violence of the Dutch régime is
by civil disobedience, boycott, collective refusal of taxes
and military service, etc.

The 64,000,000 natives who inhabit the Dutch Indies
are in no position to fight in a violent fashion with the
armed forces of the Netherlands.   And even if they
were, we should see the same thing happen there as has
already happened in the West : some years ago when
Spain was defeated in the Moroccan War, we saw
France hasten immediately to her aid, thus shattering
the armed opposition of the natives by the most up-to-
date war methods.[1]   And the Dutch and English
Imperialists are bound together even more closely.   If
Indonesia tried to free itself by violence from Dutch
oppression, England and France would immediately
come running to restore . . . order.   Because if,
in the colonial chain which stretches from Morocco

[1] *Cf.* my book, *Contre la Guerre nouvelle,* pp. 15-16.

to Indonesia, one single link were broken, all the imperialists of the West at once would feel threatened; this example will be followed, they think.

As I stated at the Congress of War Resisters, at Lyons in 1931, there has been a suspicious *rapprochement* between Dutch and French imperialism. One of its most disquieting symptoms in regard to the movement for emancipation among the coloured peoples of Asia, is the new practice of the two colonial powers in question mutually to grant extradition of political offenders, thereby entirely doing away with the right of asylum.

This brings us back to the point that Indonesia will not be able for years and years to come to defeat Western violence by violence. In resorting to it, she only shows her weakness. Everything forces her to make a virtue of necessity. That is why the promoters of the movement for emancipation there are studying very carefully the histories of Hungary, Ireland, China, of modern India, and all those historical facts which we have just given, and they rightly stress the fact that even at the beginning of the struggle the Netherlands made against Spain, strikes, boycotts and non-co-operation had a great significance.

For in the summer of 1567, the Duke of Alva came to Brussels with a picked force to stamp out heresy and to impose complete despotism on the country. The old provincial constitutions were shattered, the privileges of the towns suppressed in arbitrary fashion. The Duke ruled alone, with reference to none. War broke out and the Duke soon overcame the army of William of Orange. The leaders of the rebellion were beheaded. Hundreds of rebels and suspects were put to death by fire, by the sword or the rope. The victor imagined he had chastened the country enough to bend it to his will. But the Spanish terror repelled the Catholic majority just as much as the Protestant minority. The taxes of tenth and twentieth denier, to pay for the upkeep of foreign troops, aroused an indomitable movement of non-co-operation and boycott. " In the face of the Spanish garrisons, the towns knew that recourse to arms would only result in fruitless massacres. Therefore, they used the general strike. The artisans closed up their booths, the salesmen left the markets ; economic life was suspended and the terrible Duke, before this dumb protest of a whole people, gave himself up to impotent bursts of rage."[1]

And so, at the Anti-Imperialist Congress of Frankfurt 1929, Dr Wim Jong adjured the Indonesians, in the name of the Dutch antimilitarist movement, not to be carried away by Western methods of violence but to prepare themselves for a struggle on a much higher level and on one which offered a far better chance of success, especially if it could be begun at the right moment and coincide with strikes, non-co-operation and refusal of military service in the Netherlands. Indonesia could equally well resort to such non-violent opposition in the event of English or French intervention, all the more so as she would then see herself supported by analogous movements of civil disobedience, boycott and strikes in India, Indo-china, and elsewhere in Asia and Africa.[2]

It need hardly be said that for such an enterprise to come to something, one must choose the right moment. As if one did not always choose the most favourable time for an armed conflict ! For war, nations get ready assiduously for years on end, as much from a technical as a moral point of view, and the attack is only launched when victory seems at least probable.

[1] Henri Pirenne, *Les Anciennes Démocraties de Pays-Bas*, p. 281,
[2] See *De Wapens neder*, the Hague, September 1929.

" Even divested of legend, the history of Switzerland at her heroic period is one of the grandest there is, and the most fruitful to study," writes Raoul Privat in *Le Journal de Genève*. " Werner Stauffacher and those who with him were the real founders of the Confederation knew the day would come when, to justify its existence, this Confederation would have to undergo the baptism of blood and the consecration of victory. This future, full of threats and sufferings, they looked in the face. The war they waged had been minutely prepared. When they judged the decisive hour to have struck, they deliberately provoked the incident which was to lead them to Morgarten.[1]

Referring to the unparalleled cruelty on the part of English and French imperialists in the Near East, the Arab Abdel Karim al Rifi declared that the oppressed coloured peoples had thought themselves powerless before the ever-growing violence of modern imperialism until they discovered the weapon of boycott, and that of civil disobedience, of non-co-operation, etc., which had already proved themselves of value in Syria where they had been used against the French régime with surprising success. Abdel Karim al Rifi foresaw a decisive struggle between the imperialist Powers and the oppressed masses of Africa and of Asia, in which these latter would rise as one man from Tangiers to Australia.[2]

If only these down-trodden peoples can choose a propitious moment—for instance, when several Empires are fighting among themselves—they will then certainly be able to win their freedom with a minimum of violence and a maximum of non-violence in the conduct of their struggle.

[1] *Journal de Genève*, 1935, No. 209.
[2] This remarkable declaration is to be found in a Bielefeld periodical, *Aufwärts*, XIV, No. 53, p. 1, under the title, " The Modern Weapon of Weak Peoples ".

All hope is not lost to the world ! The time has come for the masses of the West to take courage from this new teaching.

As we are never tired of saying, there are three powerful groups who have a special interest in suppressing Militarism and war : the proletariat, the women and the exploited coloured races. All three are as it were obliged, whether by their position in society, or their vocation as mothers, or their geographical and historical situation, to use these non-violent means to an ever greater extent in their struggle for freedom. The more modern warfare is developed in scientific directions to become a real monopoly of a group, as restricted as it is powerful, composed of highly educated, intellectual men, who identify their interest with those of militarist and imperialist clans—the harder it will be for the great masses of coloured peoples, proletarians and women to make their cause triumph by violence.

It is not even necessary for *all* these proletarians, women and coloured people to band together before they obtain any results : because when, at a critical moment in history, a large number of women, international workers and coloured people adopt non-violent methods of opposition, they have a good chance of success.

Reading the declaration of the Women's Organization for World Order,[1] " *We women refuse to follow the politicians* who cannot even organize such an economic and social life as would exclude injustice and war," one would think that women are at last beginning to free themselves of the age-long masculine tutelage, and the patriarchal and violent traditions which have always gone with it. This organization insists that women should have at least a half of the power in social life, in order to defend the sanctity of human life and individual and social liberty. It demands the abolition of armies and the conversion of the murder-industries into constructive works. If the 14,000,000 women who for so many years in the past have wasted their time

[1] Address : 19 rue Henry Mussard, Geneva.

drawing up petitions which politicians look on as just so much scrap paper and addressing appeals as heart-felt as they are futile to those charming gentlemen at the League of Nations, will only combine actively behind this new programme as soon as possible, we may say that the time of the armament-makers is up.

CHAPTER VIII

VIOLENCE AND THE REVOLUTION

> The Utopians are not those who oppose
> all kinds of armed violence and wish to
> do away with militarism and war at once.
> They are those who accept certain kinds
> " for the time being ", in the hope of abolishing
> these scourges later on. For, by doing this,
> they accept military organization with its
> mechanical restraint and imposed discipline,
> war industries, espionage and all the ruses
> and lies of warfare, the appeal to brutal
> instincts and anti-social passions and even
> bloody slaughter itself—all phenomena and
> tendencies which only perpetuate war. So
> that, having got beyond the present stage of
> militarism and war, they will one day have to
> combat them in the same way as the War
> Resisters are doing already. Unless we wish
> to prolong the fight for peace indefinitely, it is
> to-day and without waste of time, that we must
> wage the *complete* war upon war.
>   CLARA MEIJER-WICHMANN.

ALREADY, for purely utilitarian reasons, the white
proletariat is forced to pursue similar tactics. The
modern technique of violence, which has created countless poisonous gases, bacteria, mysterious electric rays
and stratospheric guns which surpass the wildest dreams
of Jules Verne or Wells, rests with a comparatively
limited number of experts who, without worrying about
the consequences and because they find it pays, put the

whole resource of their knowledge at the disposal of the ruling classes to the prejudice of mankind, and above all of the people. Besides, even if the revolutionaries possessed such weapons, their use would call for the worst Fascist mentality and they would be led into doing violence not only to others but to themselves as men. To put it differently, they would come to deny the revolution itself. For the social revolution means nothing if it is not a battle for humanity against all that is inhuman and unworthy of man. That is why we have always asserted that the more there is of real revolution, the less there is of violence : the more of violence, the less of revolution. At the very most, violence may be a secondary help in the course of a revolutionary movement.

This assertion is based on long revolutionary experience and on a profound study of the history of revolutions. We are happy to say that people have arrived at similar conclusions in France. Aron and Dandieu write as follows, in the *La Révolution nécessaire* (1933) :
There is violence and violence.
There is the spiritual, doctrinal violence which for us is simply the necessary instrument of the change-over from the out-worn, oppressive order to the new order which is to be set up.
There is material violence.
Perhaps this is difficult to avoid when events follow each other at such a pace that they outrun revolutionary preparations and take it unawares, but it is only a *pis aller* and a counsel of despair, for the material violence which is a governing principle of every dictatorship in the world is never essential from a revolutionary point of view : it can only be episodic, and always to be regretted, not only from a sentimental or humane point of view, but also from that of method, because it coincides with the last convulsions of the old order

that has failed to be neutralized by spiritual means and because it always shows a lack of preparation, a character of artificial and abstract rigidity, in short, a fault of will and of faith. From this point of view, one can say :

1. That a revolution is bloody to the extent that it is badly prepared ;

2. That the blood shed in a revolution is the sign of its imperfection.[1]

In short, the great problem of revolutionary action by the masses lies in this : how to find the methods of struggle which are worthy of men and which at the same time even the most heavily armed of reactionary powers will be unable to withstand. It is precisely to such methods that the coloured peoples are now beginning to resort : civil disobedience, non-co-operation, boycott, collective refusal to pay taxes or to serve in the Army, etc. If the proletarian masses of every imperialist country in the world, including Japan, can only practise these methods at the right moment—if, also, such methods are used simultaneously by the oppressed masses of colonial and semi-colonial countries—no power on earth can resist them. In such action it would not be necessary to spill even one drop of the adversary's blood. If blood must be shed, it will be that of the non-violent combatants. But this blood would be truly consecrated : it would be in truth a sacrifice not for some abstract and outworn idea but for the idea and the reality of the human race itself.

It is of course probable that such an attitude would not come about with all the perfection prophesied by Shelley[2] and that some of those fighting for peace and

[1] See above, Chap. V, page 75. *Cf.* also, *Esprit*, November 1st 1934, pp. 182-98.

[2] See above, page 121.

justice would fall back again on mere violence. Count-less numbers of the oppressed and disinherited, besides being tormented by resentment and a thirst for vengeance, which is quite understandable, respond automatically, as we have already observed, to the suggestion of feudal, pre-feudal and bourgeois violence. But we have seen, too, in India, even among the Pathans, how the masses can raise themselves above all that. We also saw in England during the general strike of May 1926 how high a level of conduct the workers maintained. In any case, in such gigantic struggles violence will be reduced to a minimum, while the moral standard will reach its peak. What we have to do first of all is to persuade the masses in every country that violence is not their trump, but on the contrary, their weakest card, and that if, in the course of non-co-operation, boycott and strikes, the violence of the authorities may possibly destroy the masses, still it will never force them back to work.[1]

This does not mean that the methods of non-violent struggle may not have redoubtable results. Let us only study the influence of the Chinese and Indian boycotts on English economic life, the unemployment which resulted, etc. Case is perfectly right when he says that these forms of conflict have very profound social consequences. We speak here of methods which are very dangerous and which must not be used except in cases of extreme necessity, and then after great reflection. But as violence, both vertical and horizontal, grows, its consequences become more fatal for the van-quished and the victorious alike. On the other hand, as the non-violent methods of struggle spread, they

[1] See above, page 146.

become more efficacious and reach their goal sooner, while their moral and social consequences are infinitely less pernicious.

Besides the slaughter, which grows greater all the time, this more and more systematically applied violence results in the destruction of public buildings, of factories, of offices, of roads, of bridges, of railways, houses, fields, forests and—thanks to the modern inventions which make it possible to poison and burn over enormous areas—the extermination of life in whole districts.

On the other hand, the methods of non-violent resistance destroy nothing ; they leave everything whole. They know nothing of the miserable procession of infectious diseases and social and economic miseries which follow war as inevitably as the trail of light does the comet.

And to put the thing in a nutshell : modern warfare is an abominable crime against man as a moral being. The more man makes war, the more his human qualities dwindle away ; on the other hand, non-violent resistance makes calls on man as a moral being : the more he practises it, the higher a level of human value he will reach. During his last voyage to Europe, Gandhi often repeated that his experience in Africa and India had shown him that non-violent resistance enobles those who use it and that, in such a struggle, women are capable of showing a very great moral energy and even on occasion of surpassing men in their heroism.[1]

We know too from European history how, in certain circumstances, defenceless women have impulsively thrown themselves in front of the soldiers' guns, and

[1] See B. de Ligt, " Gandhi à propos du Désarmement et de la Guerre," *Évolution*, Paris, March 1932, pp. 193-211.

bared their breasts, challenging them to shoot, and how, overwhelmed by this spontaneous act of confidence, these men have been unable to play a murderer's part. We know how in Spain masses of women threw themselves on the rails in front of the trains which were to take soldiers to the front and that no driver could be found who would take his engine over this living mass. It need not be said that such acts, coming from their mothers, arouse enthusiasm and inspire courage in young men, and they rush forward to protect them. In India, the heroic attitude of the women in face of English brutality so inflamed the youth of the country that mothers became veritable Joans of Arc to their sons.

Let us now consider violence from the viewpoint of social revolution. As we know, this requires the co-action of two factors : the objective or economic factor and the subjective or moral factor.

What happened towards the end of the World War ? What happened to the economic, objective factor ? It was in the most deplorable condition. A large part of industry was utterly destroyed ; the rail-roads were worn out ; stock was exhausted, immense riches swallowed up, the whole economic life dislocated.

What had happened to the principal element, the subjective moral factor, man himself ? Mutilated, disfigured, helpless in the grip of influenza and all kinds of sexual or nervous disturbances, morally degenerate and mentally exhausted, he was in no condition to make the world over ! Even to-day, mankind is still suffering profoundly from the economic, social and moral consequences of the World War. And if war broke out afresh, it would be more horrible still. Not only the civilization but the very existence of the nations would be in danger.   To gamble on a new war, to push the nations into it if necessary, with a view to helping on a revolution which would come about as the result of the misery of thousands, such were the tactics in favour with the Bolsheviks a few years after the War, tactics as criminal as stupid.   It seems that for the present they have turned their backs on so disastrous a project, but only alas ! to fall back on the very worst kind of opportunism.   We shall return to this.

The real problem the social revolution has to face is that of the organization of labour by itself, that is, according to the principle of self-government which was at the root of the move for Workers' and Peasants' Soviets in Russia, 1917, and which we find again in the Italian workers' occupation of factories and business premises in 1919-20 and in the direct action of the Catalan workers in 1936-7.

One thing will surely be of interest to the English reader, and that is that this new method of occupying factories and workshops by workers, so important a factor in the struggle for proletarian emancipation in Europe and America since the War, had already been advocated for years by the English cobbler James Harragan.   He had a way of ending his public utterances in favour of social revolution with the words, " Stay in, don't come out."   Which means, that the workers must not strike by going home or into the streets, thus separating themselves from the means of production and giving themselves over to dire poverty but that, on the contrary, they must stay on the spot and control these means of production.[1]

In the social revolution, therefore, it is a question of creating an entirely new collective order in every

[1] See M. Nettlau, *Enrico Malatesta*, pp. 63-4.

branch of production and distribution. The masses, workers and intellectuals alike, will only achieve this in as far as they have succeeded in establishing a due relation between the methods of co-operation and those of non-co-operation : they must refuse to undertake any work which is unworthy of men and harmful to mankind ; they must refuse to bow to any employer or master whomsoever, even the so-called revolutionary State, and join solidly in the one and only system of free production. It may be that in their effort to achieve this, the masses fall back more or less into violence. But this can never be anything more than an accidental phenomenon, and, as we have said, a sign of weakness and not of strength. The readier the revolutionary masses are to accomplish their historical task, the less they will use violence. The important thing for them is in any case deliberately from now on to steer their whole revolutionary tactic towards non-violence.

For this reason we appeal to all who wish to free the world from capitalism, imperialism and militarism, to free themselves first and foremost from those bourgeois, feudal and barbarous prejudices concerning violence, which are completely obsolete, and to which the majority of men still cling. Just as it is the inevitable fate of all political or social power, even though it may be exercised in the name of the Revolution, not to be able any longer to rid itself of horizontal and vertical violence, so it is the task of the social revolution to go beyond this violence and to emancipate itself from it. If the masses of the people really raise themselves, they will substitute for the violence of the State the freedom which comes from self-government.

The traditional belief in horizontal and vertical

violence is nothing but a kind of moral enslavement to the nobility, clergy and bourgeoisie. It is nothing but a kind of blind, savage Messianism. It is the intrusion of the past into the present, to the peril of the future. He who cannot break loose from this fatal heritage is doomed to confuse it more and more with the revolution, which in turn is corrupted by it. For if the Revolution does offer a real value, it is just this, that it has shaken off barbarism and based itself on its essential principles : universal solidarity and co-operation.

" But such a conception would demand a theoretical and practical revision of the whole of revolutionary tactics ! "

Yes, a revision which will show itself in a close relationship between social theory and social practice.

" But how long will it be before such ideas take hold of the masses ? "

Years, no doubt, for it is not a small matter. But can one assert that, by employing vertical and horizontal violence, the revolutionary masses will reach their goal in a few minutes ? Recourse to violence is nothing new in the Socialist movement ! Now, we have seen that the more we become slaves to these methods, the farther we get from our goal. One thing cannot be disputed : as long as men in revolutionary circles hesitate to change the traditional tactics of violence, so long they will have to wait before they are able to rid themselves of the fatal consequences of such murderous methods.

The social revolution is a long historical process, of a kind which does not happen all at once. Marx has said that the Revolution will be a series of collective attempts, of successes and defeats, a struggle during which the rising masses will continually be changing their methods and weapons ; and at the beginning of the process all kinds of different and even contradictory tactics will be used, some of them downright obsolete. The first thing to be done, therefore, is to examine all our methods and our weapons for the struggle, as a marksman sights as nearly as he can in order to hit the target. Even if the bulk of the people, always slow of understanding, try obstinately to reach their revolutionary goal by methods which are unsuited to their cause—by methods which in a word are essentially reactionary—those who have come to see that a complete renewal of international tactic is necessary, must direct all their attention and their effort towards the new methods. They can take heart by considering that, even in military strategy, new ideas are only introduced thanks to the insistence of some daring minority !

Necessary too is the preparation of technique and organization. Gandhi has often stressed the fact that the non-violent resistance of the Indian masses was for years the subject of intensive propaganda, and its organization was carefully prepared. All that is worth having, whether in the individual's life or that of society, needs long formation, unending devotion, tireless patience. Even Hitler spent years in getting ready before he seized power. And did he not try to do it with as little violence as possible ? Often, there is much to learn from an enemy. At the outset of his movement, in any case, Hitler had the courage to stand up almost alone and risk everything for his convictions, however limited and barbarian these may be.

This does not mean that those experienced in the new tactics should hold themselves aloof from the revolutionary movement in general. They must always take part in it, everywhere, in the way which their ideas permit, and must act as unshakable *avant-gardes*. In some directions it is possible for them to co-operate with those revolutionaries who still believe in violence, for example, under certain conditions, in mass movements against Fascism, imperialism and war. If it comes to armed conflict between reactionary authorities and the revolted masses, the upholders of non-violent revolutionary action are always on the side of the rebels, even when these make use of violence. But they never join in wars, even when these are waged for their own ideals, nor do they submit to any militarism whatsoever. In the great revolutionary movement, they go their own way and try to show the effectiveness of their own tactics from both the ethical and the practical point of view. If, on the other hand, an attempt is made to force them to use methods they condemn, even in the name of the Revolution, they will refuse outright, because to obey would be to betray their own revolutionary mission. In such circumstances, they become so to speak the conscience of the Revolution, a conscience which cannot be silenced and which will speak up in spite of everything.

To come back to the question already asked above : how long will it be before the new tactics are accepted by the masses ? Let us remember how long the armed struggle of the Netherlands took against Spain. We have already mentioned it : eighty years, that is to say, that three generations of men mingled their blood in it, fathers, sons and grandsons. Then, there came to

Holland the " Golden Century ".   But, after all, what is a century ?   Against Dutch violence there rose up English and French violence.   And " the great days of Coen and Ruyter "—those representatives of national and colonial violence, which Queen Wilhelmina still holds up as an example—were gone for ever.   .   .   .

Besides, the year 1648, the memory of which is so dear to the Dutch, also saw the end of a war whose disastrous results plunged Germany into such misery that it took several centuries for her to regain her feet : the Thirty Years War.

In the beginning of the nineteenth century, Napoleon began to triumph over the continent of Europe, the last of the War Gods, but one nevertheless who distrusted war ; more than any other soldier, he understood that violence was not an ideal weapon and he tried, in vain, to get rid of it.   We know the conqueror's lamentable end : St Helena.   And the British Empire, which after the fall of the Corsican brought off a series of victories and from a distance conquered one land after another, the British Empire which seemed to tower above everything and everybody is to-day shaken to its very foundations.   This immense Empire will not be able to maintain its sway unless it shows a political sense enlightened enough to reject its violent character and offer its scattered members a loyal co-operation instead of that proud domination which once was its hall-mark.

In its turn, the German Empire also rose to seize a " place in the sun " for itself.   However, against the Reich and her Ally—already split up herself on account of the injustices caused by the horizontal and vertical violence of Vienna—there banded together in 1914 a great number of Powers, to " make an end of

Prussian militarism ". The Central Powers collapsed, but the war spirit that was supposed to have been conquered spread everywhere, even to the other side of the Atlantic. After the War, the whole of Europe was Balkanized ! The injustices of the peace which followed the war—a so-called effort on the part of the victors to abolish war and re-establish justice in the world—were such that at last they brought on the Hitlerian madness. And at the moment, we see Germany feverishly re-arming, a prey to a saddening inferiority complex, and France over-armed, anxious to keep her military supremacy, so great is her fear of her vanquished neighbour, and so guilty her conscience over the iniquitous Treaty of Versailles. Instead of finally breaking with these injustices even the Blum Government continued the policy of the encirclement of Germany begun by Barthou and Litvinoff. The German reaction to this attitude was to line up with Japan and Italy—that Italy which, by applying the methods of imperialist conquest used by so many other Colonial Powers, had drawn upon herself the cold anger of the most formidable of them all, of the British Empire, when she saw that her sea routes were threatened. Result: an armaments race as never before, which will cost the English alone hundreds of millions. Meanwhile, the more national armaments pile up, the more the nations feel imperilled by their own violence. And the whole world knows, that if we continue like this, the entire planet will be Balkanized.

So let us break this vicious circle !

Chapter IX

RUSSIA, SPAIN AND VIOLENCE

O People, how much you are capable of,
if you only knew !

GOYA.

"BUT, you will object, how could Soviet Russia exist
without an army ? "

At the beginning, the Russian Revolution broke
deliberately with all feudal and bourgeois traditions,
and manifested an anti-militarist and libertarian character. People demanded " land and peace " and set
up the Workers' Councils. The Revolution even
acknowledged profoundly moral and constructive aims.
If now it has ended by giving itself up without restraint
to the bourgeois, feudal and barbarous ways of fighting,
this is entirely because it was not ready for non-violent
resistance, neither from a technical nor a psychological
point of view. Not only did this Revolution come from
the trenches, but it was literally born of the war and
made by a people who, cowed for centuries beneath the
knout, had been dragged into modern violence for some
years past. It was also led and dominated by
authoritarian Communists who, of the teachings of their
master Karl Marx, had first and foremost retained a
fanatical belief in the effectiveness of horizontal and
vertical violence, and who were pressed on all sides by
the Imperialist Powers into the bargain.

If, however, the Bolshevists fell back on State violence and discipline through terror far more than they had ever intended at the start, the working-class movement in the West is largely to blame; owing to some curious blindness it turned its back on Russia almost to a man and put its faith in Wilson, Vandervelde, Ebert, Scheidemann, Noske and Macdonald. Instead of rushing at once into the breach for the defence of world revolution, the Western Socialists left direct action almost completely alone, took part everywhere in the restoration of national capitalism and supported directly or indirectly the White intervention in Russia and Siberia. That which happened once and once only in England in 1920 should have happened everywhere, from the beginning and continuously : the working-class movement in every country concerned should have prevented its Government by means of strikes and boycotts from shackling the Russian Revolution, and by so doing they would have begun the revolution in their own countries.

That is the view which we have held ever since the end of the War, as is shown by the first publications of the International Anti-Militarist Bureau and the reports of the Third International Anti-Militarist Congress held at the Hague in 1921. If only everyone had adopted that view, Russia would have been able to devote the whole of her energies to construction and to international solidarity, instead of destruction and violence, for many years past. But things turned out quite differently and the terrified Bolshevists, seeing themselves threatened on all sides, directed their main effort towards the armed defence of the Revolution, which soon became confused with the national defence of Russia.

Armaments and mass military training took precedence of everything, and social reconstruction came second.

Many other things caused the Russian Revolution to turn aside from its path. But the chief one was that of which we have just spoken. As far back as 1920, Bukharin began to talk of Red militarism, glorifying it as " Proletarian Militarism". Dutch Communists who before had refused to serve in the Army at all for revolutionary reasons now encouraged working-class mothers to send their sons into the bourgeois barracks so they might learn murder professionally, against the coming of the Communist Revolution ! In her pamphlet " Workers' Opposition in Russia " Alexandra Kollontay pointed out how the ex-Tsarist officers, penetrating the Bolshevist Army, had re-introduced the old spirit of blind subordination and all the hierarchy this implies into it, the servile obedience of the men and the arbitrary ways of superior officers. The military spirit spread from the Army to civilian life, combining fatally with the bureaucracy of the Party and the political dictatorship. That is to say that social life too underwent a steady militarization and was always drawing away from the free organization of labour which, according to the Spartakist programme of Rosa Luxembourg and Karl Liebknecht, is the very essence of the Communist Revolution. The Bolshevists even allowed themselves to go in for a really imperialist policy at Georgia's expense, and finally adapted themselves, in a Machiavellian, which means bourgeois, way to international political relations.

At last, all Russia was militarized, the women and youth included. In March 1935, *Pravda*, the organ of the Communist Party, sang in lyrical strain a hymn to Soviet patriotism and militarism. According to this paper, Russian nationalism differs from bourgeois nationalism except for " those sentiments which inspired the Jacobins during the French revolution and which were able to move mountains." That is why all education and all instruction must bring about a new Russian patriotism. " Every glorious or heroic memory bound up with the Red Army must be made the occasion for teaching our children never to take their eyes off our frontiers and to follow every movement of our enemies. And if the enemy falls on us, the Soviet patriots will take their weapons and, with a heroism unequalled in the history of mankind, will sweep the Fascist brigands from the face of the earth." One can understand the glee of *Le Temps* of Paris and of all the French armament Press on the occasion of this profession of patriotic faith.

"But how would you have Moscow defend itself from attack by Japan, for example ? "

Against an attack on the part of Japan, which seized Korea and Manchukuo in the same brutal way that U.S.S.R. seized Georgia, and which is now threatening Russian Siberia, the Bolshevist Government can probably only defend itself by force, since it has put its whole faith in force and since it has been preparing for years for such defence, in the systematic method proper to fanaticism. To tell the truth, the Russia of to-day has been built up by means of vertical and horizontal violence like any typically modern State, and has nothing to owe to Italy or Germany for example in this way. No doubt the military-bureaucratic pyramid in Russia has a very wide social base and the peak is not so high, but the masses of the people are nevertheless

12

heavily oppressed by the political hierarchy, above all since Stalin came to power. Still extremely weak and imperfect considered as a social organism, the Bolshevist State is, as far as violence goes, the strongest of institutions. Besides, the regrettable lack of solidarity of the workers of the world with the Russian Revolution transformed the original internationalism of Moscow into an essentially reactionary nationalism. This condition was aggravated by Stalin's policy. Let us not be astonished if such a country finds it impossible to respond to an eventual attack by Japan otherwise than by this collective and scientific organization which is called modern warfare.

Let us nevertheless bear in mind that Russia, however well-armed she may be, can less and less afford to risk a war, as all the forces which she needs for social reconstruction would have to go towards international destruction. Supposing it were possible for the Bolshevist Government to drag its people into war, it is to be feared that once the patriotic exaltation of the moment were forgotten the soldiers would turn their weapons against the Kremlin, especially if victory came slowly. The discontent of the Russian peasants—and not only of the Kulaks—is far from being over. Therefore, the Government of Moscow does all it can to avoid an armed conflict with Japan. And, thanks to this policy of moderation, dictated by prudence, the Russian Government represents for the time being at any rate a pacifist element in the assembly of nations.

Indeed, the time has come when we may speak not of Bolshevist anti-militarism but of Stalinist pacifism. At the Disarmament Conference, Litvinoff certainly made suggestions which, if carried out by the nations, might have changed this purely opportunist pacifism into a practical anti-militarism. That is why, as soon as these suggestions were put forward, we laid stress on the necessity for the masses of the people in all countries —Russia included—to force their Governments by direct action to settle the problem of disarmament in the way proposed by the Soviet representative. That is why, also, at the time when Litvinoff's first suggestions for total disarmament were rejected, the Total Disarmament Committee, aware of the dupery involved in a simple reduction or limitation of arms, submitted to every international organization interested a plan of campaign which set out to obtain total disarmament within five years at the outside, beginning with an immediate reduction by 50 per cent. of the largest armed forces ; this plan advocated, as a means of bringing pressure to bear, methods of direct action such as the refusal of military service, both individual and collective, opposition to Budget credits which would be used for military ends, and the refusal to manufacture, transport or use any war machines or material, etc.[1]

The question is not whether Litvinoff was sincere in making his suggestions or whether he simply wished to force the Imperialist States to put their cards on the table. If his propositions for general disarmament were not accepted the blame lies in the first place with

[1] Declaration of the Total Disarmament Committee, Geneva, June 1932, in La Société des Nations, XIV year, numbers 4-7, pp. 389-93. The Committee, under the Presidency of Donald Grant, was composed of the following ; Fellowship of Reconciliation, International Anti-Militarist Bureau, International of Anti-Militarist Clergymen, Quakers of U.S.A., War Resisters' International, Women's Co-operative Guild, Women's International League for Peace and Freedom.

the working class movement of every country, for not having, by means of direct action, forced their Governments to accept them immediately and in their integrity. There again, the Second International and the International Syndicalist Federation have shamefully neglected their duty; instead of urging their adherents to make their governments decide in favour of a definite disarmament —which would have greatly weakened imperialism everywhere—the leaders of these organizations lulled their flocks with false confidence in diplomatic intrigues of a feudal-bourgeois character, in parliamentary negotiations, in fruitless petitions which were nothing but scraps of paper, in the labours of bureaucratic commissions, etc.

To come back to the Russo-Japanese question, if the Bolshevists had educated the Russian people in such a way as to have developed their moral sense : if these people had been initiated into the methods of non-violent resistance : if, instead of alienating the greater part of the peasantry by their violent behaviour, they had carried the free organization of the people to its peak, they would doubtless by now be in a position to meet Japan with an effective non-violent resistance. We may indeed ask ourselves if even now it would not be possible up to a certain point. It is in any case certain that under present conditions, and in the event of having to put up a defence against an armed attack by Japan, the passive resistance of the peasant masses could play a part as important as it did during Napoleon's march on Moscow, a resistance which brought about the conqueror's retreat and meant the beginning of the end for him. The more so as neither Korea, nor Manchuria, nor China are likely to remain passive spectators of such a conflict ; and, further, we may be sure that a large part of the world's workers would implacably boycott Japan.

Already in the bourgeois world people are beginning to understand how dangerous it is to oppose a possible aggressor by violence. In *The Times* of December 19th, 1933, Lord Howard of Penrith and Messrs Grigg, Richmond and Wickham Steed, state that the Pact of Paris (Kellogg-Briand) is meaningless unless those States who are potential aggressors are threatened by an effective sanction. Such a measure of restraint, they write, which would guarantee the security of all States, is not necessarily " an act of war in itself ". A collective boycott is quite enough. The *Journal de Genève* of December 29th, 1933, admits that such a boycott is " a very powerful weapon. Put into use in its extreme form, it would end in the complete isolation and, no doubt, in the collapse of whomsoever is the object of it."

Such a collective, international method could have prevented the outbreak of the Great War and smashed German imperialism : it " would have not only prevented the war of 1914 but it would have led, without murderous hostilities, to the same results as set down by the Armistice of Rethondes ". Then who would risk such a disaster ? Lord Robert Cecil also, in a lecture he gave at Geneva, in the Reformation Hall, on October 15th, 1933, praised the boycott as the most appropriate weapon for imposing a disarmament convention on refractory States.

In the *Telegraaf* of May 7th, 1935, there was an article on a remarkable form of collective non-co-operation which has been described by General Smuts as the mineral Sanction.   In this article, Sir Thomas Holland, Principal and Vice-Chancellor of Edinburgh University, gives an account of the proposal he made in 1929 as President of the British Society of Sciences and which he discussed on January 29th, 1930, in a speech to the Royal Society of Arts.

The author states that the three usual methods of preventing war :

1. Agreed scale of disarmament.
2. Embargoes on the export of war munitions to belligerents.
3. New groups of alliances and ententes.

have all failed and that under present conditions, the disarmament conventions, the rupture of all commercial relations with the aggressor, collective pacts, etc., demand too much of the people in question, and that, besides, they risk becoming ineffective owing to the dishonesty of those whose enormous interests are at stake. That is why Article XVI of the League of Nations Covenant is doomed to remain a dead letter.

There is, however, continues Sir Thomas, one method as simple as it is effective of fighting war and bloodshed. That is to refuse to allow any country resorting to war to import the minerals necessary for the alloy of metals indispensable to armaments.   Without regular provision of these materials—above all of such minerals as iron, manganese, copper, nickel, lead, bauxite (used in making aluminium), tin, mica, platinum, tungsten, mercury, petrol, which cannot be replaced, as rubber can, for instance, by synthetic products—no war can be waged ; in time of war, a country needs these materials at least as much as from five to twenty times more than in time of peace, and it is impossible to pile up such stocks in advance.

This method is all the more effective since there is not a single country, not even Russia or the United States, which contains in itself all the raw materials necessary for making war. If we indicate by 100 a nation's chances of independence as far as raw materials go, in 1936, the situation of the chief countries was as follows :

1. United States 90
2. Russia (a) after the realization of
               economic projects .. 80
              (b) in 1936 50
3. Germany 62
4. Great Britain 55
5. France 48
6. Czecho-Slovakia 48
7. Japan 43
8. Belgium-Luxembourg 32
9. Italy (in 1936) .. .. 19[1]

Every country which is not certain of being able to procure a complete provisionment of all raw materials necessary to war would be forced to see that to rush into war would be to court disaster, for each mineral is essential : "it is useless to be able to build a motor-car if one cannot get a sparking-plug ".

In his article in the *Telegraaf*, Sir Thomas insists that the mineral Sanction used against a belligerent State would even render all forms of blockade unnecessary and would thus avoid the risk of war, which often results from such tactics. There would no longer be the formidable problem of deciding which of the exported goods were contraband. Thus, neither the means of subsistence for the population of the belligerent country, nor clothes, etc., would come under this clause.

It seems to us likely that much water will flow under bridges before capitalist and imperialist Governments will accept such rational and humane methods, and those which can so easily combine with all sorts of disarmament measures. In the meanwhile, it is up to the revolutionary movement, if it is still worthy of that name, to profit from such ideas and to render them effective by direct action.

[1] F. Friedensburg, *Die Mineralischen Bodenschätze als weltpolitische und militärische Machtfaktoren*, 1936, p. 182.

On January 25th, 1934, the French syndicalist Jouhaux admitted, before a public assembly in Geneva, that in the present circumstances the best way to prevent a war is by general strike. This strike, however, must not be put off to the last minute, since it is precisely to prevent mobilization that it must be used.

M. Jouhaux is right in insisting on the necessity of not delaying the general strike until the last minute, if we want to prevent the outbreak of war. Like Pouget, Griffuelhes and Niel, the Secretary of the C.G.T. which advocated " anti-militarism and anti-patriotism, the struggle with the State, local and general strikes, boycott, sabotage and direct action ", Jouhaux preached entire anti-militarism before the War. On July 27th, 1914, the *Bataille Syndicaliste* was still urging the workers to prevent the war by direct action. On July 29th the Government forbade a gathering of the C.G.T. at Paris, at which they were to have discussed the means whereby they might prevent mobilization. But on July 31st, the leaders of the C.G.T. gave way before the general mobilization as a *fait accompli* and on August 4th, the *Bataille Syndicaliste* was preaching the Holy War to the French and urging them to defend modern democracy, allied to Tsarist Russia, against barbarous Germany. . . .

On August 4th, 1914, Léon Jouhaux declared at the funeral of Jaurès : " In the name of the great syndicalist organizations, of all those workers who have already joined their regiments, in the name of those leaving to-morrow, of whom I am one, who will know how to do their whole duty, I salute him who was our living doctrine . . ."

Léon Jouhaux " did not, as a matter of fact, leave to-morrow nor any other day, and consented to stay at Paris and collaborate loyally with the bosses and Mgr Amette on behalf of the Holy Union ".[1]

[1] See *La Foire aux Girouettes*, Le Crapouillot, 1935, s.v. Jouhaux.

If, however, continued Jouhaux at Geneva, in January
1934, the country is attacked by an aggressive imperialism,
the workers must organize an economic boycott.
According to him, there is no doubt that if, in such a
case, the direct action of the workers took on the
character of a real demonstration of international
solidarity, one could then count on the help of a large
part of the masses in the attacking country. And
according to our way of thinking, even if Japan were the
aggressor, a country in which popular dislike of war is
much greater than is commonly supposed.

In any case, we are persuaded that the best way to
fight for the de-militarization of the U.S.S.R. outside
Russia is first of all to fight each one the militarism of
his own country. The more that the bourgeois governments everywhere are forced to reduce, limit or even
abolish their national armaments, the less the Russian
Government will need theirs, and the more they will
be able to devote themselves to the social reconstruction
dreamed of by the Russian people. At the same time,
it is the duty of these same Russian people to free
themselves from the vertical and horizontal violence
of the Stalinists, first because, as Marx and Engels
saw, true Communism cannot be reconciled with the
State, and then because, from the point of view of
proletarian revolution, according to Lenin himself, the
State could not be anything but a transitional period,
the ideal being to reach an a-political order ; thus the
State will soon have to undergo decay. But according
to the law of social inertia, bureaucratic, hierarchic
and military institutions do not " decay " of themselves :
only the direct action of the masses subjected to these
institutions will exhaust their strength to the point of

annihilation. That is to say, that it is for the Russian people itself to free itself as soon as possible from State capitalism represented by the authoritarian Communist system, and from the bureaucracy and militarism inherent in this system, and to realize free Socialism. And in this direction the Russian conscientious objectors, the anarchists and syndicalists, persecuted so cruelly by Moscow, are already accomplishing a historic task.

This all means that we do not share the view of those who go trumpeting to the four winds the motto : " Against all imperialist war ", adding on a lower note, and only for the initiated, "except for the defence of revolutionary Russia " nor of those who, declaring that " the international proletariat ranges itself without reserve (!) beside the Soviets ", extol the Franco-Russian pact of mutual assistance. Security is still based on war, and therefore remains insecure. We reject all war, even in " defence of Russia ". As we have shown, the revolution has no need of such violence and it would be a calamity if it fell back on it.

The one-time Prince Mirsky, who, after serving in the White Army under Denikin and giving lectures in the University of London, returned to Russia there to become as one of his critics said[1], " more Communist than the Commissars ", has just published a remarkable book on Lenin. According to Mirksy, one of Lenin's principal messages was that, since the working-class was the only one able to reach the revolutionary goal and its cause being that of all the exploited, however destructive it may be one should not be afraid of loosing the revolutionary energy of the masses : the revolution should conduct itself in plebeian fashion, although this may offend the susceptibilities, both aesthetic and sentimental, of intellectuals nourished by the culture of the exploiters.

As if the modern " plebs " that is to say, the industrial

[1] See *The New Statesman and Nation*, March 23rd, 1935, p. 420.

proletariat, the poorer peasants, etc., were devoid of all moral sense and as if the sentiment of human responsibility was only the attribute of intellectuals nourished by bourgeois culture. A long revolutionary experience has taught us that in general it is precisely in the mind of the people that spontaneous justice and human sensibility is to be found, more than in that of intellectuals who, with certain exceptions, have sold themselves body and soul to the ruling classes, conformably with usual capitalist morals, and have gone so far as to invent and create all the modern means of horizontal and vertical violence in the world ! Gandhi stated also that in India, whereas the masses lean instinctively towards the methods of passive resistance, the intellectuals, stuffed with all kinds of bourgeois and feudal notions, do all they can to win them over to their ideas and make them fall back into violence and war.

As for Russia, no doubt there was also there at the starting point of the Revolution, some spontaneous explosions of violence, very understandable in any case. But it was the intellectuals who, imbued with the feudal and bourgeois mentality, have systematically militarized the masses of the people and who have introduced State-ism and bureaucracy into the Revolution to such an extent that it becomes unrecognizable.

Those romantic conceptions of Lenin, so extolled by Mirsky, about the unleashing of proletarian violence, which might have had some sense in the time of Bakunin, have nothing to do with social realities nowadays and are in flagrant contradiction with the very aims of the revolution, of which one of the most indispensable factors is the moral sense of the rising masses. In the critical moments of history, it is not a question of appealing to what is plebeian in the masses ; what is needed, is to awaken in them a human personality.

If one will only reflect, it is a grave offence against the mass of the disinherited to think of them essentially as " proletarians ". It is just because they are men that they have to free themselves one and all from their state of being " proletarians " and " plebeians ".

That is why we cannot approve the thesis of Martin Hart either; this was published in the German organ of the E.S.I., saying that since every war differs from the others in many respects, and each has a different influence on the evolution of Socialism, Socialists must take only this eventual influence into account when deciding their attitude to a certain war.[1] All that we have just said has been one long refutation of this essentially Machiavellian thesis.

However, the first duty of us, the men of the West, is not to occupy ourselves first and foremost with Moscow but with our own countries ; not with the Government of the Soviets but with our own Government. The distress of modern times demands not only that we should demilitarize the nations but also that we should re-make the social order as soon as possible, in such a way that the workers perform all social economic functions in accordance with the principles of self-government. " Social revolution and reconstruction cannot be undertaken and realized except by the masses themselves . . .   the proletarian masses are called on to build Socialism stone by stone by their own efforts. Free, self-government . . .   the work of the toilers themselves. Not the acts of despair of a minority," we repeat with Rosa Luxemburg and Karl Liebknecht.

In the fight for a society worthy of men, we can affirm one thing : that is, the more Governments can be compelled by direct action to disarm and to give up conscription—even if they do so with the mental reservation that it is only for the time being—and the greater the numbers who refuse to take part in horizontal and vertical violence by either military service or

[1] *Sozialistische Warte*, April, 1935, p. 78.

economic, social and cultural collaboration, the more there will awaken a confidence in the non-violent methods of resistance, the less chance war has of breaking out, and the less the revolution risks falling back into traditional violence. It is for example obvious that in a country like England where conscientious objection and general strikes already have a certain tradition, where the significance of these methods has been admitted in congress after congress[1]—and where even the unemployed loathe military service so much that the government always has difficulty in keeping up the numbers of voluntary recruits—the great mass movements risk giving themselves up to base violence much less than in countries where they have only a vague idea of what direct action means, or where the citizens are systematically taught the art of war and where all classes of society are permeated with romantic ideas about violence.

It was Keir Hardie, as we have seen, who in 1910 declared at the International Socialist Congress of Copenhagen : " The nation that has the courage to be the first to throw away its arms will win for itself one of the greatest names in history " and in 1914 he was one of the first of the anti-war *avant-gardes*.[2]

During the War, 16,000 Englishmen refused to serve in the Army. These conscientious objectors preferred to undergo the vilest treatment and even suffer death rather than to go back on their convictions.

On December 8th, 1927, Arthur Ponsonby, one-time Secretary of State for Foreign Affairs, sent an open letter to the English Prime Minister, stating that since nowadays it is possible to settle political conflicts by diplomatic means or by Arbitration Courts, etc., he had decided to refuse to serve in any military capacity,

[1] See my book, *Contre la Guerre nouvelle*, p. 117-19.
[2] See Stewart, *J. Keir Hardie*.

should his Government resort to arms. Over 128,700 English citizens followed his example and sent the same declaration to the British Government. In 1935, the Rev. H. R. L. (Dick) Sheppard, then Canon of St Paul's, began a movement which grew into the Peace Pledge Union, whose members exceed 100,000, all signatories to the following declaration :

"I renounce War and never again, directly or indirectly, will I support or sanction another."[1]

On January 25th, 1935, Reuter announced that the number of recruits to the English Territorial Army had greatly decreased : while in 1931, the number was 31,207, in 1934 it was down to 24,000. The number of Territorial Army officers was 7,030, that is to say, 1,096 less than the required number. And yet the number of unemployed in England is more than 2,000,000.

It is the same in the Scandinavian countries, where the anti-militarist movement is deeply rooted, where direct action by the masses already has a long tradition behind it and where the masses of the people have even been able to prevent a war by direct action.[2]

That brings us back to the fact that the struggle to abolish all compulsory military service and for immediate national disarmament, when it is fought according to the principles of revolutionary anti-militarism, performs a very important function in preparing for the social revolution. It is even the first phase of this. As the struggle gains ground, not only does it seek to abolish an integral part of the equipment of violence belonging to dominant groups but it also tends to lead the great masses away from bourgeois or feudal traditions and habits, arousing more and more in each individual that self-confidence,

[1] H. R. L. Sheppard, *We say ' NO '*.
[2] See above, page 141.

that self-respect, those human sentiments without which a true social reconstruction is not possible. As Heinz Kraschutzki, a one-time officer of the German Fleet and, since the war, a convinced anti-militarist, who has made a profound study of the situation in the Spanish peninsula, stated concerning the fearful happenings of October 1934 in Spain : " The fewer arms a country has, the more rights and liberties the people have. In a completely disarmed country, revolution itself would be unnecessary, because there neither oppression nor exploitation could occur."[1]

The so-called Spanish Revolution in 1934 was put down by tanks, aeroplanes, artillery and African battalions. This revolt never had even the smallest chance of success. In any case, it was directed with a few exceptions towards political and State objectives, rather than economic or social. That is why an important article, published by *L'En-Dehors*, and entitled " Lessons to be learnt from the recent events in Spain ", ended up as follows :

" A real revolutionary movement in Spain can only aim at overthrowing the yoke of the financial powers and of *étatisme* under all their aspects. In this struggle it would be ridiculous to descend to outworn ideas of war, which have failed in any case. Only owners,

[1] Heinz Kraschutzki, one of my most faithful and devoted colleagues and friends, was for many years one of the courageous leaders of German Pacifism, at the same time as editor of the anti-militarist weekly, *Das andere Deutschland* (the other Germany), of which the title alone proves there is another Germany besides the military-minded country of which we generally speak. Some time before Hitler came to power, Heinz Kraschutzki, accused of high treason on account of publications dealing with Germany's secret armaments, had to leave his country, and established himself at Majorca where he continued his struggle against all forms of militarism and war, and for human society based on self-government. He was one of the first to be deprived of his German nationality by Hitler. After Franco's troops entered Majorca, Kraschutski was soon imprisoned and, if he is not dead already, the worst is to be feared for him.

statesmen—even those in the Bolshevist State, which owns property and money—and others of that sort continue blindly to believe in violence. A real revolution would not only be anti-capitalist and anti-*étatiste*, but it would develop all along according to the non-violent method of which the Gandhi movement has given an undying example. So, ' absolute refusal to carry arms or obey the laws, to defend or protect any form of the State whatever. Only then, a United Front could come into being and be successful.' In the present circumstances, the armed can only constitute a minority. To put arms into their hands, is to make it possible for them to despoil, bully, assassinate the people. While armed men still remain, it will never be possible to secure absolute solidarity, nor even complete socialization. The rights and privileges of the men at arms will drown all the rest. We can, in the West, make fun of Gandhi's teaching but it is the only hope for the revolution, and this in spite of the turn which Gandhi himself has thought fit to give it."

So there is nothing surprising in the fact that for years past the Dutch syndicalists Albert de Jong and Arthur Müller-Lehning, without being non-violent on principle, have been preaching the systematic use of non-violent methods to the International Working Men's Association ; methods such as strikes, non-co-operation, boycott, to be used in the fight for social emancipation since the development of the technique of warfare demands a complete revision of revolutionary tactics. This propaganda encountered a strong opposition among the Spanish syndicalists and anarchists, which was all the more regrettable since the Spanish working-class movement, especially the C.N.T. and F.A.I., has for a long time been giving striking proof of the effectiveness of such methods as are described above. But in Spain, there exists a tradition of violence, both collective and individual, which it seems extremely difficult to overcome. Further, the people of this country seem to incline fanatically towards extremes— as Juan Donoso Cortès wrote, *el caracter historico de los Españoles es la exageración en todo*— ; and to understand them, we must always remember that they are Torquemada, Loyola and Don Quixote.

However this may be, the Spanish working-class movement, particularly the left wing, did not adapt itself to these new military techniques, which require of the workers either that they become more militarized than the reactionary forces or else that they conduct their battles in nobler fashion, with humaner methods. While the Spanish military caste systematically modernized the army and entered into sinister relations with foreign Fascist powers, the syndicalists and anarchists, drawing their inspiration from the romantic revolutionary ideology of the bygone century, secretly armed themselves to be " ready " for a decisive battle which they assumed to be imminent, but all in a distinctly primitive way.

Even in Catalonia, with its remarkable working-class movement which, according to *The New Statesman and Nation*, is distinguished by its " pervading sense of freedom, of intelligence, justice and companionship ", the powerful C.N.T. and F.A.I. with their hundreds of thousands of members remained on this point almost . . . conservative.

Further, instead of forcing the Government of Madrid by means of direct action to suppress the Spanish military caste, only too tragically notorious, they allowed it with amazing *insouciance* to exist even after

13

they knew that these reactionaries were hatching a *coup d'état*. The result was the terrible event of 1936. Armed in the most effective way and assisted by the most up-to-date military powers, Franco and his gang flung themselves on the country and attacked the masses, who in the beginning almost had to defend themselves with their naked hands. Let us remember the heroic resistance made by the Catalan population, which shattered the first onslaught of the Fascists. Then there came the long struggle, in the course of which the reactionaries advanced but slowly, for all their great military superiority, while the Popular Front, defending itself as best it might, had to adapt itself to the exigencies of modern war with the help of the hyper-militarized Russia and all kinds of foreign aid. While on one side Germany, Italy and Portugal—as formerly, England and France in Russia—systematically intervened in Spain in a counter-revolutionary way, on the other side, the English, French and even Russian Governments did all they could to restrain the efforts of the masses, fighting for the Government, towards social reconstruction.

Indeed, the most interesting feature of the Spain of 1936 was the vigorous attempt made by the F.A.I. and the C.N.T. to subordinate the war to this reconstruction. Spanish and Catalan lovers of freedom did not wish to sacrifice themselves in war except for a society which should be truly worth defending. For this reason Catalonia, where they formed the majority in the working-class movement, was a ferment of constructive activity, the creative activity of social revolution.

" The entire social, political and economic structure of this most important region—wrote Norma P. Jacob in *Reconciliation*, January 1937,—is being transformed with almost unbelievable speed and thoroughness, and the anarcho-syndicalist society is rapidly coming into being. Anarchism is a word not usually associated with peaceful activities, and yet it has points which should commend themselves to the absolute pacifist. Anarchism or Libertarian Communism, is defined in a pamphlet called " Arms of the C.N.T." as : ' The organization of Society without the State and without private property. The nucleus of organization, about which will be built up the economic life of the future, exist already in society ; they are the Syndicate, the spontaneous grouping of workers in factories and all kinds of collective undertakings, and the Free Municipality, the spontaneous grouping of the people in towns and villages. These organizations take collective possession of private property and regulate the economic life of each locality.' Each of these economic units is bound to consult with other such units about matters regarding the good of all, but there is no central authority nor any outward link binding individuals together beyond that of economic necessity. The principle of ' from each according to his ability, to each according to his need ' is to be strictly observed. Already the public services in Barcelona and other towns have been running for several weeks under workers' control and a recently published Decree of Collectivization provides for the ultimate extension of workers' control to the whole of industry."

The author states that Spanish anarchism is anything but a creed of non-violence, " but violence is not an essential part of the system. It proceeds simply from the belief that man must be set free from external bondage at whatever cost. The axioms and advice offered to the anarchist man-in-the-street are indications of an idealism which is certainly not assumed. ' Comrade,' says the daily newspaper, ' while the enemy is destroying, your mission is that of construction. Reconstruction is the common task of the workers. Put away all egoism and consider the necessities of others.' The writer of a recent eye-witness account of Barcelona in the *New Statesman and Nation* points out that anarchism should be an ideal not unsympathetic to the English, who have always honoured freedom and individual eccentricity and whose liberalism and whiggery might well have turned to something very similar had they been harassed for centuries, like the Spanish proletariat, by absolute monarchs, militant clergy, army dictatorships and absentee landlords. . . . It is as if the masses, the mob in fact, credited usually only with instincts of stupidity and persecution, should blossom into what is really a kind of flowering of humanity."

But here begins a real tragedy. Strongly opposed to any form of military conscription, like all convinced anti-militarists, the Spanish anarchists accepted at the most " spontaneous violence for the revolution ", and organized a free militia, in which the union methods of collaboration were to be used and in which everything would be controlled from the bottom upwards. But the necessities of modern warfare made it imperative for the Revolutionary Army to be systematically militarized, the command to be centralized, conscription to be introduced and so on. Besides this, total warfare could only be waged if supplemented by the totalitarian State. So that the longer the Civil War persisted, the more militarism and *étatism* began to grow, even in the most libertarian circles. The Spanish syndicalists and anarchists were decoyed by false hopes even to the extent of allowing themselves to become involved in an essentially bourgeois system of government.

In the Spanish Popular Front, two tendencies could be distinguished : the one, of those who wished to make war only in service of the Revolution (C.N.T.,

F.A.I., P.O.U.M.) and the other, of those who made war only in order to defend the existing " democracy ", which was actually no such thing, but a mere camouflage and a poor one, for the realities of a capitalism as pitiless as brutal.   The defenders of this self-styled democracy (bourgeois Democrats, Catholics, Socialists and Stalinists), inspired by conventional political and military ideas, systematically encouraged the militarization of the country, supported materially and morally by Moscow, whose political influence was gaining more and more weight.   At one time, the Stalinist Government, in agreement with the British on this point, demanded the suppression of certain libertarian and revolutionary tendencies in return for its technical and material assistance.   To disobey the orders from Moscow would have meant for the Spanish Government doing without a moral and technical support indispensable for the continuance of the war.   So that the libertarians were suddenly expelled from the Government and, in May 1937, in the midst of one civil war there broke out another, so to speak : between one side of libertarians who wished to defend their rights and their liberties, and the Stalinist-bourgeois government. If the C.N.T. and the F.A.I. agreed to a compromise which put an end to this new fratricidal conflict after a few weeks, it was only because they found themselves in a painful dilemma : either they must break with the Popular Front and, waging a civil war within a civil war, increase, however involuntarily, the chances of victory of Franco and his Fascists, or they must accept their defeat from the point of view of social revolution in order that military victory might be assured to the Popular Front.   And even then, this eventual victory might mean defeat for the revolution ; indeed, what hope would there be of a victorious " democratic " Government reconstructing society ? Such a Government would inevitably be conditioned by its own new militarism, and would incline towards a dictatorial and even Fascist régime rather than towards a libertarian.

Considering the ideological traditions and the social, political and moral conditions under which this civil war broke out in July 1936, the Spanish anti-militarists could do nothing else than resort to arms before the military invaders. But by so doing, they found themselves on the same level as the Fascist Generals : they found themselves obliged to use the same weapons as their enemies. They had to engage in a devastating war which, even in the event of victory, must bring about conditions both objective and subjective as unfavourable as could be to the realization of the social revolution. If we look at things closely we see here again a kind of dictatorship : if men wish to defend themselves against a violent invader on the level of violence, it is the invader who dictates to the defender what methods of combat he shall use. On the other hand, if the defender can rise immediately above violence, he is free to use his own, and really humane, methods.

It goes without saying that we would rather see victory go, if only partially, to those who fight for justice, peace and freedom, even with gun in hand, than to those who can only prolong injustice, slavery and war. But we must admit that the Spanish people, in its fight against Fascism, has chosen the most costly and ineffective methods it could, and that it did neglect to get rid of the military clique at the proper time, which is to say, long before the Civil War broke out. " Nowhere is the officer class more honoured and looked up to than in this country, where it has become the classical example of a military clique, and the sole victim of all this glorious institution has been, O irony ! not even a foreign enemy but the Spanish people itself."[1]

" But even if all this is true, there still remains the question of how else than by violence the Spanish people could have defended itself against the Fascist invader ? You yourself admit that Franco was helped from the start by certain foreign powers. Would you prefer to see the Spanish masses subjected to the reactionary forces without the smallest resistance ? "

In the first place, I am not advocating here either passive resistance or non-resistance, but an active defence from a moral as well as a material point of view. The best way to fight Franco would, no doubt, have been for the Spanish people to allow him to occupy all of Spain temporarily and then to let loose a great movement of non-violent resistance (boycott, non-co-operation and so on) against him. But our tactics also include, and far more than modern military tactics do, an effective international collaboration. We are no party to the deceitful idea of non-intervention : wherever humanity is threatened or attacked, all men and women of good will must intervene in its defence. In this case also, from the very beginning, a parallel movement of non-co-operation from the outside should have been organized to support that of the inside, in an

[1] Ellen Hörup, " La caste militaire," in *La Patrie humaine*, special number, November 1936.

endeavour to prevent Franco and his friends from getting the materials for war or, at least, to keep these down to the minimum.

And even in the situation as it is at present, all sincere war-resisters should have intervened systematically on behalf of the Spanish people and especially of the libertarian revolution, by fighting Franco with the methods indicated above. Nothing is more wrong than to put the invaded Spanish people and Franco, the obvious aggressor, on the same level—as nearly every State has done, in flagrant contradiction of the League of Nations Covenant—and to practise a so-called policy of neutrality, such policy being decidedly in favour of the aggressor and against the attacked, and worse still, conniving in all sorts of ways with those Fascist Powers who either openly or secretly were supporting Franco and his gang. Whatever the methods used by the Spanish people to defend itself, it is in a legitimate state of defence, and this is truer still of those revolutionaries who—during the Civil War—are striving to bring about the social revolution.

Once again, the international working-class movement has neglected one of the noblest of its historic tasks by falling in with the deceitful measures of Imperialist Governments, either self-styled democracies or actually Fascist countries, and abandoning those who fought in Spain with unequalled heroism for the emancipation of the working class and for social justice. If it had intervened in time, the masses of Spain would still have been able to dispose of the military clique in 1936 and to concentrate on social reconstruction. If it had only done so, violence would have been kept down to a minimum and the possibility of a real revolution would have been so great as to change the face of the world.

Franco's appearance on the scene shows another danger to the social revolution, to which we drew attention as long ago as in 1921, at the Third Anti-Militarist Congress at the Hague : if those in power are no longer able to maintain the capitalist and imperialist order at home, they will use not only the national army and the foreign legion, but also coloured troops, in the service of reaction against those who are fighting for justice and liberty, including liberty for the coloured peoples. Which only shows once again the necessity of winning over the coloured peoples to non-violent methods of struggle.

So that the tragic events in Spain teach us that to total war, which sucks up all individual and social life and requires as its natural counterpart, the totalitarian State, we must oppose total peace and its natural counterpart, a free and supernational society. And this demands a permanent mobilization not only against war and the possibility of war, but against all its causes, whether moral, political, social or economic. As long as people will submit to conscription and allow themselves incessantly to be mobilized for slaughter, even if it were for the social revolution, there is not a hope of seeing a really humane society come about. If, however, becoming aware of their collective moral force, the peoples break with militarism and war and mobilize for the service of peace, they will create at the same time such subjective and objective conditions as are most favourable to social reconstruction. The vanguard of this new mobilization is made up of those who have already refused as individuals to participate either in war or in its preparation.   By the example of their attitude, these conscientious objectors are pointing out to the masses their only way of safety.

It is characteristic of modern society—this real civilized barbarism—that in most countries the Governments have not known what to do with such men other than to imprison them, if not torture or kill them.   Even in times of peace, in our own day, hundreds of young men, profoundly conscious of their responsibility in what concerns justice and peace, are imprisoned ; many of them, as in Jugo-Slavia, for ten and more years.

So that there is nothing more topical and more pressing than the programme of the International Pacifist Group, founded on the International Congress against War and Militarism in Paris (1937), which urges the masses of the people on to an immediate and continual struggle in every country, Russia and Spain included :

1. for moral and military disarmament.
2. for political, economic and social justice between the nations, as an essential condition of total peace.
3. against compulsory military service, and every other form of militarism.
4. against military, industrial and social preparation for a totalitarian war.
5. for the immediate liberation of hundreds of conscientious objectors at present in prison in different countries.

CHAPTER X

THE NEW ARMY

Our choice is to go on to a new state of being
or to end.

GERALD HEARD.

"BUT by abolishing the army are we not destroying
at the same time a certain kind of physical and moral
education which will be very difficult to replace?
However formidable nowadays the function of the army
and of war, ought we not to admit that a certain
heroism and devotion is found in the army which has a
great deal of social significance? Was not Auguste
Brachet right when he said, 'The soldier has this
superiority over other men, that he puts his skin on the
table as stake'? In several countries, it has been
noticed that while judicial and parliamentary systems
have completely broken down, the military circles
alone retain a sense of honour. And are not even the
Nazis right when they say: 'Politics are history in the
making. And who is more the shaper and mover of
history than the Soldier?' "[1]

The reader will already have seen that I do not
ignore the important part played by certain moral
factors in military life and the organization of an army.
In my speech delivered at the W.R.I. Congress at

[1] Politik ist werdende Geschichte. Wer aber ist mehr Gestalter
und Beweger des geschichtlichen Geschehens als der Soldat?
Frankfurter Zeitung, January 30th, 1935.

Welwyn, 1934, I even based the methods of anti-militarist fighting on, amongst others, *La Psychologie du Combat* and *La Psychologie sociale de la Guerre*, by the French Commandant Charles Coste. When—by a reasoning so naïve as to be worthy of censure—one really does still believe that a country and even humanity itself can be served by a war, the military servitude retains a relatively moral worth, at least from the subjective point of view. We have always distinguished between those who on the one side, impelled by a certain idealism or by inclination, have imposed on themselves voluntarily a great discipline, that of service, and who give themselves up enthusiastically to the military calling and, on the other hand, those masses of the people who are called up to do compulsory military service if even a profound instinct warns them that they are acting against their own true interests. A large part of the people, enlightened by anti-militarist propaganda, is already well aware of the pernicious rôle it would be forced to play in a modern war.

We are not overlooking the relatively high value of the armed revolutionary struggle, either. In fact, with Gandhi, we must distinguish three different levels :

1. That of non-violence in the negative sense of the word—lack of courage and heroism, cowardice and so on.
2. That of violence, at the service of all justice and freedom.
3. That of non-violence in the positive sense (the sublimated struggle).

We have already said several times in this book that however great the moral worth of armed warfare in the service of justice and liberty, considered from the subjective point of view (as regards the mentality and the intentions of the fighters) may be, from the objective point of view (historical and cultural) such armed fight even for the noblest of ideas becomes more and more meaningless, being inappropriate to the goal in sight.

Many sociologists have already predicted that humanity will have to pass once and for all the military stage of their development. Inspired by the ideology of the bourgeois revolution, several nineteenth-century French Socialists advocated the transformation of military armies into industrial and social armies. They thought that what was good in the organization, mentality and education of the soldiery should be preserved and raised to a higher level than that of wholesale carnage. There is nothing to wonder at in this, for it is well-known that in France, the soldiers of the Revolution too readily confused the idea of a struggle for the liberty and the rights of the people, with that of armed force and national defence. It is very different in England, for example, where public opinion is not favourable to conscription of any sort and where military ideology has always been identified with the reactionary spirit, since in general the British Army is used either against the English people themselves or to subjugate other peoples.[1]

In Holland, the armed struggle of the Netherlands against the Spanish oppression, the Battle of Waterloo and the desperate defence made by the Boers against the British Empire, have brought about a great admiration for all spontaneous armed defence. But with us, what is hated and detested is compulsory military

[1] Russell, *Freedom and Organization, 1814-1914*, p. 143.

service, that fatal form of State slavery, which was imposed on the Dutch people by a foreign ruler, Napoleon. It is not surprising that since the World War, the conscientious objectors in this country number hundreds, despite the severe punishments inflicted on them. For the rest, it is notorious that even in France the institution of military recruiting has met with a strong opposition from the masses of the people. When, under the old régime, in order to fill the gaps in the front-line troops of professional soldiers, each commune had to furnish a new contingent every year by drawing lots, the number of dispensations was so great that the burden came to rest on the countryside workers. We must not be astonished if the authorities met with opposition from the peasants, who sometimes rose in real revolt, and if at the end they had to register a good number of desertions. When, later on, the bourgeois Revolution tried to extend compulsory service to all citizens, it was met with a lively resistance which showed itself by all kinds of illegal acts. The popular instinct, which distrusted such measures, was justified in the event : at the end of a few years, the army for the defence of the Revolution was seized by a spirit which grew more and more aggressive, and the consequences proved disastrous for the great mass of the people. Anyhow, in September 1798, of the 200,000 people called up, only 24,000 joined their regiment.[1] And again, did not the bourgeois Republic follow exactly the same foreign policy, in essentials, as the old régime ? In his *Napoleon*, Jacques Bainville has shown that a straight line passes from Louis XIV to Bonaparte, through the *Convention* and the *Directoire*. We can easily understand therefore

[1] Coste, *La Psychologie sociale de la Guerre*, p. 143.

that the opposition to compulsory military service should have remained very strong during the whole Bonapartist régime, that it should even have appeared among certain elements in the War and that, far from being dead, it seems more active to-day than ever before.

On the other hand, we have no objection to the transformation of military armies into industrial and social armies if in the first place all State control, which means political and social slavery, is abolished. We have even insisted more than once on the importance of not suppressing the impulses to struggle, to conquer, to sacrifice and to rise higher than the self—impulses so typically human—but of sublimating them. For a long time we have promulgated the idea of converting compulsory military service into a free civilian service, which is part of our social plan for organizing a system of communal production. Let us remember in this line of thought the initiatives already taken by the Swiss Pacifist, Pierre Cérésole.[1]

In brief, all that might be borrowed from military service for adaptation to the new, and truly humane, order would have to be subjected to serious revision. As for the preparation of a non-violent army of labour, which will have to play an ever greater part in the future, no doubt on various points the Boy Scout movement would be very instructive. But let us not forget that the physical training of the new youth will have a very different character from the military training of to-day ; it will work for the harmony of the whole man, which includes not only the body but the mind and spirit too,

---

[1] Cf. A. Danan, L'Armée des hommes sans haine and other pamphlets published by the International Civil Service. Also see Les Soeurs du Service Civil, on the part played by women in this noble war.
See too my book, Contre la Guerre Nouvelle, p. 212-14.

and this can only be achieved in an atmosphere of free collaboration.

Economic, industrial and technical experts say that if we eliminate from the world's production all superfluous and harmful work, and all that is poisonous or destructive, and if we distribute products for consumption efficiently enough, the work necessary to satisfy the elementary needs of man would only require one or two hours work per day per person. It goes without saying that if the whole attention, energy and devotion that thousands of intellectuals give at present to perfecting the engines of war, to organizing armies and fleets and elaborating strategical plans, if all this intellectual force could be centred round the reorganization of social life and the complete rearrangement of domestic life—first as regards dwelling-places, housekeeping, hygiene, heating, lighting, etc.—we shall be able within a short time to assure to all individuals in civilized countries conditions of life that are worthy of human beings.

The World War cost about 400,000,000,000 gold dollars.

According to the *Congressional Record*, quoted by Mr Nicholas Murray Butler in 1934, in his annual report to the Division of Intercourse and Education at the Carnegie Foundation, with this sum one could have built a $2,500 house, furnished it for $1,000, and surrounded it with five acres of ground at $100 the acre, for every family in the United States, of Canada, of Australia, of England, Wales and Ireland, of Scotland, of France, of Belgium, of Germany and of Russia.

After that, there would still have been money enough to give every town of 20,000 inhabitants and upwards in all these countries, a library worth $5,000,000 and a University worth $10,000,000.

Then with the balance, we should still have had enough left of our 400 milliards to buy the whole of France and Belgium together, that is to say, all which exists in these two countries in the form of houses, farms, factories, churches, railroads, roads, in short, everything which represented value of some kind in 1914.

We must remember that in 1914 the total fortune of France, according to official French figures, amounted to 62 milliards of dollars. For Belgium, the official Belgian figures were 12 milliard dollars. For the two countries that means a total reaching to about 74 milliard dollars.

Put otherwise, the price that the rulers and statesmen of the Entente, including the United States, have made humanity pay for the victory over Germany, represents the value of five countries like France plus that of five countries like Belgium.[1]

The havoc wrought by the next war will be greater still. Which led Bertrand Russell to write : " Modern war is practically certain to have worse consequences than the most unjust peace "[2] and to affirm that not one of the evils we wish to avoid by war is so great an evil as war itself. Pierre Boivin has declared that war can no longer be looked on as a legitimate means of defence. It is high time indeed that the enormous work of destruction which war is should be converted into a really creative work.

Unless we prefer the solution of the French royalists. The *Sunday Chronicle* of April 7th, 1935, having stated :

that a German engineer had invented a bullet, Halger Ultra, which can pierce a plate 1 m. 80 thick.

that Krupp had bought in Holland a rotary cannon which contains five rotating arms, firing 1,000 projectiles per minute.

[1] See Décugis, pp. 9-10.
[2] Russell, *Which Way to Peace ?* p. 212.

that the Nazis' national defence possesses some " Stratospheric guns " which can be loaded with high explosives, poisonous gases or noxious germs and have a radius of 320 km. (a single movement is enough to make the gun project where required) ;

that, with their Z ray, the German experts can from a distance destroy bridges, melt the mouths of cannon, dismember the motors of aeroplanes, pulverize wireless stations, railroads and the plating on tanks, etc., etc.

L'Action Française of April 9th, 1935, exclaims, without even asking if these statements are true :

" But the Germans need not worry ! The French, English and Italian laboratories are also preparing a few pleasant little surprises for use in the event of war being thrust on them. Soon we shall be able to destroy a whole town . . . and that won't stop war ! See the book by Alphonse Séché, called *Les Guerres d'Enfer*."

This only shows once again how Brachet's words, quoted above (p. 203), become daily more meaningless through the evolution of the technique of murder. People who understand modern war recognize that in the next the civilians will be the primary " war material ", the recent manœuvres over London and Paris having shown that in the battles of to-day the protection of the civilian population is impossible and bombardment of the great towns inevitable.

For this reason, we soldiers of peace will put our skin on the table as stake, not to make war but to render it impossible, once and for all. In this struggle, the new fighters need as much heroism, discipline and self-denial as in an armed battle. As much, did I say ? far more, for it is necessary for them to remain on a constantly high moral level—a thing which would never be asked of a soldier—and give battle without the exaltation of a barbarous romanticism and all kinds of other artificial stimulants : alcohol, religion and deceitful music, without the unanimity of hatred or the unleashing of all the brutal passions, so characteristic of traditional warfare.

Commandant Coste himself admits that in war " bestiality enters largely into certain acts of courage, which strangely recall the fury of the wild beast and suddenly occur, like mad fits of rage " ; that, in modern war, all human acts go towards working a gigantic mechanism which " has, morally, its awkward side " because man is subordinated to the machine which he serves ; that, in armed conflict, where one comes up against such brutal realities, one must deliberately " put all delicacy aside ", " triumph over physical and moral sensibility ". . . . " Is it not necessary to destroy one's memories, so to speak ? "[1]

One thing is certain. That is, that self-sacrifice and the other moral qualities called forth by armed conflict are subordinated to a collective violence. As Marshal Foch said, in war, it is a question of kill or be killed ; it is a barbarous enterprise, devastating, homicidal : from this fact proceeds the equivocal character of all military " glory ".

The glory of the new army is quite different. While according to the official formula, the " value of the soldier becomes social as it is de-individualized ", the value of the fighter for peace is social to the extent that he affirms his intellectual and moral individuality ; while, in armed warfare, the *res publica* crushes the

[1] Coste, *La Psychologie du Combat*, pp. 189, 196, 197, 209, 211.

vita individualis of the soldier beneath the weight of its imperatives, in the non-violent struggle the soldiers of peace bring all their energies into play in a free and spontaneous collaboration.

It is only then in war without arms that the whole conception of human nature, after which modern youth so ardently strives, can be realized in all its plenitude.

Dr Karl Willing may quote the ancient writers who hold forth on Sparta, and praise Spartan history, customs and laws as an example to Nazi youth, as much as he likes, but he will not be able in the smallest degree to modify the judgment of the great German historian, Edward Meyer, who says that, compared with Athens, Sparta—however great her military training—was behind in nearly every field of human activity.[1]   No doubt, at one moment, the Spartans were able to dominate ancient Greece, but they were very soon corrupted by the wealth gained from their victories. Living from the work of others, exploiting their slaves and tributary peoples without pity, they rapidly degenerated and even became unfertile : at the beginning of the fourth century B.C. the 9,000 Spartans of Lycurgus's time had dwindled to 1,500.   Fifty years later, to 700.   Aristotle came to the conclusion that if Sparta perished, it was for lack of men.[2]   Which bears out what the great English pacifist Bruce Glasier has to say : namely, that it is rare for nations or races to be destroyed or eliminated by conquests coming from the exterior.   The victorious nation falls more often than the vanquished, by the very fact of its conquest.   Weakness in social solidarity, corruption and tyranny have been the chief reasons for the degeneracy of the different nations and races.   That which constitutes the real spirit of a nation or race, its liberties, its virtues, its genius, cannot be destroyed by an outside conquest.

[1] Edward Meyer, *Geschichte des Altertums* III, p. 265.
[2] Décugis, p. 309.

Dr Willing can also compare the Spartan customs with those of the Prussian Junkers as much as he likes, but he cannot deny that as far as human civilization is concerned, Germany was much greater when comparatively feeble from the political and military point of view than in the period from Bismarck to Hitler. Let us remember the almost desperate protest made by Nietzsche against the cultural degeneration of Germany which accompanied the feverish evolution of her imperialism and militarism. Even the fact that Germany owes almost nothing to Prussia on the cultural side—literature, arts, sciences, philosophy—means nothing to this fervent believer in the ideal of authority and military obedience, who has written his book on the Spirit of Sparta in the hope that it will be read chiefly by young people and grown-ups enthusiastic about Nazi ideals and that " it will rapidly win a place in our public and school libraries ".[1]

As for the Nazi declaration that the warrior will be the shaper of mankind's history, this means that from the point of view of civilization, the Assyrians surpass the Egyptians, the Macedonians, the Athenians and all the peoples in Alexander's empire as far as India : the Romans, the Greeks : the Tartars, the Chinese : the Arabs, the Persians : the Turks, the Byzantines : the Aztecs, the Mayas and so on. Napoleon himself came to see that in the end the sword does not win the victory, but the spirit. And the modern soldier, so far from shaping history, can only deform and pervert it, as each war renders political, economical and social problems more complicated.

Even in Germany, they are preaching ideas on the nature of the soldier which can easily be put at the service of the new non-violent army. For instance, in the official organ of the Hitler Youth, Dr Stellrecht,

---

[1] Willing, *Der Geist Spartas*, p. viii.

sectional chief for the physical training of the youth of the Reich, opposes a pre-military education for boys on principle. He says that Germany is one of the rare countries where the youth is not exercised in the profession of arms, which is left to the men. Because we must avoid the danger of allowing young men to imagine that their vocation is to kill : Germany, says Dr Stellrecht, does not automatically connect the idea of killing with the word " soldier ", as the French do, for example. For Germans, the word means nothing more at bottom than the highest type of man (*Höchstform des Mannes*). For that reason, it is possible for Germans to conceive of a " political soldier " (*Begriff des politischen Soldaten*) who does not even carry a weapon. One thing is certain, that is that the physical education of youth should have the nature and the spontaneity of a game. It is not a matter of creating miniature soldiers. Dr Stellrecht believes that this conception of physical training for young people is best understood among the English Boy Scouts.[1]

But in any case, where could the constructive, dynamic tendency and enthusiasm hidden behind the Nazi theory in question be better satisfied than in this new army, whose soldiers have to re-make not only political life, national and international, but also social and moral life ? Even the famous *furor teutonicus* has a wonderful opportunity here to sublimate in all kinds of cultural enterprises. The same is true of the taste for conquest, the practical empiricism and the sense of fair play typical of Britons, and of the feverish activity and *buchido* of the Japanese. I have heard that great Japanese man, Ianazo Nitobe, state several times at Geneva that the time was past for the soldier's code of ancient Japan : but that it should not disappear

[1] " Keine Miniatursoldaten ! " *Frankfurter Zeitung*, April 18th, 1937.

but be transformed into a higher code. "The State
. . . is falling rapidly into the hands of squabbling
lawyers and talkative politicians, armed with a pernicious
logic. . . . The morality of *Buchido* which came
into being to the sound of drums and trumpets is bound
to disappear. Life has widened itself amazingly in
the present era. Nobler and larger missions than those
of the men of war claim our attention to-day. Men
have become more than subjects, being raised to the
level of citizens : what did I say ? They are more than
citizens : they are men."[1]

For the formation of the new army, a new individual
and social education is necessary, based on a new code of
honour—an education which corresponds intimately
to the conclusions of modern pedagogy (Montessori,
Russell, Boeke, etc.) and of modern psychology (Freud,
Adler, Jung) and which is opposed to all kinds of compulsion and cruelty.

After the W.R.I. Congress at Copenhagen (July 23rd-
27th, 1937) I met Dr Maria Montessori, who had arrived
to attend the Sixth International Montessori Congress.
She was much concerned with the fact that the modern
military State was assailing more and more the divine
possibilities inherent in the Child, this "new world
citizen without any rights". She laid the stress on
the necessity that, in view of the emancipation of
mankind, the new education of the child, so essentially
directed towards world peace, should have as a
complement the new education of the masses, and
vice versa.[2]

In this same spirit Boeke created at Bilthoven, near
Utrecht, a school whose first aim is to educate the children in such a way that they become free human beings,

[1] Nitobe, *Buchido*, 1927. *Cf. La Paix Créatrice*, pp. 50, 101-3.
[2] See the *Message to the International Congress against War and
Militarism* by Maria Montessori, Appendix I, p. 286.

and conscious of their responsibility :[1] in the new school, the whole of life is nothing but preparation for a new society which shall be worthy of man.[2]

M. Jean Piaget, Director of the International Bureau of Education at Geneva, has summed up with remarkable clarity the result of an international inquiry concerning self-government in schools. We have only one objection to his *exposé* and that is, that he has not drawn the social conclusions which follow. According to M. Piaget, " it seems that self-government is plastic enough to be used in no matter what kind of social or political organization."[3] The question is if many forms of this method of education are not perhaps actually serious abuses, since the method used is not directed towards the essential goal of all self-government : liberty. In his essay on the school co-operatives in France, published in the same volume, M. Colombain states that active collaboration pre-supposes free adhesion, and M. Piaget himself has shown, in his book on *Moral Judgment in Children*, how young people, having passed a primitive stage of obligation, of heteronomy, of legalism or " moral realism ", tend to unite amongst themselves in a co-operation where all restriction disappears and the respect which once was accorded unilaterally to adults, becomes a mutual respect between all those who are freely working together. Which means that an ethic of solidarity, of reciprocity and of justice develops in Man from about his eleventh year onwards. So that children become capable of self-government in the course of their school life.

It seems to us, then, that Professor Claparède was right when he said, with regard to the publication in question, " Self-government is certainly the method *par excellence* for democratic education."[4] It goes

---

[1] See Boeke, *Kindergemeenschap.*

[2] See also Russell, *On Education ; Education and the Social Order.*

[3] Heller, *Le Self-Government à l'École*, p. 107.

[4] Ed. Claparède, *Le Self-Government à l'École, Journal de Genève,* 1935, No. 197, Causerie Psychologique.

without saying that he meant a true social democracy, the self-styled democracy of to-day having as a rule nothing to do with the real self-government of the people. It is even impossible to use this educational method integrally, if we wish to prepare for a social life dominated by political or social dictators, and completely militarized, since such regimes are bound to throw people back to the stage of social constraint, of unilateral respect, of the imperative obligation, of heteronomy and of legalism. That is to say, into social infantilism. Briefly, such régimes which, from the psychological point of view, show a real regression to primitive mentality and which display a nationalism which is nothing more than a barbarous collective selfishness, instinctively averse from all kind of international solidarity, reciprocity and self-government, are shown up by their inability to draw the inevitable conclusions of the new education in the international field.

At the last dinner of the *Revue des Deux Mondes*, Marshal Pétain exclaimed, " A people's destiny is settled on the school benches before ever it is played out on the battle fields ! " and he was right. Neither the school nor pedagogy itself is neutral in character.

Modern pedagogy cannot but realize that it is a real corrective to present-day society, that of Russia included, and that as regards the militarism and autocracy which are so much in vogue in our time, it maintains a view which is downright revolutionary.

The more this new education—characterized not by automatic obedience, but by self-realization, the physical, intellectual and moral growth of human personality[1]—is recognized and practised, the less we shall need sanctions and imposed obligations, deliberate non-co-operation with all warlike destruction and murder being no more than the negative side of an enthusiastic co-operation in the construction and glorification of life.

[1] Holmes, *What is and What Might Be.*

CHAPTER XI

THE LEAGUE OF NATIONS, THE KELLOGG PACT AND SANCTIONS

> Much, however, has been gained if only the workers can see now that where imperialism enters, international justice goes out, so that they will no longer support a League dominated by imperialist governments and which has never been and can never be a League of peoples.
>
> ELLEN HÖRUP.

" YOUR theories are excellent ! But you seem to be in the clouds, or even above them. Leave your heights and come down to earth, to reality. You will then see that there exists to-day in the world at least two instruments of peace, first, the League of Nations and then the Briand-Kellogg Pact."

For many years the supporters of official pacifism have been reproaching the revolutionary anti-militarists with a deplorable lack of realism. According to them, we supporters of direct action, individual and collective, are just naïve idealists and deficient in all practical understanding. Meanwhile, the realists—these practical men and women—have had every opportunity of demonstrating the efficacy of their own methods ! The time has come to take stock and see how things stand.

First, twenty years ago it was the " realists " themselves who reproached us with a lack of . . .

idealism. It was at the time when Wilson had promulgated his famous Fourteen Points—rather like a new set of Commandments. Then the realists reproached us for being sceptical of this modern Moses' good intentions. The truth was, that we saw through them only too well. We said in so many words that the appearance of this new people's legislator on the scene was all the more dangerous on account of his " good intentions ". The frank *naiveté* of Woodrow Wilson only served to conceal the realities of the imperialism of Versailles. As President of the largest capitalist republic in the world, he was himself an official representative of imperialism. That is why from the word go we were constantly putting all men of good will on their guard against this childish historian, who from his very function could not do otherwise than mislead his people. All that he seemed to promise was unrealizable in an imperialist world, where the strongest powers were striving frantically to find a new balance of power and where the victorious States were dividing up the booty among them, like robbers.

Sooner than lend an ear to the seductive messages of such a Messiah, the revolutionary anti-militarists preferred to appeal direct to the masses themselves to throw off the capitalist yoke which threatened to weigh more heavily than ever before. Instead of pushing the people along in the politicians' way, they urged them to fraternize among themselves. The moment was propitious : in Russia, Hungary, Italy, Germany, social revolution was fomenting. Alas ! the vast majority of the masses in the West soon chose the guidance of those who, beneath the Wilsonian camouflage were arranging the most imperialistic, and so the more precarious peace that was ever concluded. They stood by the iniquitous Peace of Versailles, which proved more fatal to the evolution of European history, and to that of the whole world for that matter, than the famous Congress of Vienna. Instead of signing a peace which, as the official promise ran, would put a stop to all war, we fell into political chaos, a veritable hornet's nest from which nothing but fresh armed conflicts could ensue.

"So we must admit that the revolutionary anti-militarists of that time had foresight. However, Wilson's efforts were not all in vain, for out of them arose the League of Nations, the first attempt at a real commonwealth of nations."

Let us remain realists. The so-called League of Nations has nothing to do with the nations themselves. It is nothing more than a sort of Trust of capitalist, imperialist and colonial Governments, that is to say, in essence it is an attack on all the nations of the earth. To-day everyone knows what twenty years ago might not be said, namely, that the League of Nations was really a political instrument in the hands of the victorious European States, chiefly France and England, that the political activity of the League could only disgust the masses of Germany and the coloured peoples, seduced in the beginning by Wilson's fallacious promises and that in this way it created the possibility of all kinds of mis-understandings and new wars.

"Nevertheless, the League of Nation's aim was to abolish war!"

What blind idealism on the part of those who were defending political realism! For our part, the so-called idealists, we held from the beginning that the creation of the League could never abolish war, but, on the contrary, would maintain and sanction it. It is true that the League prohibits certain kinds of wars, that is to say, such wars as are declared illegitimate by itself. Nevertheless, it allows others, so that at Geneva they distinguish between legal and illegal wars, just as in Paris they distinguish between legal and illegal prostitution. And just as these distinctions will never abolish prostitution in France, so they will never banish war from the world.

So far from liberating mankind from this plague, the League has even introduced new forms of it. For the ultimate sanction brought into use against a State which has been declared the aggressor is still war. And so, in the name of all kinds of peace measures, war is sanctioned by the League as a war for Peace. By the irony of things, savage Mars receives his wreath at the blessed hands of Pax.

Further, the League recognized the right of national defence, to the great delight of the international armament manufacturers, and consequently upheld the fallacy that peace can be based on force. In several countries, the Government has made this an excuse for changing the name of their War Minister to that of Minister for National Defence—doubtless, he will soon receive the title of Peace Minister ! Of course we all know that from the day the Romans began their conquests, no State has ever attacked another and that it was only " in defence " and from a simple love of peace and justice that the great Empires were ever built up on earth.   .   .

Moreover, the League allows its members to conclude treaties and alliances for collective security among themselves, so that this security is once again based on force and a general feeling of insecurity is produced. And it does not worry at all about colonial wars, since the colonial powers believe them to be necessary for the maintenance of their authority.

Having carefully analysed the League of Nations Covenant, I stated in my book *Contre la Guerre Nouvelle*, Paris, 1928, that the results of the pacific measures of Geneva had been as follows :

1. War allowed on principle :
    (a) if executed by the League (sanctions).
    (b) to help those illegally attacked (and members must be sufficiently armed for this).
2. War is tolerated :
    when " order " has to be maintained in colonies.
3. War is forbidden :
    (a) If a dispute between two States, members of the League has not been previously dealt with by an *ad hoc* body (such as the Arbitration Committee, the International Court, the Council of the Assembly).
    (b) If three months have not elapsed since the publication of judgment.
    (c) Against a State which accepts such judgment.
    (d) Against a State which submits to the decision of the majority of the Assembly.
    (e) Against a State which has itself the power to decide certain questions.
4. War is permitted :
    (a) If a State is illegally attacked.
    (b) If the Council cannot arrive at a unanimous decision. In this case " the Members of the League reserve to themselves the right to take such action as they shall consider necessary for the maintenance of right and justice ".   (Art. XV, § 7.)

If in certain questions to which the answer lies with the Council of the League, its members are unable to agree unanimously, war is, according to this Covenant, the most laudable way out. It is clear that only the great Powers could resort to such a method, after having first prepared it most carefully beforehand, either openly or covertly, unless of course the smaller Powers were egged on to it by the great.

"But you are forgetting the Pact of Paris, whose aim was to outlaw war and to which the Governments of over sixty States were signatories ! "

I have not forgotten it. But neither have I forgotten that, with the Briand-Kellogg Pact, we entered the realms of pure talk, or if you prefer, the most misleading idealism. No doubt, it sounds fine to declare " that the time is come when a frank renunciation of war as an instrument of national policy should be made " and that all adjustments in political relations " should be sought only by pacific means and be the result of a peaceful and orderly process ",—that the High Contracting Parties " condemn recourse to war for the solution of international controversies " and that they " agree that the settlement or solution of all disputes or conflicts shall never be sought except by pacific means ". To this ideal Pact, however, the international politicians hastened to add the following reservations :

1. *League Obligations*, i.e. freedom to co-operate in sanctions against a Covenant-breaker ;

2. *Existing Treaty Obligations*, France reserving her system of exclusive alliances against private enemies with their secret military conventions, all declared compatible with the Pact ;

3. *The British Reservation :* " There are certain regions of the world the welfare and integrity of which constitute a special and vital interest

for our peace and safety. His Majesty's
Government have been at pains to make it
clear in the past that interference with these
regions cannot be suffered. Their protection
against attack is to the British Empire a
measure of self-defence. It must be clearly
understood that His Majesty's Government
in Great Britain accept the new treaty upon
the distinct understanding that it does not
prejudice their freedom of action in this
respect." (Sir Austen Chamberlain.)

4. *Self-defence :* " Every nation is free at all times
and regardless of treaty provisions to defend
its territory from attack or invasion and it
alone is competent to decide whether circumstances require recourse to war in self-defence,"
declared Mr Kellogg in a note of June 23rd,
·1928, to the Governments which first signed
the Pact of Paris.

It is therefore not surprising that never since the
beginning of the world, have the peoples armed against
each other as much as since the Disarmament Conference of 1932. And, as we have seen, these armaments
were primarily intended to maintain the *status quo* laid
down by the Treaty of Versailles which simply teems
with injustices and errors.

Apart from the defeated nations, it was chiefly the
unsatisfied, victorious Allies, such as Japan and Italy,
who objected to the existing arrangement, whose
maintenance was Geneva's first care.

What was the actual, historical result of all this ?
It was this, that hardly had the Peace Treaty been

signed when the world started off once again along the bloody road to war. From the beginning, the revolutionary pacifists grasped this historical reality and stated that the very nature of the so-called pacific measures of the League would prevent their effective application. As to the Article XVI of the Covenant, we might quote the proverb, "Who attempts too much, accomplishes nothing". For the application of this article against possible aggressors would have catastrophic consequences.

In the first place, it is certain that if one or more of the Great Powers decided it was to their interest to break the Covenant, no one would be able to stop them unless he were willing to risk a world war. Even if, in such a case, the League did risk a world war, such a step would not necessarily be repeated in other cases where the Covenant was violated. It is easy to see that humanity cannot go on indefinitely from one world war to the next.

Besides, in present-day political conditions, it is most improbable that the most powerful members on the Council who would be called on to judge the case of one State violating the Covenant, would not themselves be implicated, at any rate indirectly, in the conflict in question, and so become both judge and party.

The nature of the capitalist, military and imperialist States of to-day, as well as their violent, Machiavellian methods, resemble each other so much that no one among them has the right to judge the others. The whole idea of imposing sanctions is out of date. In modern education, we have completely given up both the principle and the practice of punishment, the worthlessness of which from a human point of view is universally

15

recognized. In the criminal field, also, people are beginning to break with the ancient tradition of retaliation and retribution, the whole object of criminal law to-day being merely the protection of society and the re-education of the malefactor. Shall we see the principle of retaliation, revenge and punishment creep back into the sphere of international law, which we had hoped was going to carve out a new path for humanity ?

For this reason, ever since the end of the Great War, we have been warning international public opinion against the inevitable consequences of such an attitude towards Germany, who was officially labelled as guilty of the Great War. This could lead to nothing else than a vicious circle of accusations and counter-accusations, of which none was entirely just and none entirely unfounded.[1] It goes without saying that even the most imperialist, military nation in the world will not consent for ever to be the scapegoat of the other imperialists in the world ! The proof of this, the Hitlerian reaction of a maddened Germany in face of the crazy attitude of the Allies, stares us in the eye.

History, then, has amply fulfilled our most gloomy prophecies. By a stroke of irony, just at the time of the Disarmament Conference in Geneva, Japan followed on the colonial, imperialist footsteps of Europe and threw herself on China.

At that moment, nothing could have been easier than to state which side was the aggressor and which had violated the Covenant. But nothing was harder than to apply sanctions. Although Japan had infringed

[1] See among other Harry Elmer Barnes, *La Genèse de la Guerre mondiale. Introduction au problème des responsabilités de la Guerre.* Paris, Rivière, 1931.

the League Covenant as well as the Kellogg Pact and the Nine Power Treaty, Geneva simply did not know what to do. And while dozens of ships left England, as other countries who were members of the League, laden with arms for Japan, and the French Press, came out brazenly pro-Japanese, China was sacrificed.

The only way in which to try and bring Japan to her senses would have been another world war. And we emphasize the word " try "—because how do we know we should succeed ? And even if we had succeeded, at the price of what sacrifices would it have been ? And should we have been ready to apply these terrible sanctions again in another violation of the Covenant ? The result would be a permanent state of world war, until the physical and moral strength of all mankind was exhausted.

Before the impossibility of doing anything, then, things were left to take their course. Perhaps this was all for the best. For, according to the great Catholic moralists of the Middle Ages and to all great liberal thinkers of to-day, it would be foolish, and hence immoral, to try and fight an evil by a far greater evil.

These difficulties appeared all the more clearly at the time of the Ethiopian conflict. As in the Sino-Japanese conflict, many great Powers who officially confirmed the guilt of the aggressor State were involved in the affair, particularly France and England. And on being accused, the Italian Government replied with a veritable torrent of counter-accusations and cleverly exploited the idea of sanctions to give the Italian people the feeling of having been chosen as the scapegoat of the powerful victors in the World War, who, in their ferocious egoism, were clinging on to their enormous booty.

Rightly wishing to avoid a new European war, which might easily have become a second World War and more murderous than the first, the Governments decided only to apply certain economic sanctions. But these measures—applied in the half-hearted way that they were—so far from preventing the war, only hit the Italian masses, who were far more the victims than the instigators of Mussolini's colonial escapade. Instead of depriving the aggressor of certain indispensable war materials, which as we have shown would have been simple enough, especially if at the same time an appeal had been addressed to the Italian people by means of the wireless in every country and pamphlets dropped by airmen, the men at Geneva began a series of economic sanctions which only alienated a large part of the Italian population from the League of Nations. Sole victims of the sanctions, they immediately gave their support to Mussolini who was in no way hindered by these intentionally ineffectual measures : the League of Nations did not even forbid the export of cars and tractors, petrol, steel, rubber and other essential materials to Italy. So that the Italian Government was able peacefully to continue its murderous enterprise for months and that consummate demagogue, the Duce, was able to arouse the old Messianism of the masses by appealing to the " Italian proletariat " to come to the help of the " Italian proletarian State ".

Apart from the obscure influences of armament manufacturers, petrol kings and steel kings, the reasons for these half-measures and shilly-shallying were the following :

In the first place, the well-known divergence between French and English policy.

Next, the " Lavalism " : the impudently pro-Italian policy of the French Government under Laval.

Then the contradictory policy of the Colonial Powers in general, especially that of the British Empire who, having regard to the hostility of its own colonial masses to the rule of the Whites, were unwilling to see an overwhelming victory on the part of an African Emperor over a European power just as much as that of Italian imperialism over a semi-barbarous State, situated in a country of vital interest to the British Empire.

And, finally, the great majority of the Governments represented at Geneva wished to avoid too crushing a defeat for the Italian dictator, afraid that this might bring about his downfall, which in turn would lead to a revolutionary movement involving the whole of Europe.

However, a system of ineffectual sanctions did come into play, and in every country " sanctionists ", as naïve as they were whole-hearted, urged their Governments, happily in vain, to take military measures until suddenly, the Nazi dictator having observed what success Japan and Italy had with the policy of the *fait accompli*, tore up the Treaty of Locarno and occupied the Rhineland.

Quite unable to operate the famous sanctions system and possibly war as well against two great Powers at once, and terrified of an attack on the part of Germany, France did everything she could to restrict the measures against Italy in order that she might not lose a possible Ally against the Reich, and also concluded her military pact with Russia. Then the chaos of international politics was complete and Abyssinia was the first victim : she, who ought to have been protected by fifty-two members of the League against the Italian aggressor, was abandoned in cowardly fashion.

The only thing in the world capable of preventing this disastrous state of affairs would have been the direct action of the popular masses who, by following the few spontaneous examples given here and there by workers aware of their historic task, could have stopped the export of necessary war materials to Italy. In spite of countless resolutions in favour of a strike against the war, passed by International Socialist, Communist and Syndicalist Congresses, the working-class movement preferred to follow the line of least resistance and supported the deceitful measures of Geneva.

Foreseeing the futility of the League as an instrument of Peace, the War Resisters' International was the first to try to organize some kind of anti-war action on the part of the international proletariat when the Italo-Abyssinian war threatened to break out in 1935, with a view to stopping the Italian aggression if possible, or at least holding it up. As far back as July 1935, the International Council of the W.R.I. stated that :

1. The most effective method whereby the Italian Government could be prevented from going to war would certainly be the mass resistance of the Italian workers themselves.

2. Since such mass resistance seemed at present unlikely to materialize, it was the duty of the working-class movement in all countries to deprive the Italian Government of those raw materials which were necessary for the war-industries.

Similar ideas were propagated by the International Anti-Militarist Bureau (I.A.M.B.), the International Anti-Militarist Commission and its Press Service.

For this reason the International Council of the W.R.I. hastened to send one of its members to the secretariats of the Socialist and Syndicalist International, to various official representatives of the Communist International, to try to organize an effective collaboration of the working-class movement in all countries against the possible Italian aggression. In their view it was necessary to organize this action independently of the League, as it was only too probable that the League's motives would be partially at least of an imperialist nature and that it would try to betray the cause for which it was officially fighting. Besides, the measures taken by the League in accordance with Article XVI of the Covenant were liable to turn the Italian masses against the masses of all other countries, and to bring about another World War. Since the vital thing was to continue to ask the support of the Italian people against the Italian Government, nothing could have been more stupid than to take economic measures which, besides upsetting the economic and social balance of international life, struck first of all at the Italian workers, already exploited by the Fascist Government up to the hilt. The only possible way in which the Italian Government might have been prevented from waging war was to withhold the necessary materials for it.

Obviously, if the international working-class movement had taken such a view and had explained the reasons for their action to the Italian workers by means of the wireless, and if, at the same time, airmen, heroes of peace indeed, had scattered pamphlets showing how this action was undertaken in the first place for the sake of the Italian workers themselves, the results would have been immense ; especially if Russia had cut short all petrol supplied to Italy and joined in the international movement whole-heartedly. Even had it not been completely successful, the repercussions would have spread through the world, and the way cleared for a solidarity that was truly international and profoundly revolutionary.

In the course of meetings which our delegate had with various high officials of the Internationals in question, it was admitted by these that the mentality of European workers was favourable to such an enterprise. But the Socialist International did not wish to start without being sure of the Communist International, and the International Transport Federation did not wish to act alone either, finding it unjust that it was always left to pull the chestnuts out of the fire. Further, it was thought unlikely that the enterprise could succeed unless the commercial relations between Russia and Italy were severed. And finally, they were afraid that it would be difficult to stop the export of war and raw materials to Italy, in countries whose railways were in the hands of the State.

When our delegate presented the suggestion to the representatives of the Russian Government at Geneva, he received a most evasive reply, in which emphasis was laid on the fact that relations between Russia and Italy are particularly friendly, because the Italian Government had been one of the first to acknowledge the Moscow Goverment officially. Further, the Soviet Government could not act independently of Geneva, as this would constitute a *casus belli* for Italy.

So that Mussolini was free to spring on his prey. For, in line with Stalin's disastrous policy, the international working-class movement deliberately stood aside and fell in with the corrupt policy of Geneva.

In theory, the League would have been able to take effective measures against Italy, the aggressor, in the very beginning. Since it is not obliged to apply Article XVI immediately, it could have followed the line of conduct laid down by the War Resisters. It should never have lost sight of the fact that its aim was not to starve Italian people, to upset its economic and cultural relations with the rest of the world, nor uselessly to disorganize international trade. As we have said, it should merely have made it materially impossible for the Italian Government to wage war or at least, to continue so doing. If the Italian people had, by means of refusing military service and going on strike, obliged its Government to give up this bloody enterprise, it would have been greatly to its honour and certainly a large part of the workers of the world would have come to its aid. But the War Resisters have never been willing, either by boycott or absolute blockade, to cut off a people from the rest of humanity because it goes to war, even if this people, deceived by its Government and religious leaders, participates in so frankly imperialist an enterprise with the craziest enthusiasm. It is only a question of taking effective measures against collective murder and its disastrous consequences and of healing the people in question of the collective malady which enthusiasm for war is. Nevertheless, we could not follow the example of that British Government which organized a " cordon of death " against a whole people at the beginning of the Russian Revolution.

To prevent a bellicose Government from going to war, it is enough to deprive it of its principal means of fighting. It is not even necessary to deprive it of all of them. The question of the embargo on petrol which, at the time of the Italo-Ethiopian conflict, occupied public opinion for long months and caused whole floods of ink and eloquence, this question gives an indication of the direction in which we have to find the solution of the problem. If at the very outset the petrol supplied to Italy by various members of the League had been stopped, the Mussolini gamble would have come to a full-stop. Even the argument that America is not a member of the League and could have continued her petrol exports to Italy does not carry much weight, as the transport of petrol is largely in the hands of the companies whose headquarters are in countries who belong to the League.

" You forget that the American petrol exporters, who were not obliged to join in the anti-war measures against Italy, might have increased their supplies to such an extent that Mussolini would still have had enough to carry on ; besides which, the Government of Italy itself began from the beginning to exploit the petrol sources of Albania."

But these sources were inadequate, both from the quantity and the quality point of view, and as to the import of petrol from America, we have already stated that this was dependent on companies in countries belonging to the League : we speak in particular of England, Norway, Holland. Even if Italy had at her command all the tankships of America, Japan and Italy which could be used for this traffic, it would not still have been enough for her complete revictualling. Besides, if America had contravened the embargoes of the League in this way, its members could have retaliated by boycotting all American petrol, so that the American exporters of this raw material would have lost the market for millions of tons. And before rushing into an adventure of this sort, they would have reflected. . . .

" But we must admit that throughout the war with Ethiopia, Italy was able to get sufficient supplies of petrol."

There is nothing astonishing about this, since the petrol sanction which, as everyone recognised, would have stopped the war and which should therefore have been put into force at once, was not even applied.

What really happened has been described by the Danish anti-militarist, Ellen Hörup, as follows, in the newspaper *Politiken* : " While England rigorously demanded that the sanctions should be carried through, oil from the Anglo-Persian Oil Company was flowing straight into Mussolini's tanks, aeroplanes and cars in Ethiopia. While Laval got them postponed, France in November exported 500,000 gallons more than the whole amount exported by France to Italy from January to November.

" On December 4th news came from Rome of a contract between the Italian branch of the American Standard Oil Company and the Italian Government. As soon as oil sanctions came into force the Company was to supply Italy with all the oil necessary in return for a thirty year monopoly on delivery. On the 29th England declared that oil sanctions were of no interest at the moment, since it depended upon the United States who would come to a decision thereon on January 15th. Mussolini need scarcely be afraid of the decision.

" The events of the autumn have shown us financial imperialism hand in hand with political imperialism. None of the Great Powers have the slightest interest in overthrowing Mussolini. On the contrary, they all prefer Fascism to Socialism whether it be a question of Mussolini or Hitler. They are investing capital in the two dictator-countries and supporting them economically even if they are apparently attacking them politically.

" The action of the League of Nations was bluff; sanctions broke down. Mussolini's fear of oil sanctions was bluff ; the Laval-Hoare-Baldwin fear of Mussolini's threats about war was bluff. And during all this bluff the war is being continued in Ethiopia unaffected, in Fascist style, with bombs upon the defenceless and unarmed, upon villages and Red Cross hospitals."[1]

[1] *Ethiopia Member of the League of Nations?* Ellen Hörup. This pamphlet can be obtained from the author, 19 rue Henri Mussard, Geneva.

Further, the integral pacifists have never said that measures should be restricted to one raw material. *The Times* of February 24th, 1936, was right in saying that in certain circles the importance of the petrol sanction was being ludicrously over-estimated and made into a veritable fetish. We, however, are not fetishists of petrol ! And in no way do we wish to apply anti-war measures drop by drop but massively. According to our ways of thought, it is as effective as it is important to put a stop to all financial assistance being given to a warlike enterprise, and to the import of all which might be considered arms and munitions, and especially of all raw materials indispensable for war and which the belligerent does not possess in its own country : because neither war-industries nor war itself can carry on if a certain number of raw materials are lacking. And, as we have seen,[1] by a happy chance, there is not a single Power in the world, not even Russia or the United States, these gigantic States so rich in minerals, which possesses all the materials necessary to war.[2]

In the case of Italy, for example, the embargo on the export of arms would not have been the most important, as Italy herself exports them. But to produce arms and to transport and make use of them a certain number of raw materials were necessary to her, for which she is completely dependent on foreign countries, as the following statistics show :[3]

[1] See above, pp. 182-3.

[2] See also Evans Clark, *Boycotts and Peace* ; Brooks Emeny, *The Strategy of Raw Material* ; Alfred Plummer, *Raw Materials or War Materials*, 1937.

[3] Taken from the Dutch edition of the above-quoted book by Sir Thomas Holland, which appeared in 1936. Of course, after the conquest of Abyssinia, which is very rich in minerals, these statistics must be modified.

RAW MATERIALS	Annual Consumption during the years 1925-1929	Percentage of Production in Italy
Chromium	2,800 tons	—
Coal	12,965,000 tons	3·17
Copper	70,934 tons	1·58
Cotton	1,052,660 bales	0·06
Iron, steel and alloys	1,749,000 tons	37·05
Manganese	31,978 tons	14·52
Mica	273,000 tons	0·00
Nickel	854 tons	0·12
Petrol	6,903,000 barrels	0·70
Phosphate	281,105 tons	0·00
Potassium	11,883 tons	25·54
Rubber	27,504,000 tons	0·00
Tin	3,385 tons	0·00
Leather	150 tons	0·00

In 1935 the heel of Achilles in Italian imperialism could be seen by a glance at such statistics. Deprive a country of such indispensable products and the whole of its war preparations go up in smoke.

"But you forget that a State which prepares for war will have the foresight to lay up stocks of these materials which have to come in from outside."

To wage war the quantity of materials required is so enormous that it is quite impossible to lay up sufficient stocks. According to experts, modern States need from five to twenty times as much of them in time of war as they do in time of peace.

" You know, too, that in time of war the Government needs a far greater quantity of things which serve the ends of war either directly or indirectly, for example, wheat, potatoes, etc."

The other countries must restrict exports of such things to the same amount that they would supply in times of peace, in order to injure the population of the belligerent State as little as possible without helping on the warlike plans of the Government.

If you still like to call such measures " sanctions " you may do so, on condition that all thought of punishment, vengeance and war is eliminated from the conception.

We are glad to say there is perfect agreement on this point between the integral pacifists of both America and Europe. The American monthly, *New History*, of February 1936, published a lecture which was given by the famous American disciple of Gandhi, John Haynes Holmes, before the Assembly of the Community Church at New York. He too asserts that there is nothing to gain and everything to lose by risking another world war in order to defend peace. Further, he recognizes that military measures against a bellicose Government are quite unnecessary if financial assistance, arms and raw materials are refused to it and if other products are kept down to the quantities imported in times of peace.

Taking into consideration the present-day political and economic conflicts, and the character of those capitalist and imperialist States which form the immense majority of the League membership, it is highly improbable that this institution will become humane, especially since Russia also has accepted the methods of armed national and collective security and those of military sanctions. If, however, as Léon Jouhaux said at the Assembly against War and Fascism, at Geneva on February 21st, 1936, the different peoples have to prevent their Governments from going to war, the moment has come when they are faced with the following alternative :

Either the peoples in question force their Governments to act in the way described above.

Or if the Governments continue to undermine the struggle for peace in their usual manner, the international working-class movement must immediately free itself from the Geneva authority and pass straight to direct action on its own account.

How well the working-class movement is able to effectively act in this way was shown in 1920 when the French, English and Irish workers in the ports refused to load arms on to ships destined for Poland and other States intervening against Soviet Russia and when the French and English workers even set up Committees of Action to put a stop to the Polish invasion.

At Antwerp, Rotterdam, Danzig, everywhere the workers joined in with action of this sort and every endeavour to send raw materials to Poland came up against stubborn resistance on their part. At the same time, the English miners and transport workers joined together to fight the bellicose attitude of their Government. Working in with the whole Socialist and syndicalist movement of the country, they forced the Government to give in to the following demands :

1. The withdrawal of the Conscription Bill then before Parliament.
2. The withdrawal of all British troops from Russia.
3. The release of all C.O's. then in prison.
4. The raising of the Blockade.[1]

[1] See Gerald Gould, *The Coming Revolution in Great Britain*, London, 1920.

And, at the Congress of Red Syndicates in Moscow, 1921, the People's Commissar Rykov declared that Russia was saved not by arms but by the direct action of the international working-class movement ; for this act of true human solidarity the Congress expressed its gratitude.

The international pacifist movement which now numbers hundreds of thousands of men and women of good will, as much of the Right as of the Left, and tens of millions of workers, must take the responsibility of following the directives of the War Resisters rather than of obeying the orders of opportunist politicians.

It need hardly be said that on our side there is no objection to working in with the League of Nations in as far as it uses measures which are both effectual and humane.   But in such cases it can only be a matter of a wise and prudent co-ordination of the international pacifist movement with the States who are members of the League.   Unconditional subordination to Geneva must be avoided at all costs, the character of the Governments in question, and that of the present-day politico-economic conflicts, being too suspect to allow of our giving up ourselves blindly to the direction of the official " sanctionists ".   The international pacifist movement must preserve its moral and tactical independence absolutely and integrally.

This movement, which might be so powerful with its immense resources of unused energy, must now act according to the proverb : " God helps those who help themselves."

Yet we know too well that a true world peace can only be the result of a true world revolution.   But we look on the struggle for peace as part of the great revolutionary struggle.   Every time that the masses of the people are successful—as they have often been—in preventing the bellicose enterprises of their rulers, they become more aware of their own strength, increase their own self-confidence and undermine the foundations of the capitalist pyramid.

At this epoch of hyper-imperialism, which is liable to bring the world to ruin, it is more than time for the world movement for peace to rise up and show the real worth of its moral and physical energies, so that even if the League does tend to disorganize the world instead of organizing it for peace and justice, the pacifist movement will act in spite of it and, if necessary, even against it.

For at all costs the masses of the people must not be sacrificed again in wars caused by the moral and practical impotence of a political institution setting itself up as the guardian of Peace.

CHAPTER XII

ARMED DEFENCE AGAINST HITLER?

> Better fall than hate and fear, and twice
> better fall than make ourselves hated and
> feared.
>
> NIETZSCHE.

"BUT, people are always asking me, if Hitler attacks Holland to-morrow, what would you do?"

In reply to this question, which since the advent of the Nazis to power has often been put to me, I have already declared that Hitler would not "attack us to-morrow". Even if it were his intention to conquer the Netherlands, he would have to make full moral and technical preparation. For the moment, his hands are tied in any case, for he is involved in all manner of interior difficulties. In the meantime, we Dutch have the opportunity of getting ready for the fray morally and practically on a far higher level. "But if, all the same, Hitler were to invade Holland, then do only what you cannot help doing! But do nothing that you do not will to do!"

Supposing that the Netherlands were physically capable of defending themselves by arms against Hitler Germany, could we do so morally? During the World War, having recognized that to be able to resist Prussian militarism by force we should have to become more Prussian than the Prussians, we, the Dutch anti-militarists, preferred to prepare for a fight on a higher plane. And now that Prussian militarism is returning to life, are we going to sink back to its level ? We cannot sustain an armed struggle with the Third Reich except by surpassing it in cruelty and destructivity of method. And even if this were to lead to success, what would be the outcome ?

As we have said before more than once, the Allies, having succeeded in destroying German militarism with the help of the United States, themselves possessed with a belief in violence, showed such injustice in preserving their privileges as victors—they imposed a Peace Treaty so brutal and created a League of Nations so arbitrary—that, as a counter-blow, the German love of war was soon aroused. Besides which, militarism, once confined to the Continent, has since the World War been introduced with dire results into the British Isles and the United States ; in the Anglo-Saxon world, the intellectual youth has become more and more militarized, and conscription, once generally hated, has been maintained in principle ever since the Great War even if it is not actually applied in times of peace. As for France, she is over-armed. So that nowadays, we are witnessing a kind of Prussification of the universe. Another war like that of 1914, which they said was " the last ", to " defend the independence of the smaller States ", to " protect Western democracy ", to " uphold the right ", " to establish the freedom of peoples ", and what will be left us of independence, of democracy, of right, of freedom, of justice, going by what we have already lost since 1914 ? The civilizing values which are at stake cannot be defended by means of modern warfare. What we Dutchmen have to defend against a foreign invader is our best national tradition : individual and social liberty, toleration, individual and collective responsibility, the respect for human dignity and all it implies : liberty of conscience, of thought, of organization and of action.   Well, the whole system of modern violence, once it is accepted, even in the service of real national defence, would require us to destroy all these typically Dutch traditions with our own hands, without knowing if we should ever see them again !   And, at the same time, what evil might we not do to others, our so-called enemies ?

What is more, in taking part in a war against Germany, whose allies should we be, we Dutch war-resisters ? Of Mr Colijn and of all our colonialists and imperialists —in fact, of the pillars of Dutch capitalism !

And what " enemy " is it we should be blindly attacking ?   Another people, the whole German people. But if among the sixty-eight million Germans there was one single anti-militarist comrade—and there are many men and women there who have not bowed the knee to the Nazi Baal—this one comrade would be nearer to us than all the members of the Government at the Hague and all the Dutch militarists and imperialists.

Das andere Deutschland, that is, the other Germany, the pacifist and anti-militarist Germany which has been eclipsed for the present by the Hitlerian violences, is really far from being utterly crushed.   It goes without saying that now those who oppose war in all countries must stand more solid with her than ever before !

According to the inspired press, writes *Le Semeur* of June 19th, 1935, the news that conscription was to be reintroduced into Germany was acclaimed with frenzied enthusiasm.   According to the *Weltbuhne*, however, this was not precisely true and there are numerous mal-contents in Germany.   Tangible proof of this discontent was given when, during the anti-war attack manœuvres in which Berlin was plunged into total darkness, thousands of leaflets were thrown into the streets.   The next morning, the police and the Storm Troops set to work to pick up these leaflets, which had on them in large letters : *Krieg dem Kriege !* (War upon War !)

Which proves that although many of their fighters are in prison or shot, the German pacifists are not giving up the struggle.

For us, this is a source of comfort and one more reason why we must oppose the Germanophobia which is raging at the moment.

Our own frontiers are not those traced by the diplomatic hand : they are everywhere and nowhere, since we are first men, cosmopolitans, internationalists and then Dutchmen.   Doubtless, we love our country, the Dutch art and science, all the great civilizing tradition from which we have sprung and which lives in us as we live in it.   We are specially grateful to her because she has instilled into us a taste for independence and the will to keep those good things we have conquered, in the cultural domain and the moral to an equal extent[1] and we by no means feel obliged to deny them. In any case we could not, for the Dutch spirit is in a manner of speaking second nature to us.   But above our country, we put humanity : above our essentially bourgeois nation, the Socialist International.   There is no question here of an official, organized Church, as for instance the Second or Third International, but of the universal brotherhood of those who, starting with opposition to the iniquities of their own Government, fight in a way worthy of man's dignity by using new methods in the effort to bring about a truly humane society.   The more we act in this way, the more faithful

[1] See Henry Asselin, *La Hollande dans le Monde.*

we shall be to the noblest of Dutch traditions : those of Erasmus, of Multatuli, of Domela Nieuwenhuis, of Herman Gorter, of Henrietta Roland Holst, of Clara Wichmann, those of the many " reformers " of the seventeenth century and of hundreds of Dutch con- scientious objectors now living.

In a possible war with Germany, the matter at issue would not in the final analysis be these civilizing values, but capitalist interests : a new division of the world's riches according to the rules of the imperialist game. If we should subordinate ourselves, in these circumstances to the idea of nationality, if we accept the fairy tale about home defence, and if we consent to play some help- ing rôle in a modern, scientific war, not only should we be traitors to the best in ourselves and in our country, but we should be making ourselves responsible too for all the consequences proceeding from such a war, in which we had been accomplices.

The Dutch Government itself has admitted that in the event of war with Germany, Holland would never be left to fend for herself, which means that our country would have to enter into some anti-German imperialist coalition to which all interests, strategic as well as economic and moral, would be subordinated. In this way, the Netherlands might find itself in relation to England, for instance, in much the same position as Belgium to France, of whom, since her participation in the World War by the side of the Allies, she has become more than ever the vassal.

Modern war is no longer able to resolve the smallest problem, whether economic, social, moral or cultural. It does nothing but add to complications and aggravate difficulties. International interests demand in any case not the shifting about of political frontiers, but their abolition, and national traditions are of altogether secondary importance : they are worth nothing except in as far as they do not stand in the way of humanity's unification. In Switzerland and the U.S.S.R. they are well advised to allow the different national tendencies a chance to express themselves. For the freer national traditions are left, the less risk of their dividing the nations and the greater likelihood of their re-uniting them.

To take the Flemish question, it can be clearly seen that this will cease to exist the moment that the Flemings are granted all their rights. It will then be up to them to show how far their national traditions correspond to the norm of humanity. As long as the Government at Brussels persists in ignoring these rights, or in not giving them full recognition, the Flemings will continue their struggle with the same bitterness. And this struggle will become nobler as it is fought on a human plane. The plane on which the Flemings fight the imperialist ways of Brussels is already relatively high, and above violence of any kind. Would they inspire any greater respect if they resorted to brute force, if they tried to destroy Brussels, to exterminate hundreds of thousands of Walloons, and to expose their own towns, Antwerp, Bruges, Louvain, Malines, to complete destruction ? Would this not be a proof of their blindness, their irresponsibility ? The mediaeval Catholic moralists would surely have condemned such a war as worse than the evil. As for the modern moralists, what would they think of it ?

The same would hold good for Holland were it invaded by the Third Reich. What sense would there be, anyhow, in this minute country entering into armed conflict with a great nation endowed with a most formidable war equipment ?   It would be a short-lived comedy, a gesture of seeming heroism but really a blind escapade which would leave this cultivated little country open to ruthless destruction.   Everything would be wiped out in this constricted space : the fields and well-kept meadows, the farms, the wonderful herds and flocks, the gardens and greenhouses, the canals, the factories, the ports and all the countless treasures of art and of science, and with them of course, the population itself, so dense.   .   .   .

We have another conception of national defence. If Hitler dares, let him come and occupy the country right up to the North Sea.   What could he do, finding before him a people of obstinate tenacity, knowing what they want and doggedly applying the non-violent methods of struggle against his military régime ?

" But you are not sure of winning this struggle : it may be that you would lose ! "

Yes, and no.   It is not impossible that in such a case Germany might be able to impose for a time her politico-military domination over the country.   But would this domination take hold so easily of the Dutch *spirit ?*   Would it not turn back on itself, in order to concentrate on its own best traditions ?   If not, this people would not deserve its freedom.   If so, its moral force would radiate ever more intensely and would attract sympathy even among the German people.   It might quite well be that the violent annexation of so free a people might be the right remedy for the Nazi disease !

There is no question, then, of bowing in servile fashion before a foreign conqueror.   On the contrary, it is certain that a people is in much better shape for resisting all kinds of tyranny and oppression on the part of an invader in a country which has not suffered the ravages of modern violence and where, from an intellectual and moral point of view, the population is sane and sound, than in a country defeated in war.

And even if, victims of foreign violence, we should lose our political independence, there would be no grounds for despair. The great thing is that the best Dutch traditions should remain intact and spread themselves more and more throughout the world. The greatest shame a people can know is to be beaten, not physically but morally. About the middle of the seventh century, the Persians who were passing through a decadent period, were utterly subjugated by Arab conquerors. "These conquerors were absolute barbarians," says Keyserling; "in the whole history of mankind, I know of no event comparable to the *auto-da-fé* of the Alexandria library, burnt down on the pretext that ancient wisdom was useless. Yet, at the end of a few decades, Persia experienced an incredible renaissance. Every decadent symptom disappeared : and there was a superb flowering of truly Persian poetry and mysticism, though it was partly hidden by an Arab cloak.[1]

Another example, which is not widely enough known, and which it is good to bear in mind, is that of the Mayas : the barbarous Aztecs, who in the seventh century had begun to attack the Mayas and finally defeated them altogether, were themselves conquered by the Maya civilization which they had overthrown, for the Mayas

[1] Keyserling, *La Révolution mondiale et la Responsabilité de l'Esprit*, p. 36.

were an agricultural people who had already reached a high standard of cultural development.[1]

To go back to antiquity, from the tenth to the seventh century B.C., it was the Assyrians, those terrible fighters, who dominated the whole of Asia Minor. But everywhere they made themselves masters, it was the great tradition of conquered Babylon which imposed itself. From this point of view, these so independent conquerors were " dependents of Babylon " themselves.[2] Ages before, the victorious Semites were conquered by the Sumerian civilization which they had thought to overthrow.

It is to the everlasting glory of Greece that she triumphed over her invaders in the cultural domain :

> Graecia capta ferum victorem cepit, et artes
> Intulit agresti Latio.

" Vanquished Greece defeated her savage conqueror and brought the arts and sciences to the untutored Romans," as Horace admits. The German writer Nestle states that from the second century B.C. Rome became, from the point of view of civilization, a *Provinz des Hellenismus*. The Greeks, " rendered powerless in political matters became by the spirit alone a ruling people."[3] The Hellenist spirit filtered through the whole of European thought. St Augustine declared as much, quoting the memorable words spoken by Seneca concerning the Jews in the Roman Empire, *victi victoribus leges dederunt*, (the vanquished gave laws to the victors).[4]

[1] Ellwood, p. 137.
[2] Rohrbach, *Geschichte der Menschheit*, p. 5.
[3] Nestle, *Griechische Religiosität*, III, 1934, pp. 5, 7-8.
[4] St Augustine, *De Civitate Dei*, VII, p. 11.

What is it, indeed, which constitutes the undying glory of the Jewish race? It is not to have defended their country against the invader with weapons, thousands of years ago, as every nation did, and without success for that matter. But it is that no violence, horizontal or vertical, has ever destroyed their belief that they have a universal mission to fulfil, and that they have always possessed outstanding gifts in every branch of human civilization.

Whatever objection one may have to the Jews' assertion that they are the chosen race, we must admit that, having been for centuries the butt of cruel persecutions and ferocious attacks, they have been able to survive without resorting to violence. No people has ever been the object of a persecution so persistent and cruel as that suffered by the Jews. Forming in every land an infinitesimal minority, they have been obliged to give up all idea of resistance by force. But their non-violent attitude is largely a matter of choice, for their best and most typical men have always realized that the Jewish race can only fulfil their national mission by making a virtue out of necessity. Jewish influence has made itself felt to an extraordinary degree in every branch of human civilization and in every direction, favourable and otherwise. One thing is indisputable, and that is that mankind owes infinitely more to the Jews than to all the war-like peoples, Assyrians, Spartans, Aztecs, Huns and Prussians together.

It is again the glory of China that even the most violent rivals who invaded her have rapidly succumbed to the native, pacifist civilization. Krause has stated that in spite of the relative non-violence of Chinese civilization, it has dominated the whole of the Far East from the earliest times until to-day : " the civilization of Eastern Asia is that of China."[1]

The Dutch Chinese scholar Duyvendak, at the University at Leyden, has just published a remarkable book on the history of China. Concerning the Japanese invasion of Manchuria, he states that this invasion of Chinese territory by foreign barbarians is one of the most typical events of Chinese history. The occupation in 1931 and the creation of Manchukuo, a State whose independence is only a semblance, seems to be a complete victory for Japan. And indeed, we cannot foresee the time when China would be in a position to reconquer this country by force. " But there is something on which China can rely with confidence : thanks to the heavy influx of Chinese into Manchuria, this country has already become an essentially Chinese land : the Japanese can do what they will to establish themselves in the country, they will never be able to modify the Chinese character of it. They run the risk rather of becoming absorbed by Chinese tradition themselves."

However deplorable China's situation may be at present, her spacious traditions are still alive. " How could a civilization live for over 2,000 years if it did not carry within it some great creative forces ? The most radical revolution will never reject this past. There are some things against which it is useless to struggle. A lock of hair, for instance, can never be combed in a different way from that in which it grows. No government which is not impregnated by Chinese tradition can hope to achieve anything of lasting value."[2]

Let us remember, too, that the most famous centre of the Italian Renascence, Florence, never excelled from the military point of view. . . .

And in the long run, what has Holland come to, this so " highly cultivated and humane country ", this " fortress

[1] Krause, *Geschichte Ostasiens*, 1925, I, p. 34 ; II, p. 244. See also my book, *La Paix Créatrice*.

[2] Duyvendak, *Wegen en Gestalten der Chineesche Geschiedenis*, pp. 341.

of liberty ", which we are to defend, even with weapons
in our hands, against foreign attack ?   She is headed for
decline, the object of continual attacks not from outside
but from within, not on the part of foreign governments
but on that of her own Government, she is not dominated
by rulers from without but oppressed by her own ruling
class.   Endeavouring to maintain before anything
else its imperialist régime, the Dutch bourgeoisie has
had to own that the political and social liberties which
it once won from the feudal powers for itself, have in
their turn become the formidable weapons of the
oppressed classes and must be done away with, by
resorting to all kinds of semi-Fascist and even frankly
Fascist methods.

In Indonesia, Holland, who at the opening of the
century, seemed willing to follow a liberal policy, and
one of emancipatory tendencies, has for some time past
set up a veritable régime of vertical violence, with a view
to smashing the powerful movement for emancipation
on the part of the coloured peoples once and for all.

In the Netherlands themselves, an imperialist Government Calvinist-Catholic-Liberal-Radical in make-up,
under the sway of a strong reactionary crisis, has set about
limiting and reducing Dutch liberties, even the most
classical, such as the liberties of conscience, of thought,
of association, of press, etc., with a zeal equal to that
with which it brings its armaments in Europe and Asia
up to date.   It is to the Colijn Government that we must
concede the glory of having introduced a pre-Fascist
mentality into the Netherlands.

A real Fascist wave is sweeping over the Dutch dikes
already !   The more this mentality spreads in our
country, the more the Dutch character will weaken.

The masses are in danger of becoming a prey to a nationalism calling itself Socialist, which is really nothing else than a neo-capitalist nationalism with a pronounced leaning to State capitalism, in the Italian and German style, two countries whose civilizations are fundamentally foreign to ours !

If, on the other hand, we can oppose to the international waves of reaction such a resistance that our strength grows daily and the knowledge of our freedom spreads ever farther, what Fascism or National-Socialism will be able to cross our frontiers ?

What we, the War Resisters of Holland, have to defend does not coincide in any way with what the Dutch Government wishes to protect above all against a possible German invasion. We defend humanity—not only the spirit of the best Dutch traditions but also the very essence and the aim of the International revolutionary movement—against all those who attack it and above all, against our military fellow countrymen and those of Fascist mentality. We defend it with our own weapons and our own methods. Since the Dutch bourgeoisie is bound by its capitalist and imperialist function always to resort to violence both horizontal and vertical, it is for the oppressed masses in the West and the East—whose real interests are those of mankind at large—as well as for all who care about the struggle for peace and freedom, to undertake the task of doing away with violence.

Further, if the Dutch people should unhappily allow itself to be carried away by the official anti-Hitlerian ideology, that which puffs up the Western imperialism, Holland will never be more than a secondary part of the politico-strategical system of the British Empire,

whose official representatives have just declared cynic-
ally that their frontiers are on the Rhine nowadays and
that they consider the Netherlands an indispensable
element in the   .   .   .   British defences.   Indeed, the
international position of Holland in relation to England
has already become that of Belgium to France, a position
which is at bottom a caricature of national independence !
Anyhow, the attitude of Lord Hailsham and Mr Baldwin
towards the Netherlands has, since 1934, become essentially the same as that of Bethmann-Holweg towards
Belgium in 1914.[1]   If Holland should go to war with
Germany, she would automatically be incorporated
in the imperialist anti-German bloc and would fight
to protect the interests of London.   .   .   .

The truth is that the Dutch people are threatened
by two imperialisms[2] and that they will not be able
to protect themselves against both except by breaking
with the modern politico-military system.   For Holland
it is the only way to maintain her independence, not
only as regards Germany, but also England, a possible
occupation by whom would have to be met with the
same non-violent opposition as a possible occupation by
the Third Reich.

The fighters for freedom and peace will have nothing
to do with " national defence ", whether it be of the
Netherlands, of Germany, of the British Empire or of
Russia :   they will form an International of all who
resist horizontal and vertical violence, and who fight
for the transformation of the international-imperialist
system into an international and truly humane society.

---

[1] See B. de Ligt, " La Paix Menacée, la situation politico-
strategique de la Hollande," *Rouge et le Noir*, Brussels, March 2nd,
1935.

[2] If not by three, the third being Bolshevist Imperialism.

CHAPTER XIII

THE JAPANESE DANGER

> By force, the smoky torch of violence,
> We shall not find the way.
>
> TOLLER.

"BUT if Japan were to attack the Dutch Colonies?"

Such a possibility is envisaged in all the War Offices, the Parliaments and the newspapers of the world. The British Naval Conference of Singapore in 1934 dealt with this question among others. We ourselves drew attention to it already during the World War. As a Colonial Power in the East, Holland finds herself in the same politico-strategical relation to the British Empire and the other great Colonial Powers neighbouring (France, the United States, Japan) as Belgium in Europe the imperialist France and other bordering States (England and Germany). If war breaks out in the Pacific, " Holland cannot be neutral ", say the English, French, American, German, Italian, Russian, Swiss papers. Indonesia is only a very fragile link in the politico-strategical chain of the British Imperialism which extends from India to Australia. On some geographical maps of England, the Dutch Indies are already coloured red ! The Dutch Government is watching all this, just as the Japanese Government is, and all the more so because the Dutch Indies are one of the greatest of petrol sources, controlled by the formidable Royal Dutch Shell. That is why—when in 1921, during the hunger-strike endured by the conscientious objector Herman Groenendaal (the heroic act of a single man, which stirred a nation) the Imperial Prince of Japan, Hiro-Hita, paid a visit to Queen Wilhelmina—we confronted our fellow countrymen with this choice : Hiro-Hita or Herman Groenendaal, war or peace. For we Dutch war-resisters must also keep awake.

Since the Dutch Government is not in a position to defend her immense possessions in the East, as other great Powers can, she has given up her neutral policy as regards Japan and other Eastern powers in favour of an Anglo-Dutch understanding for mutual assistance in Europe and in the Far East. " If the Netherlands do not side with Great Britain, then the British Navy and Air Force will have to take necessary measures to prevent any possibility of Java or any other Dutch East Indies and their oil and other resources from falling into Japanese hands. Therefore, it is safe to assert that the part of the Netherlands in the Far East must necessarily be pro-British."[1]

So it will easily be understood why we will not take part in a war against Japan, under any pretext whatever, not even if Japan deliberately attacks the Dutch Colonies. If we have broken once and for all with the classic methods of national defence, even when it is a question of the independence of the Dutch State, it is certainly not in order to take up arms to safeguard her " possessions " overseas. The system of vertical violence that the Dutch Colonial administration stands for shall not be

[1] Taraknath Dass, *Foreign Policy in the Far East*, New York, 1936, p. 188.

17

upheld by the horizontal violence of war. The truth is, that the native populations have had more than enough of it. The Dutch Colonies represent the interests of bourgeois-imperialism, and not those of social revolution.

Analysing the situation of international imperialism and particularly the colonial question with Mr Quincy Wright, author of *The Causes of War and the Conditions of Peace* (1935), we agreed how applicable the following conclusion reached by Grover Clark is to Dutch colonialism :

" The struggles to get and keep colonies have been appallingly costly in suffering and money, both directly in the colonial parts of the world and indirectly in the home lands. The tangible profits which the nations have received or can receive from political control over the colonies cannot compensate the common people for all they have paid so that their governments might have that control and a few private interests might make money.

" The ledgers of the past have been posted, with their entries of staggering losses written in the red blood of the peoples. The ledgers of the future are open. Has the lesson of the past been learned ? "[1]

"And if the Indonesians prefer the Dutch Colonial administration to that of Japan ? "

This is a question worth asking. Nevertheless, it is not for Holland to answer it, but for the coloured peoples. Let the Netherlands withdraw from the Indies, as an imperialist Power. Let them do away with their armies of occupation, their submarines, their cruisers, their fleet of military planes. If the natives then wish to form an alliance with the Dutch in perfect freedom, of a humane and civilizing nature, there is nothing against

---

[1] Grover Clark, *A Place in the Sun*, New York, 1936, p. 224.

it. All white people who feel a special inclination for such work may follow profitably the example of Albert Schweitzer with the negro peoples. Our motto, *Indie los van Holland!* (entire separation of the Indies from Holland) does not only mean the absolute break away of exploited Indonesia from imperialist Holland, but also : Indonesia to be bound more closely than ever to the movement of world revolution, and to that in the Netherlands themselves first and foremost. To fight for the independence of coloured peoples is in any case the best way in which we whites can avoid alienating them. It is high time we did so, too, for the reactions to the violence of Western methods of colonization are already making themselves felt and the coloured populations are turning back upon and into themselves. One thing is certain, and that is that as long as the present colonial system prevails, universal disarmament will be impossible and that as long as Holland holds on to her prey, the Dutch people will have to go on arming.

"But if Holland withdraws from the Indies, will not the Japanese imperialists immediately seize this rich and coveted archipelago ?"

Supposing that Dutch imperialism did retire in this way, that Japan wishes to succeed her and that the natives do not want this to happen. The 64,000,000 natives have enough weapons of a non-violent sort to prevent it. For even the Japanese imperialists are not all-powerful. They have their hands full ! For, as Japanese imperialism spreads, so will her strength decrease in relation to the conquered peoples and the more chance the latter will have of effectively applying the non-violent methods : against a movement of non-co-operation, of civil disobedience, of boycott, reaching from Korea to Manchukuo and Indonesia, no power on earth, not even that of the Rising Sun, would be able to prevail. And still less if such an enterprise was upheld by a world-wide movement on the part of the workers, which might penetrate to the heart of Japan itself.

"But is not boycott a blind and cruel weapon, seeing that the disinherited classes of the Japanese people would be the first, and the innocent, victims ? "

For this reason, one must always distinguish clearly between the interests of the Government attacked and certain social and economical forces which it represents—those which constitute the real enemy—and the interests of the mass of people, drawn compulsorily into the system of national imperialism. Even by making itself the accomplice of such imperialism, it is acting against its own best interests, led on to it by the political and social powers which stand to gain from its so doing. It is therefore a question of organizing the non-violent struggle against such imperialism in a way which least injures the mass of the people. And again, we can show our respect for life even to the benefit of our bitterest foes. This is a luxury which the adepts of non-violent struggle can allow themselves : their tactics show a chivalrous spirit by far in advance of that boasted by the Middle Ages. They could never, for instance, harbour any intention of starving hundreds of thousands of women, children, old people and invalids, as England did towards the end of the World War with regard to the peoples of Central Europe and later to Russia, by a complete blockade. That is a cruel act by which we could not fail to estrange a great number of the people who suffered from it and who would naturally regard us from then onwards as their worst enemies. Far from us, above all, to make attempts on the life of Kagawa and other Japanese anti-militarists !

The *Vredes Pers Bureau*, under the direction of Pastor J. B. Th. Hugenholz d'Ammerstol (Holland) says in its issue of April 23rd, 1935, that Japan, whose press is more and more under the thumb of the militarist party, is waiting to hear any moment that the writings of Kagawa, are officially banned on account of their anti-war tendencies. Even if this did not happen, such a bulletin is significant of the influence that the great pacifist Kagawa has on the minds of his countrymen. However powerful the warlike tradition may be in Japan, it is a mistake to suppose that militarism is inborn over there.

We wish only to starve violence and war, and this by depriving them of what gives them life. That is to say, as regards Japanese imperialism, by depriving it in the first place of petrol, zinc, rubber, cotton and all the engines of war, munitions and equipment used in the army, and the naval and air fleets.[1]

As very often happens when the workers are called upon to fulfil their historic mission and prevent collective murder, it is upon the transport workers that the duty falls first and foremost : for, by the nature of their function, they hold the keys of heaven and hell and can open or shut the hellish gates of war as they choose.[2]

For the rest we cannot put the burden on to the shoulders of the few, since it is the duty of all mankind. We must therefore think out and put in use a kind of universal system for peace.

[1] See Harriet Wanklyn, " Instead of an International Police Force," *Reconciliation*, February 1934, pp. 50-1 ; Clark, *Boycotts and Peace* ; Holland, *The Mineral Sanction*.

[2] See *Contre la Guerre Nouvelle*, pp. 104-5.

In his excellent book, *Which Way to Peace,* Bertrand Russell has rightly stressed the necessity of systematically applying other methods than war to establish the universal peace. But in a chapter entitled " The Conditions for Permanent Peace ", he demands " a single supreme world Government, possessed of irresistible force, and able to impose its will upon any national State or combination of States," able to compel obedience to international law. To this end, he proposes to confine national armed forces to the older weapons and to make air warfare the exclusive prerogative of the world Government.

Are such measures, which are in obvious contradiction to the moral tenor of Russell's book, really necessary, if in future the education of the masses proceeds along the lines we have laid down and if, in case of failure, the people act against a belligerent State in the way we have suggested several times in the course of our *exposé*? War is war, even when waged in the cause of peace. In maintaining air warfare, as a weapon for international justice, we should be sanctioning one of the most repulsive features of our civilized barbarism which, although used possibly for noble ends, would certainly end in disaster. Since it is now imperative to begin a profound re-education, both individual and collective, national and international, for the establishment of peace—which is closely bound up with the world struggle for political, economic and social justice—we must definitely exclude war from now onwards. Besides, the more the conditions for permanent peace are realized, the less war is likely to occur. We must recognize that the military method is inherently ill-designed to yield good results. In a remarkable article in the review *Nature,* of June 12th, 1937, on " Science and Peace ", the editor affirms that men of science know better than any others how " the judgment is warped by bitter passions such as prevail in war, that difficult problems are best attacked by earnest, dispassionate search after understanding

and truth, with prolonged patience and resource ",
and that they have therefore " a special duty to urge
the application of these methods to international
problems ".   History having become more and more,
as H. G. Wells put it, a race between education and
catastrophe, we war-resisters must make every effort
to help on the cause of education.   If only because,
by advocating a " war for international Justice " as an
exception to our pacifism, we should be giving the
present-day governments a good excuse for all kinds
of " transitional measures " with a view to this imagined
future, and for indulging in all kinds of real wars at
the present time !

Chapter XIV

DON'T WAIT FOR THE ELEVENTH HOUR!

When shall the saner, softer politics,
Whereof we dream, have play in each proud land,
And patriotism, grown God-like, scorn to stand
Bond-slave to realms, but circle earth and seas?
                                HARDY.

WE must not wait till the last minute, till the moment of mobilization for war, to oppose this butchery. We have explained more than once how, when the war-machine is set in motion and the people maddened with fear and carried away by false patriotism and all kinds of religious fairy tales, a mobilization against war is apt to fail. So instead of waiting till the last moment, why not begin to mobilize at once against not only war but mobilization for war itself? Why not fight at once, by non-co-operation, civil disobedience, boycott, both individual and collective, all preparations for war, so as to make it—this obsolete method of settling political conflicts and regulating the affairs of the nations—impossible once and for all? Why not definitely refuse to make, transport or handle the engines of death, war having been officially outlawed ever since the Kellogg Pact. The thing we have to do is to banish it altogether!

"But what would happen then to the hundreds of thousands of men who earn their living in professions on which national defence depends, especially in times of economical crisis ?   We may be quite sure that the war-resisters will never win these workmen over to them ! "

That is another question that must be answered. Let us bear in mind that, according to Lehmann-Russbuldt, there are not more than 1,000,000 workers engaged in the manufacture of arms, munitions, etc., in the whole world.   A relatively small fraction of the total number of the world's workers.   There must spring up in the working-class such a solidarity that the more men and women voluntarily withdraw from the permanent service of death, the greater the enthusiasm and loyalty with which they will be received and economically supported by their international comrades. If the working-classes still feel a scrap of responsibility, there is nothing more urgent for them to do than to demand with one voice the immediate abolition of all war preparations and the transformation of these murderous activities into peaceful ones.   It goes without saying that this demand must be backed by every possible means of direct action.

As to the international, economic aspect of the matter, it would be fairly easy to solve the financial problems which would arise as soon as all the workers stopped their service of death, as long as the total number of these workers does not exceed 4 per cent. of the 25,000,000 now actually unemployed.   One might go so far as to say that it would even be an advantage to pension off all those who have an interest in the technical preparations for war—the munition-makers included—than to allow them to continue their evil work which, in any case, precedes certain bankruptcy for the whole world.

After the war of 1914, the conquerors forced the Krupps organization to transform itself from a factory for war material into one for useful goods in the space of a few months. Why cannot the working-class force the ruling-class to do the same thing ?

The battle for total and immediate disarmament must no longer consist of sending futile petitions to all sorts of Disarmament Conferences and Commissions. It is wasting time to go in for parliamentary and verbalist tactics which come to nothing : the example of Geneva is there to prove it.

Mussolini, who at least has the merit of absolute candour where the realities of imperialism are concerned, declared frankly on October 6th, 1934, that the Disarmament Conference had failed : " No doubt Mr Henderson is very dogged, like all self-respecting Englishmen, but he will never succeed in raising the Lazarus of disarmament from beneath his tombstone of cannon and armour-plating."[1]

Arthur Henderson, the unlucky President of the Disarmament Conference at Geneva in 1932, one of those rare souls who really did desire peace at that time, issued before his death a last appeal to the working-class to put an end to war. In his *Labour's Way to Peace* (1935), he declared that the only way to organize peace is to place all national armaments, reduced to a minimum by agreement, at the service of the League of Nations and international justice. National wars must be universally prohibited. If, in spite of this prohibition, some State resorts to it to obtain justice for itself, it must be subjected to the League's Sanctions. Since loyalty to the world community must take precedence of all national duty and obedience to national Governments, if the latter flout international law, conscientious objection becomes a way in which such Governments may be induced to give up their crimes. It is for the

[1] *Cf.* " Ecco il Duce ! " *Journal de Genève*, October 9th, 1934

working-class movement to make the first move in this direction, by calling a general strike.

Henderson's idea of conscientious objection corresponds to that of Professor Wehberg, which was given publicity some years ago.[1] According to this conception war, and all that war is, however remains, with all its inevitable, fatal consequences, in so far as one continues to make wars at the service of international justice. Instead, would it not be infinitely more effective to outlaw war once and for all ? Then, against a possibly warlike Government, financial, economic and social sanctions would come into force, making the conduct of such a war difficult without endangering the life of the people or risking a fresh world-wide conflagration.[2]

Besides, the struggle against war will never be effective until it forms an integral part in the struggle for a new society. Marshal Pétain was absolutely right when he said that as long as an international solidarity does not replace the political game caused by imperialist, national and social rivalries, we can only regard peace as a more or less durable interval between wars.[3]

There is one remarkable thing about Henderson's work, and that is that he does not share the fashionable deification of the State. From this point of view, Mussolini could learn a great deal from him ! Henderson opposed the conception of the State as an absolute power (" power State "), according to him the State must be the servant and not the master of the people (" welfare State ") : it should serve their interests and they themselves are charged with a human responsibility far in excess of all political authority. The respect for personality which characterized Henderson's work shows a degree of political and social maturity which are far from being reached in the countries of Hitler and Mussolini.

[1] Wehberg, *Grundprobleme des Volkerbundes*, pp. 70-2.
[2] See above, pp. 181-83, 236-38.
[3] Marshal Pétain, in his Preface to *La Guerre Moderne*, by General W. Sikorski, p. V.

The Anti-War struggle must be a non-violent, economic, social, moral and cultural struggle, waged by the masses of the people themselves—a part, secondary though important, of a far wider struggle—that for social liberty and justice.

We have shown what in our view constitutes the individual and collective tasks to be undertaken against War in our " Plan of Campaign against all War and all Preparation for War ", submitted to the International Conference of War-Resisters, held at Welwyn (Herts) in July 1934, which deals with the strategical and tactic side of the non-violent struggle and which the reader will find at the end of this book (pp. 269-285). This struggle extends into every branch of human civilization and demands a systematic, intellectual and moral readiness that we have not by any means reached.[1]

Now is the time to concentrate on this formidable struggle. For one thing is certain : if our forces do not rise from a deeper source, if our horizons are not wider, if our goals are not nobler than those of all the imperialisms of the world, our enterprise is foredoomed to failure.

Let all those who say " no " to war grasp the great responsibility that the noblest struggle in the world imposes on them !

---

[1] *Cf.* Braatoy, *Labour and War.*

PLAN OF CAMPAIGN AGAINST ALL WAR AND ALL PREPARATION FOR WAR, PROPOSED TO THE INTERNATIONAL CONFERENCE OF THE WAR RESISTERS' INTERNATIONAL, HELD AT WELWYN (HERTS, ENGLAND), JULY 1934, BY B. DE LIGT.

This plan for the mobilization of all anti-war forces is not based on any kind of compulsion, compulsory service or conscription. The anti-militarist movement is entirely composed of volunteers, every one of whom is called upon to act as energetically as possible according to his conscience but without being obliged to go beyond his strength. The deeds to be accomplished and the attitudes to be taken up under the following plan are dictated to no one. They are instanced in order that individuals and collective bodies may become conscious of the numerous possibilities within their reach to-day, to make all and every war impossible. The cases mentioned below should especially stimulate men to put into the service of this new fight their maximum of energy, devotion and courage.

A. IN PEACE TIME

I. Direct INDIVIDUAL action to prevent war and all preparation for war.

A. Refusal of military service :
   1. as conscript.
   2. as soldier or sailor.
   3. as reservist (return your military papers to the state).
   4. as citizen called to arms :
      (a) for the purpose of manœuvres.
      (b) on the occasion of a strike.
      (c) on the occasion of political and social conflicts.
B. Refusal of non-combatant military work (even in the Red Cross or the Army Medical Corps which both are by their nature subordinated to the military system).

C. Use every possible means for making anti-militarist propaganda in the army or in the navy in order to create nuclei of resistance and establish relations between these and the anti-militarist movement with a view to mass refusal of orders.

D. Refusal of industrial, technical and social service :
1. refusal to make war materials, munitions, etc.
2. refusal to take part in military aviation.
3. refusal to construct barracks and fortifications.
4. refusal to make :
   (a) military clothing.
   (b) military boots.
       etc.
5. refusal to make optical instruments, instruments of precision, etc., destined solely for war purposes.
6. refusal to set up type for or to print articles, pamphlets, books, manifestoes, tracts, etc., of a distinctly military, militaristic, jingoistic or imperialistic tendency.
7. refusal to make military toys.
8. refusal to handle, forward or transport anything used for war and its preparation, etc.

E. Refusal to put trade at the service of war (as employer or employee) :
1. banks.
2. co-operatives.[1]
3. publishers.
4. clothing trade.
5. saddle makers, harness makers.
6. shops for technical, optical and precision instruments, etc.
7. bookshops.
8. bazaars (children's toys).
   etc., etc.

---

[1] (See III E 2, p. 282). It may be surprising to find mention made here under the heading of indirect individual action, of an organization such as the co-operative movement, the characteristic of which is so distinctly collective and so fundamentally pacifist. Already in 1913 the International Congress at Glasgow declared that the International Co-operative Alliance should seek to prevent the war which was smouldering. None the less during the world war the co-operatives of every country became quite simply incorporated into the system of national defence. In France the co-operator Albert Thomas, was even entrusted with the administration of the Ministry of Munitions ! " The sumptuous hotel in which this ministry was established, Claridge's Hotel in the

F. Refusal to pay taxes.

G. Refusal to put up soldiers billeted on you. (Or they may be received hospitably and as imposed guests may be subjected to a judicious anti-militarist propaganda while the indemnity paid by the State may be used in favour of anti-war propaganda.)

H. Refusal of intellectual and moral service :

1. Abstentionist methods :

   (a) direct (i.e. refusal to undertake research work which aims at creating means for war purposes or to draw up plans connected therewith, and refusal to direct any

2. Constructive methods :

   (a) direct (i.e. the endeavour to place at the service of peace and human civilization alone those technical and intellectual inventions and means which are actually

Champs Elysees, had almost become a branch of our Co-operative Federation, so great was the number of co-operators, theoretical or practical, who held leading posts in important services " as was recognized in 1926 by Charles Gide (*Les Coopératives françaises durant la Guerre*, Association pour l'Enseignement de la Coopération, 1927, p. 8).

After the World War the governments of Italy, Russia and others officially incorporated the co-operative distributive system into the system of national defence. Only in England and the U.S.A. have the co-operative associations shown themselves to be conscious of the fact that their very nature obliged them to refuse any economic or social service which might contribute to war.

Wherever the co-operative organizations still allow themselves to become cogs in the wheel of the " totalitarian war " every co-operator who is conscious of the essentially anti-war and humanitarian character of his organization should consider it *his individual* duty to use every endeavour to bring about a clean break between the latter and all war slavery. He should continually place on the agendas of his local, national and international organization the formal refusal of all participation in any war whatsoever.

With regard to the staffs of the co-operatives and in so far as every individual is conscious of the essentially pacific and universal rôle which these associations should fulfil it should be every man's duty as far as lies within his power, to refuse *individually* every war service to which his organization would constrain him and seek to win over to his cause the whole of the collectivity.

Cf. B. de Ligt, *La Coöpération et la Guerre*, " Les Affranchis de toutes les Guerre," Genval (Belgium), September 1927 ; *La Coöpération et la Guerre*, " Evolution," Paris, October 1927 ; *Contre la Guerre Nouvelle*, Paris, 1928, p. 144-56.

technical or intellectual work of preparation for war) :

1. as physicist.
2. as chemist.
3. as bacteriologist.
4. as civil engineer.
5. as technician.
6. as speaker, orator or broadcaster.
   etc., etc.

(b) indirect (i.e. refusal to prepare a war-like mentality) :

1. as parents :

   (a) by keeping the children as far as possible away from all nationalistic, militaristic, jingoistic and imperialistic influence (by watching over the influence exerted by their reading matter, their teaching, festivals, etc.).

   (b) by refusing to hand over to the State children who have not yet attained their majority, for the purpose of military training or of compulsory military service.

placed at the service of war ; the endeavour not to pervert science in its applications) :

1. as physicist.
2. as chemist.
3. as bacteriologist.
4. as civil engineer.
5. as technician.
6. as speaker, orator or broadcaster.
   etc., etc.

(b) indirect (i.e. by preparing a humanitarian and international mentality) :

1. as parents :

   (a) by leading as harmonious as possible a family life, inspired by a truly universal spirit (the home atmosphere exercising a capital influence on youth).

   (b) by educating youth in as free and wide a spirit as possible, and especially indirectly by awakening in youth a sense of respect for others, love for the inorganic and organic kingdoms, for plants, animals and man; by awakening sympathy for foreign peoples and races ; by awakening the sentiment of social justice and admiration for all forms of courage and heroism, even in war—by a constant direction of the attention of the new generation to that which rises above all violence.

(c) by sending one's children to schools where they are sure to receive modern and up-to-date instruction in the widest sense (and if such schools do not exist, establish same) remaining in constant touch with the teachers, the parents of the other pupils and the pupils themselves by taking part in parents' circles, teachers' and pupils' meetings, etc.

2. as schoolmaster, teacher and professor by refusing to educate youth in a national, imperialistic and militaristic spirit.

2. as schoolmaster, teacher or professor by educating youth in a truly universal spirit according to the method of self-government (and with this aim in view seeking to keep up regular contact with the parents).

3. as journalist, publicist, lecturer or man of letters by refusing to influence public opinion in a nationalist, militaristic or imperialistic spirit, by showing up modern politico-economic life, etc.

3. as journalist, publicist, lecturer or man of letters by directing public opinion as much as possible to the ideals of justice and freedom and teaching the readers to appreciate foreign nations and races.

4. as religious or moral leader, by refusing to sanctify or to glorify national defence and war.

4. as religious or moral leader by awakening by word and deed the sentiment of universal solidarity and a sense of responsibility to mankind generally, seeking to sublimate the fighting habit and war.

5. as chief of a movement or a political group or party by refusing to prepare public opinion in any manner whatsoever for national defence.

5. as chief of a movement or political group or party by inciting the masses to work for a new civilization, giving them confidence in the method of non-violent struggle.

6. as jurists by refusing both to subordinate international law to national interest and to interpret the law with a bias in favour of one's own country.

6. as jurist by directing law towards a harmonious international world in which individuals, groups, nations and races would entertain free relations and exchange all their products (material, intellectual and spiritual) according to their nature and need.

7. as historian by refusing to commit the common error of making the history of one's own nation the starting point of world history by elevating it as the chosen one above any other nation and by refusing exclusively to glorify one's own race.

7. as historian, by taking universal life as a starting point, pointing out the qualities of every nation and race, demonstrating the relations and influence which each has with and upon the others and showing according to universal history the existence of an undeniable tendency towards a social life which would be as free as it would be varied, offering to every individual the greatest possibility of free development.

8. as artist, by refusing to place one's services at the disposal of nationalism militarism and imperialism.

8. as artist by directing every effort towards a truly human and universal harmony.

9. as sociologist by showing up nationalism, militarism, imperialism, pride of race, etc.

9. as sociologist, by recognizing the relative meaning of war and showing why and by what means the nations may rise above it and pass out of the stage of violence and barbarism.

10. as medical man, psychologist or psychiatrist by revealing the unconscious and subconscious tendencies which make for war, the retrogressive character of military discipline, and by showing that modern war is an odious crime against life, the physical, moral and mental health of man as well as against his aesthetic sense (millions of dead, mutilated, unbalanced, sexual illnesses, consequences of undernourishment, rachitis, tuberculosis, etc.).

10. as medical man, psychologist or psychiatrist:
    (a) by analysing the pathological phenomena of society with a view to individual and social self-cure and the establishment of moral hygiene.
    (b) by demonstrating the possibilities of canalizing and sublimating the instincts and passions which formerly found their outward expression in war.

11. as philosopher, by showing up all forms of dogmatism and absolutism, especially in the field of the history of civilization of religion and of comparative philosophy.

11. as philosopher:
    (a) by recognizing the relative value of all traditions of thought and civilization and by permitting them all full expression and in showing how they complete each other mutually.
    (b) by making universal philosophy a force of social dynamics.

12. by organizing effectively from the points of view of science, propaganda and action in respect to the above mentioned aims and by associating on a federal basis with other

12. by organizing effectively from the points of view of science, propaganda and action in respect to the above mentioned aims and associating on a federal basis with other

organizations for direct action against war and its preparation.

organizations for direct action against war and its preparation.

II. Direct COLLECTIVE action to prevent war and all preparation for war.

1. THEORETICAL

A. Propaganda by public and open meetings, etc.

B. Propaganda by congresses, courses, schools, etc.

C. Propaganda by study circles, etc.

D. Propaganda by writing or by pictures.

E. Propaganda by plays, pageants, etc.

F. Propaganda by cinema.

G. Propaganda by wireless.

H. Propaganda by processions and demonstrations.

J. Propaganda by house to house canvass (a far too neglected method).

K. Youth organization :
1. Children : Do not moralize ; borrow what is good from the Boy Scout Movement ; awaken above all a sense of respect for others and for oneself and a sentiment of responsibility and of human solidarity.
2. Adolescents : Should organize themselves according to their own methods to discuss the subjects in question.

L. Women's organizations.
(These are chiefly needed where women do not yet or have only for a short time taken any interest in social questions and where in connection with their maternal and social functions they require special education. The central idea must here be *their responsibility towards the new generation* in respect of physical, moral and intellectual health ; it is of the greatest importance that women should become conscious of the fact that in modern war the industrial, intellectual and social work of women behind the front is as necessary as the men's work at the front ; that if the system of national defence is to work well, at least 20 per cent. of the mobilized men should be replaced by women and that without the constant collaboration of millions of women the making of munitions would be paralysed. In this connection house to house canvass by women to women is of the highest importance.)

M. Anti-militarist propaganda in the army and navy (see I. C).

N. Special propaganda amongst the workers adapted to every kind of trade, especially *those of first necessity for war purposes*, in order to explain to these workers the technical function of their trade and what can be done individually or collectively—by each on his own ground—in order to undermine and to prevent war by refusing to serve and by systematic and reasonable sabotage :[1]

1. transport (goods and material, men) :
   (*a*) by rail.
   (*b*) by autobus.
   (*c*) by car.
   (*d*) by tramway.
   (*e*) by boat.
   (*f*) by aeroplane.
   (*g*) by beast.
   (*h*) by men.

2. minerals :
   (*a*) coal.
   (*b*) iron.
   (*c*) lead.

---

[1] in this respect a first attempt has been made by J. Verlinde in Holland in *Bevryding* of August 1931, in which he analysed the immense role played by coal in modern war. Below is the chief abstract of his conclusions concerning this industry which is fundamental to all war.

| | *Raw Materials.* | *Intermediary Product.* | *War Material.* |

AGRICULTURE
- grain ————→alcohol
- potatoes————→acetate
- beetroot————→ether
- cotton, wood——→cellulose

MINERAL EXTRACTS
- coal ————→gas ————————→explosives.
- lignite ————→tar ————————→war gas.
- ore ————→iron, steel, etc.———→guns, rifles, etc.
- oil ————→petrol ————→transport

This statement by Verlinde in combination with an analysis of the whole war system by Han Kuÿsten was published later by the Dutch Youth Movement for Peace in a pamphlet entitled *Dooft de Vuren!* (Put the Fires Out!).

Such pamphlets should be published in every country for every calling or trade which is basic to war so that every worker may have in his hands precise information concerning his own branch of work and may therefore know exactly what he should do or not do in the fight against war.

(d) aluminium.
(e) zinc.
(f) tin.
(g) nickel.
(h) mercury.
(i) copper.
(k) manganese.
(l) sulphur.
(m) pyrite.
(n) tungsten.
(o) chrome.
(p) antimony.
(q) graphite.
(r) mica.
    etc., etc.

3. Iron and Steel Industry (engines of war material, munitions).
4. Chemical Industry (asphyxiating gases).
5. Mineral oils, petroleum, heavy oils, petrol (gasoline), wells, refineries, pipe lines, tanks, etc.).
6. Alcohols.
7. Cotton.
8. Wool.
9. Rubber.
10. Leather.
    etc., etc.[1]

2. PRACTICAL

A, B, C, D, E, F, G, H (see I. A-H, p. 276).

J. Organization of a movement based on direct action for the immediate abolition of military slavery (compulsory military service).

K. Organization of a movement based on direct action for the immediate liberation of all objectors to military service.

L. Organization of special movements for direct action connected with special events of an anti-military character (such as f.i. the 1921 movement in Holland on the occasion of the hunger strike by the objector Herman Groenendaal and the one of 1932 in Belgium on the occasion of the hunger strike by R. A. Simoens).

---

[1] In order to prepare and develop this propaganda consult chiefly : Halle and Ache *La Défence Nationale et ses conditions modernes*, 1932, *Boycotts and Peace*, a report by the Committee on Economic Sanctions edited by Evans Clark, 1932, and *Wie wuerde ein neuer Kreig aussehen* (What would be the character of a new war, published by the Interparliamentary Union). Untersuchung eingeleitet von der Interparlementarischen Union, 1932.

M. Organization of a popular movement with the aim of eliminating immediately from the laws of one's country the right to declare war.

N. Unarmed mass opposition to the imprisonment of objectors in own town or village and organization in connection with such injustices of demonstrations, meetings, strikes of protest, etc.

O. On the occasion of parliamentary decisions or special governmental measures (such as a vote for the increase and the modernization of war material, manœuvres, dispatch of military or naval forces to a place where a strained situation has arisen, dispatch of military forces to some colony), to prevent such measures from being carried out by demonstrations and strikes.

P. Wide distribution of manifestoes inciting to refusal of service in which thousands of men and women—giving their names, callings and addresses—declare openly that they refuse to take any part in war or in its technical and moral preparation whether it be in the army, the navy or in social life.

Q. Creation of funds in aid of the victims of refusal to take part in war :
  1. in favour of those objectors who have lost their work in consequence of their anti-military attitude.
  2. in favour of propagandists in a similar situation.
  3. in favour of those who refuse to make war material or to participate in the technical, intellectual or moral preparation of war.

R. Compelling the governments to renounce all forms of national defence (if f.i. reasonable plans for universal disarmament are proposed the masses must compel the governments by direct action to accept the same).

S. Organization of international itinerary peace crusades (this campaign lasting several weeks or several months begins at the same time in different countries and in the most important centres. The crusades pass through towns and villages holding meetings and march to a designated spot where a grand international demonstration is to take place).

Should political tension between two countries threaten to lead to the danger of war :

T. A common front of all organizations who are opposed to war and its preparation should immediately be established in order to :
  1. create a Committee and a special fund for any proposed action.

2. inform public opinion of the threatening danger through :
   (a) the press.
   (b) lectures and meetings.
   (c) manifestoes, tracts and pamphlets dealing with the political difference in question in an objective and anti-war manner.

3. appeals should be launched by wire or express letter to all pacifist, anti-militarist and workers' organizations, etc., to exert pressure upon the government and parliament to avoid war at all cost.

4. leading personalities of the country should be supplied with full particulars concerning the point in dispute, with a request that they should influence public opinion, the government and parliament, to avoid war at all cost.

5. appeals should be addressed to all teachers, journalists, religious or political leaders, lawyers, historians, etc., that they may use all their influence to avoid war.

6. the government and parliament should be warned that in case war is declared the masses will refuse to take part in it and this all the more since modern states dispose of political and juridical means—such as arbitration—for settling any political difference and so to avoid all war.

7. in the country which might become the enemy country manifestoes should be published declaring clearly that should war break out the masses will refuse to take part in it and inviting all human beings worthy of the name, on the other side of the frontier, to act in a like manner.

8. enter into immediate contact with kindred movements, committees and organizations in a prospective enemy country so that parallel action may be taken in both countries in peace time as well as when war threatens to break out.

9. in towns and villages situated on the frontiers of both countries in question conferences and meetings should be organized at which the war resisters of both countries should meet in order to
   (a) examine the political dispute in question and devise means for a pacifistic solution.
   (b) examine all possible means to be employed for preventing the outbreak of war.
   (c) examine all means to be employed to oppose mobilization and prevent the outbreak of war.

10. a general strike, the collective refusal of military service and non-co-operation, etc., should be prepared in advance and if necessary commenced at once and any other steps taken to render the threatened outbreak of war impossible.

U. All things and persons having any connection with militarism
    —particularly officers—should be boycotted in social
    life.

Since it is likely that in case of a mobilization or on the outbreak
of war the members of the directing committee of anti-war organizations and the best known propagandists of the anti-war movement
will be arrested and the documents, archives, etc., of these organizations confiscated, it is necessary

V. to take the following preventive measures :

    1. educate the members of the organizations in question in
    such a way as to enable them more and more to continue
    their illegal work even should all their leaders be arrested,
    banished or killed.

    2. to keep several duplicates of membership lists in different
    places in order to avoid the consequences resulting from
    confiscation.

    3. bear in mind the possibility that the funds of the organizations
    in question which may be deposited in official institutions
    (Savings Banks, Banks, etc.) may be confiscated by
    the state and avoid the danger of being deprived of means
    at the moment of action.

In order to be able to act effectively at the given moment and to
forestall possible proclamations launched by the government it is
necessary :

W. to have prepared already in advance proclamations of different
    sizes and colours, drawn up in clear short terms, inciting
    to direct action, individual as well as collective, against
    war and its preparation and calling upon all to mobilize
    their forces in the service of humanity, to meet the following
    cases :

    1. state of war.
    2. state of siege.
    3. rumours of mobilization.
    4. mobilization.
    5. rumours of war.
    6. civil war.
    7. colonial war.
    8. international war.

B. IN THE TIME OF MOBILIZATION AND WAR

III. Direct INDIVIDUAL action to make war impossible.

A. Refusal of military service.

B. Refusal of non-combatant military work (even in the Red
    Cross or the Army Medical Corps, which both are by
    their nature subordinated to the military system).

C. Use every possible means for making anti-militarist propaganda in the army and the navy in order to create nuclei of resistance and establish relations between these and the anti-militarist movement with a view to mass refusal of orders.

D. Refusal of industrial, technical and social service :
    1. refusal to make war materials, munitions, etc.
    2. refusal to take part in military aviation.
    3. refusal to construct barracks and fortifications.
    4. refusal to make :
       (a) military clothing.
       (b) military boots.
         etc., etc.
    5. refusal to make optical instruments and instruments of precision, etc., destined solely for war purposes.
    6. refusal to set up type for, or to print, articles, pamphlets, books, manifestoes, leaflets, etc., of a distinctly military, militaristic, jingoistic or imperialistic tendency.
    7. refusal to make military toys.
    8. refusal to handle, forward or transport anything used for war and its preparation.
    9. refusal to place at the disposal of war everything connected with the postal, telegraph, telephone and wireless services. etc.

E. Refusal to put trade at the service of war (as employer or employee) :
    1. banks.
    2. co-operatives (see I. E 2 note, p. 270).
    3. publishers.
    4. clothing trade.
    5. saddle makers, harness makers.
    6. shops for technical, optical and precision instruments, etc.
    7. bookshops.
    8. bazaars (children's toys).
         etc., etc.

F. Refusal to pay taxes.

G. Refusal to have soldiers billeted upon you (or they may be received hospitably as imposed guests and subjected to a judicious anti-militarist propaganda while the indemnity paid by the state may be used in favour of anti-war propaganda).

H. Refusal of intellectual and moral service by abstentionist and constructive methods :
    (a) direct methods :
       1. as physicist.
       2. as chemist.

3. as bacteriologist.
4. as civil engineer.
5. as technician.
6. as speaker, orator or broadcaster.
   etc., etc.
(b) indirect methods :
   1. as parents.
   2. as schoolmaster, teacher or professor.
   3. as journalist, publisher, lecturer or writer.
   4. as religious leader or moral leader.
   5. as leader of a movement or political party.
   6. as jurist.
   7. as historian.
   8. as artist.
   9. as sociologist.
   10. as physician, psychologist or psychiatrist.
   11. as philosopher.
      (See I. H 1b and 2b.)
   12. notwithstanding the most deplorable circumstances and
       the most disastrous events, seek to maintain, to create
       or to restore the local, national and international
       relations which are indispensable for individual
       and collective direct action against war.

J.   Render impossible the requisitioning of your horses, mules
     or any of your cattle by the military.

K.   Render useless for mobilization and war service any bicycle,
     motor car, boat, aeroplane or other means of transport
     requisitioned by the military.

L.   Render useless for mobilization and war the telephone, tele-
     graph, wireless, etc.

M.   Render useless for mobilization and war : bridges, railways,
     etc. (not forgetting to place *danger signals* on roads and
     railway lines in order to avoid any accidents and save
     human life).

etc., etc., by practising in every sphere of social life the most effective
non-co-operation boycott and sabotage without ever damaging
or destroying instruments, machines, bridges, roads, etc., to a
greater extent than is strictly necessary.

If the choice is left open it is always preferable to convert the means
of war—in time of mobilization and war everything is so to say a
means of war—into means of peace rather than to destroy them :
f.i. by using your aeroplane to shower down upon town and countryside of your own as well as of a possible enemy country anti-war
manifestoes and leaflets, by placing your wireless (ordinary or secret
installation) at the service of the anti-militarist mobilization and
of the war against war movement in order to appeal to the people
of the countries in question to join the fight against all war, etc., etc.

IV.   Direct COLLECTIVE action to make war impossible.

A, B, C, D, E, F, G, H : the same as under III—Direct Individual action.

J.   BOYCOTT, NON-CO-OPERATION AND GENERAL STRIKE SHOULD BE EMPLOYED :

    1. In time of war danger *to oblige the government to give up its disastrous plan.*

    2. In time of war *to stop the slaughter.*

WHERE THE ANTI-WAR MOVEMENT IS NOT SUFFICIENTLY STRONG TO RENDER A NATIONAL MOBILIZATION IMPOSSIBLE ATTEMPTS MUST BE MADE :

K.   To create a united anti-war front :

    1. *in time of mobilization but when war has not yet broken out* to put on foot the most active propaganda campaign throughout the country and by making use of all available means to prepare for the general strike and mass refusal of military service.

    2. *in time of war* to act in a like sense but secretly and with tact, a task which, however, should already be prepared for in peace time.

L.   To attempt to win over to the anti-war mobilization soldiers, sailors and workers still mobilized for war by :

    1. demonstrations.

    2. house-to-house canvass.

    3. picketing in front of barracks (in this sphere *women* can act to great advantage), etc., etc.

M.   To disorganize as much as possible the great mechanism of war, chiefly by seeking to paralyse transport (and here again women have a special task to accomplish, for instance by placing themselves in their thousands on the railway lines or on roads in order to prevent the departure of military transports, in one word by practising methods of passive resistance as has been done in these recent years in India by all the women who have fought so heroically against the police and the Imperial British Army).

N.   Wherever it is possible to do so without the risk of endangering human life, arms, munitions and all war materials should be destroyed, etc., etc.

If the choice is left open it is always preferable to convert the means of war—in time of mobilization and war nearly everything is so to say a means of war—into means of peace rather than to destroy them ; f.i. by using aeroplanes to shower down upon town and countryside of your own as well as of a possible enemy country anti-war manifestos and leaflets, by placing your wireless (ordinary or secret installations) at the service of anti-militarist mobilization and of the war against war movement in order to appeal to the peoples of the countries in question to join the fight against all war, etc., etc.

O. The collective opposition to war should be converted into SOCIAL REVOLUTION (in this revolution it will likewise be the duty of all anti-militarists and radical pacifists to carry on their fight by such means only as may be worthy of man, by rising above any bourgeois, feudal or pre-feudal methods of violence, such methods being in strict contradiction to any rebirth of human civilization).

APPENDIX I

(see page 215)

MESSAGE TO THE INTERNATIONAL CONGRESS AGAINST WAR AND MILITARISM AT PARIS, 1-5 AUGUST, 1937

A war would be such an undoubted danger for mankind that it is the duty of every one of us to act with energy to prevent its coming. The method which you have chosen is the most direct and, if adopted, would bring an end to all danger of future war. To work for the abolition of armaments, to refuse to take part in a war : this is the most direct course towards the goal. By this method you hope to make "Heroes" of the countless individuals who form humanity. But resistance to the command of the State demands tremendous strength, strength to oppose ideas universally accepted, to resist public opinion, to renounce your country, to give up your posses- sions, and, eventually, even your life. Its call for a spontaneous heroism is one to which only a few rare individuals can reply.

To spread your ideal widely you must for this, as for all other ideals, good as well as bad, take into consideration that part of mankind which to-day is so little appreciated. Such heroism as you call for exists naturally in few persons, and cannot be instilled in those who do not have it ; this ideal calls for a long moral training, an Education for Peace which will develop in the individual those moral, spiritual, and social values which make him a personality who recognizes the " Mission of Mankind ".

If at some time the Child were to receive proper consideration and his immense possibilities were to be developed, then a Man might arise for whom there would be no need of encouragement to Disarmament and Resistance to War because his nature would be such that he could not Endure the state of degradation and of extreme moral corruption which makes possible any participation in war.

You, the Peace Volunteers, the shock troops of the fight for Peace, may be able, by your resistance to furnish the example and provide the time necessary for the willing volunteers of the rear guard, as yet untrained, to organize and to prepare themselves to take their posts.

MARIA MONTESSORI

Copenhagen, 29th July, 1937

II

(see page 10)

Protect us, Mother of God,
From our first days to our death ;
In the paths of this life
Everywhere, always, lead our steps.

We will have God in our army,
So that our valiant soldiers
Fighting for the beloved Motherland
Shall be heroes in the battle.

Stretch out your blessed hand over Belgium,
Our prayers rise to you, O Mary,
That under your care, She may remain
Faithful to Christ, to the Church, to the Cross.

The world knows what heroic battles
Our ancestors fought for the Faith ;
To be worthy the name of Catholics
We will fight to the death as they.

III

(see page 112)

You, who are bowed to the earth
Your forehead pale with suffering ;
Rise, proud worker,
The future appears brighter.
Not by the roar of guns
Will you overcome Capital,
No, for to win the battle
You have only to cross your arms.

Chorus

For the downfall
Of the exploiting tyrants,
The General Strike
Will give us the victory.

The best weapon to smash
The capitalists—
Those parasites—
Is for all to stop work.

BIBLIOGRAPHY

ALLEN, Devere, *The Fight for Peace*, New York, 1930.

ALLEN, JONES, FENNER BROCKWAY, NIEBUHR, *Pacifism in the Modern World*, 1929.

ALLENDY, Dr R. et Y., *Capitalisme et Sexualité*, 1932.

ANDREWS, C. F., *Mahatma Gandhi's Ideas*, 1929.

ARON, R. et A. DANDIEU, *La Revolution nécessaire*, 1933.

ASSELIN, Henry, *La Hollande dans le Monde*, 1931.

BAINVILLE, J., *Napoleon*, 1931.

BAKER, BARTLETT, BROWN, HAMILTON, HUXLEY a.o., *Challenge to Death*, 1934.

BASCH, Victor, *L'Individualisme anarchiste*, 1928.

BAUER, Ludwig, *La Guerre est pour Demain*, 1931.

BEER, Max, *Histoire du Socialisme*, I., *L'Antiquité*, 1930.

Bericht über den I.A.M. Kongress im Haag, 1921.

BERKMAN, Alexander, *What is Communist Anarchism*, New York, 1929.

BIJ, T. S. VAN DER, *Ontstaan en Ontwikkeling van der Oorlog*, 1929.

BOÉTIE, Etienne de la, *Freiwillige Knechtschaft*, edited by Felix Boenheim, 1924.

BOÉTIE, Etienne de la, *Vrijwillige Slavernij*, edited by Bart. de Ligt, La Haye, 1933.

BON, Dr G. le, *La Psychologie et la Défense sociale*, 1910.

BOSE, Subhas C., *The Indian Struggle*, 1935.

BOJER, HUIZINGA, HUXLEY, MAUROIS, WAELDER, *L'Esprit, l'Ethique et la Guerre*, Correspondence III, 1934.

BOUILLET, Susanne, *Comment réaliser la Paix*, 1936.

BOVET, P., *L'Instinct combatif*, 1917.

BRAATOY, B., *Labour and War*, 1934.

BREYSIG, K., *Vom Geschichtl. Werden*, I-III, 1925.

CAMPION, L., *Le Noyautage dans l'Armée*, Brussels, 1934.

CASE, C. M., *Non-Violent Coercion, a Study in Methods of Social Pressure*, 1923.

LES CATHOLIQUES EN FACE DE LA GUERRE, Consultation internationale, W.R.I., 11 Abbey Road, Enfield, Middlesex.

CECIL, MURRAY, FORSTER, LLOYD, NORMAN ANGELL, LASKI, BUXTON, *The Intelligent Man's Way to Prevent War*, 1933.

CLARK, Evans, *Boycotts and Peace, a report by the Committee on Economic Sanctions*, 1932.

CLARK, G., *A Place in the Sun*, 1936.

CONSTANTINESCO BAGDAT, Elise, *La " Querela Pacis " d'Erasme (1517)*, 1924.

CORNEJO, M. H., *La Lutte pour la Paix*, 1934.

COSTE, Charles, *La Psychologie du Combat*, 1929.

COSTE, Charles, *La Psychologie sociale de la Guerre*, 1929.

CURTI, Merle-Eugene, *The American Peace Crusade 1815-1860*, Durham, 1929.

DAMAYE, Henri, *Problèmes sociaux et Biologie*, 1929.

DAMAYE, Henri, *Sociologie et Education de Demain*, 1931.

DAMAYE, Henri, *Psychiatrie et Civilization*, 1934.

DAMAYE, Henri, *Paix et Morale par la Science*, 1933.

DASS, Taraknath, *Foreign Policy in the Far East*, 1936.

DAVIE, M. R., *La Guerre dans les Sociétés Primitives*, 1931.

DECUGIS, Henri, *Le Destin des Races blanches*, 1935.

DEVALDES, Manuel, *La Maternité consciente*, 1927.

DEVALDES, Manuel, *Croître et multiplier, c'est la Guerre !* 1928.

DREVET, Camille, *Peut-on contrôler les Industries de Guerre*, Geneva, 1932.

DREVET, Camille, *Désarmons d'abord les Profiteurs de Guerre*, Geneva, 1932.

DUPRAT, C. L., *La Contrainte sociale et la Guerre*, 1928.

DUYVENDAK, J. J. L., *Wegen en Gestalten der chineesche Geschiedenis*, 1935.

EINSTEIN und FREUD, *Warum Krieg*, 1933.

ELLWOOD, A. Charles, *Cultural Evolution*, 1927.

EMENY, B., *The Strategy of Raw Materials*, 1934.

ENDRES, Franz-Carl, *Giftgaskrieg die grosse Gefahr*, Zurich, 1928.

Enquête sur les Livres Scolaires d'après Guerre, Carnegie, 1926.

ERMEMONVILLE, *Les Munitions du Pacifisme*, 1933.

ESSERTIER, Daniel, *Les Formes inférieures de l'Explication*, 1927.

L' Evolution humaine des Origines à nos Jours, I-IV, sous la direction de M. LAHY-HOLLEBECQUE.

FENNER BROCKWAY, *A New Way with Crime*, 1928.

FERRERO, Guglielmo, *Le Militarisme et la Société moderne*, 1899.

FLÜSSER, E., *Krieg als Krankheit*, Heide in Holstein, 1932.

FRIED, A. H., *Handbuch d. Friedensbewegung I*, 1911.

FRIEDENSBURG, F., *Die mineralischen Boodenschätze als weltpolitischen und militarische Machtfaktoren.*

FREUD, S., *Beschouwingen over Oorlog en Dood*, Utrecht, 1917.

FÜLOP-MULLER, R., *Lenin en Gandhi*, Utrecht, 1928.

FULLER, Col. J. F. C., *The Reformation of War*, 1923.

FUNCK-BRENTANO, F., *La Renaissance*, 1934.

GANDHI, *The Story of my Experiments with Truth*, Ahmedabad, 1927.

GANDHI, *Speeches and Writings*, Madras, 1922.

Gewalt und Gewaltlosigkeit, Handbuch des aktiven Pazifismus, published by FRANZ KOBLER, Zurich, 1928.

GILTAY, Mr H., *Sociaal-cultureele Vernieuwing en Psychoanalyse*, Arnhem, 1933.

GLASIER, J. Bruce, *The Meaning of Socialism*, 1919.

GLASIER, J. Bruce, *James Keir Hardie*, London.

GLASIER, J. Bruce, *William Morris and the Early Days of the Socialist Movement*, 1921.

GLOVER, Edward, *War, Sadism and Pacifism*, 1933.

GOULD, Gerald, *The Coming Revolution in Great Britain*, 1920.

GREGG, B. Richard, *The Power of Non-Violence*, 1934.

GUYOT, Yves, *Les Causes et les Consequences de la Guerre*, 1916.

Handwörterbuch der Soziologie, published by A. VIERKANDT, 1931.

HEARD, G., *The Third Morality*, 1937.

HEERING, G. J., *Dieu et Cesar*, 1933.

HELLE ET ACHE, *La Défense nationale et ses Conditions modernes*, 1932.

HELLER, PIAGET, ZIELENCZYK, KANOVA, et COLOMBAIN, *Le Self-Government à l'Ecole*, 1934.

HIRSCHFELD, Magnus, *Sittengeschichte des Weltkrieges*, I, II, 1930.

HOLLAND, Sir Thomas H., *The Mineral Sanction as an Aid to International Security*, 1935.

HOLMES, Edmond, *What is and what might be. A Study of Education in general and elementary education in particular*, 1917.

HUZELLA, Théodore, *L'Individu dans la Vie Sociale en Temps de Paix et en Temps de Guerre : Essai sur la Sociologie médicale*, Paris, 1922.

IHERING, Rudolf von, *Der Kampf ums Recht*, 1877.

JONG, Albert de, *Oorlog tegen Hitler Duitschland ?* Nieuwe Niedorp, Pays Bas.

JOUHAUX, L., *Le Désarmament*, 1927.

JUDET, Ernest, *Le Vatican et la Paix, de Léon XII à Pie XI*, 1927.

KEYSERLING, Hermann de, *La Révolution mondiale*, 1934.

KIRK, Walter-W. van, *Religion renounces War*, Chicago, New York, 1934.

KRAUS, Dr Oskar, *Der Krieg, die Friedensfrage und die Philosophen*, Prague.

KRAUSE, F. E. K., *Geschichte Ostasiens*, I, II, III, 1925.

LABRIOLA, A., *Le Crépuscule de la Civilisation*, 1936.

LANDAUER, Gustav, *Die Revolution*, 1919.

LECAT, M., *Contre la Guerre avec Einstein*, Louvain, 1931.

LECAT, M., *L'Objection de Conscience est-elle soutenable*, Brussels, 1932.

LEHMANN-RUSSBULDT, Otto, *Die blutige Internationale des Rüstungs-Industrie*, 1929.

LEHMANN-RUSSBULDT, Otto, *Die Revolution des Friedens*, Berlin.

LIDDELL-HART, Captain B. H., *Paris, or the Future of War*, 1925.

LIEBKNECHT, K., *Militarismus und Antimilitarismus unter besonderer Berücksichtigung der internationalen Jugendbewegung*, 1907.

LIGT, B. de, *Gandhi over Oorlog, Ontwapening en Volkenbond*, Utrecht, 1932.

LIGT, B. de, *Vrede als Daad*, I, 1931, II, Arnhem, 1933.

LIGT, B. de, *Contre la Guerre nouvelle*, 1928.

LIGT, B. de, *La Paix Créatrice*, I, II, 1934.

LORWIN, Lewis L., *L'Internationalisme et la Classe ouvrière*, 1933.

MACKAY, John Henry, *Die Anarchisten*, cheap edition, 1893.

MACLAGAN, D. F., *International Prohibition of War*, 1915.

MALTHUS, Thomas Robert, *An Essay on the Principle of Population*.

MELLOR, William, *Direct Action*, 1920.

MÉRIC, Victor, *La Guerre qui revient : fraiche et gazeuse !* 1932.

MEIJER-WICHMANN, Clara, *Mensch en Maatschappij*, Arnhem, 1923.

MEIJER-WICHMANN, Clara, *Bevrijding*, Arnhem, 1924.

MEIJER-WICHMANN, Clara, *Misdaad, Straf en Maatschappij*, Utrecht.

MIRSKY, D. S., *Lenin*, 1935.

MITCHELL, Dr Chalmers, *Evolution and the War*, 1915.

MONTESSORI, Dr Maria, *Pédagogie scientifique*, I, II, Paris.

MOREL, E. D., *Truth and the War*, 1916.

MORRETTA, R., *Wie sieht der Krieg von Morgen aus?* Berlin, 1934.

MORRIS, William, *News from Nowhere or an Epoch of Rest, being some chapters from an Utopian Romance*, 1931.

MORRIS, William, *Stories in Prose, Stories in Verse, Shorter Poems, Lectures and Essays*, New York, 1934.

MOUNIER, Emmanuel, *Révolution personnaliste et communautaire*, 1935.

NAINE, Charles, *Plaidoirie*, Le Locle, 1931.

NAINE, Charles, *Sa Pensée socialiste*, I, II, La Chaux de Fonds, 1928.

NEHRU, J., *India and the World*, 1936.

NETTLAU, Max, *Der Vorfrühling der Anarchie*, Berlin, 1925.

NETTLAU, Max, *Errico Malatesta*, 1922.

NICOLAI, G. F., *Die Biologie des Krieges*, Betrachtungen eines Naturforschers den Deutschen zur Besinnung, I, II, Zürich, 1919.

NITOBE, Ianazo, *Le Buchido, L'Ame du Japon*, 1927.

PAGE, Kirby, *National Defense, a Study of the Origins, Results and Prevention of War*, New York, 1931.

PELISSIER et ARNAUD, *La Morale internationale, ses Origines, ses Progrès*, 1912.

PELLETIER, Doctoresse Mad., *Dépopulation et Civilisation*, 1928.

PFISTER, O., *Zum Kampf um die Psycho-analyse*, 1930.

PHILIP, André, *Sécurité et désarmament*, 1932.

PIAGET, J., *Le Jugement moral chez l'Enfant*, Paris, 1932.

PIRENNE, H., *Les Anciennes Démocraties dans les Pays Bas*, 1905.

PLUMMER, A., *Raw Materials or War Materials*, 1937.

PONSONBY, Arthur, *Now is the Time*, 1925.

PONSONBY, Arthur and Dorothea, *Rebels ànd Reformers*, 1919.

PRIVAT, Edmond, *Le Choc des Patriotismes*, 1931.

PROUDHON, P. J., *La Guerre et la Paix*, 1869.

QUACK, H. P. G., *De Socialisten*, I-VI, Amsterdam.

RAGLAN, Lord, *The Science of Peace*, 1933.

READE, W., *The Martyrdom of Man*.

RELGIS, Eugen, *Wege zum Frieden*, 1932.

REYNOLDS, Reginald, *The White Sahibs in India*, 1937.

ROHRBACH, Paul, *Die Geschichte der Menschheit*, 1914.

ROLAND HOLST, Henriette, *De Strijmiddelen der sociale Revolutie*, Amsterdam, 1918.

ROLAND HOLST, Henriette, *Sterft, gij oude Vormen en gedachten*, Bevrijding, 1934.

ROLAND HOLST, H., *Revolutionaire Massa-Aktie*, 1918.

ROLLAND, ROMAIN, *Mahatma Gandhi*, 1924.

RONCIÈRE, Ch. V., *Nègres et Négriers*, 1933.

RUSKIN, John, *Fors Clavigera*, New York, 1882.

RUSKIN, John, *Time and Tide*.

RUSSELL, Bertrand, *On Education*, 1928.

RUSSELL, Bertrand, *Roads to Freedom*, 1923.

RUSSELL, Bertrand, *Education and the Social Order*, 1932.

RUSSELL, Bertrand, *Freedom and Organization, 1814-1914*, 1934.

RUSSELL, Bertrand, *Which Way to Peace*, 1936.

SCHOLTZ, Gerhard, *Die Allgemeine Wehrpflicht in Deutschland und in der Welt*, Hamburg.

SEILLIÈRE, E., *Le Romantisme*, 1925.

SIKORSKI, General W., *La Guerre Moderne*, 1935.

SHEPPARD, H. R. L., *We Say "No"*, 1935.

Sociologie de la Guerre et de la Paix, containing the report of business at the Tenth Congress for Sociology, held at Geneva, in October 1930. Vol. XVI.

SOREL, Georges, *Réflexions sur la Violence*, 1930.

SOROKIN, P., *Soziologie der Revolution*, 1928.

STEINBERG, J., *Als ich Volkskommissar war*, 1929.

STEINBERG, J., *Gewalt und Terror in der Revolution*, 1931.

STEWART, William, *J. Keir Hardie*, 1921.

STIRNER, Max, *Der Einzige und sein Eigentum*, Reclam.

SUMNER, W. G., *Earth Hunger and other essays*, 1914.

TAGORE, Sumyendranath, *Gandhi*, Paris, 1934.

THEVENIN et COZE, *Moeurs et Histoire des Peaux-Rouges*, 1929.

TUCKER, Benj. R., *Instead of a Book*, New York, 1893.

UMILTA, Angelo, *Histoire d'une Utopie, l'Idee de la Paix à travers les Siècles*, Neufchatel, 1911.

VERGIN, F., *Das Unbewusste Europa*, 1931.

WEIL, Simone, *Oorlog en Revolutie*, I.A.M.V., Nieuw Niedorp, Holland, 1934.

WELLS, H. G., *An Outline of History*, London, 1920.

WELLS, H. G., *Mankind in the Making*, 1914.

Western Samoa, Imprisonment, Deportation, Shooting? W.R.I., Enfield.

Wie würde ein neuer Krieg aussehen? Untersuchung eingel. v. d. Interparlementarischen Union, 1932.

WILCOCKS, M. P., *Towards New Horizons*, 1919.

WILLING, Karl, *Der Geist Spartas*, 1935.

LE WITA, Henri, *Autour de la Guerre chimique*, 1928.

WOKER, Gertrud, *Der Kommende Gift-und-Brand-Krieg*, 1932.

WRIGHT, Q., *The Causes of War and the Conditions of Peace*, 1935.

INDEX